FUTURES
conditional

other books by robert theobald

The Rich and the Poor *1959*

The Challenge of Abundance *1960*

Free Men and Free Markets *1963*

The Guaranteed Income (ed.) *1966*

Social Policies for America in the Sixties (ed.) *1968*

Committed Spending (ed.) *1968*

An Alternative Future for America *1968*

The Economics of Abundance *1970*

Teg's 1994 *1971*

Habit and Habitat *1972*

robert theobald

FUTURES
conditional

THE BOBBS-MERRILL COMPANY, INC.
indianapolis
new york

to those who
choose to cooperate in
creating the better future
which is within our grasp

contents

three/refining
your view
of
the future

four/basic tools
for your
future
imagining

preface

This book is designed to help you perceive your future more vividly. It has been written because we can, for the first time, choose the future we desire.

Each of us has a view of the future—although we may hold it subconsciously. What is your view?

Is the future determined by forces over which you have no control? Must you adapt to forces which have been created by others and which they still can force upon you?

Do you see the future as a chaos of forces which interact in unpredictable ways? A world in which each individual can do what he wants without affecting others? A world which is so unknowable that you cannot decide where you stand or where your future will take you?

Do you believe that your future is created out of your past and your dreams of the future? Do you believe that there are real options and that you can choose what you want to achieve? Do you believe that your actions have consequences, that these consequences can be predicted and that you are therefore responsible for your actions?

In the last year, the future has become one of the major concerns of America. Two books on the future stayed at the top of the best-seller list for several weeks. More and more people are trying to discover the options they and the society have in creating the future.

Three views are being expressed at the present time. The first holds that the future is fixed and, with it, our overall patterns of living. Those who hold this view believe that present trends will inevitably continue to develop whether we desire this or not and that there is no way to alter our future.

Most of the best-known futurists—Herman Kahn, Daniel Bell, Alvin Toffler—believe that the future is determined. They argue that the future will be a continuation—or extrapolation—of the past. They state that we must expect more science, more technology, continuing economic growth, continuing urbanization, and ever-greater complexity to life.

The second view of the future finds man free to act in any way which seems good to him. There are no genetic or cultural limitations which cannot be immediately and successfully overcome. Man can change—indeed is changing and this change is irreversible.

Charles Reich is the best known of this school of futurists. He argues that we are caught up in a historical transformation which will automatically create a better society. He believes that we are already creating a new consciousness which will change the way the world works. He sees no reason to be concerned with the strains that such a transformation of consciousness will inevitably create—both within the rich countries of the world and even more critically in the scarcity-regions; an invisible hand will solve the problems.

Both the extrapolator view of Bell, Kahn, and Toffler and the romantic view of Reich deprive men of the freedom to act. In the first case, we are forced to remain within the existing social system and structure; in the second, we are being forced into a new consciousness and a new world and our actions are not essential to bring it about. The actions of individuals and groups are essentially irrelevant; history is predetermined.

I cannot accept either of these views—I find them neither logical nor attractive. I hold a third view—that of the system thinkers—which differs fundamentally from both of those set out above. I believe that we are in urgent need of a transformation toward a more human society, but I believe that we shall not achieve it unless we make far more effort than presently seems probable. I believe that the transition toward a more human society can be achieved if, and only if, we will take the time to discover the real forces operating at this point in human history, to imagine the future we want, and to create the methods by which we can move from the present future into the conditional future that we choose.

It is for this reason that I have been speaking to campus and other groups on a continuing basis for many years. I believe that the educational process can be recreated so that the student ceases to be involved in the ingurgitation of information and its subsequent regurgitation. I believe that the college, the university, and the society are capable of creating the new knowledge which we need if we are to insure the survival of the human race.

I am aware that it is unusual for an author or editor to state his subjective views. The academic is supposed to be objective and dispassionate. I personally do not believe that such a stance is possible. I believe that each of us has his own biases and beliefs and that the best we can do is to state them clearly.

This does not mean, however, that the purpose of this book is to convert you to my point of view. I believe that each person must develop his own world view in terms of the reality that he himself perceives—not the world view of another. I have tried, therefore, to provide you with fiction and science fiction, poetry and songs, social science and physical science, cartoons and pictures which will make it possible for you to decide which view of the future makes most sense to you. Are you an extrapolator—a person who believes that the future is determined by the past and cannot be altered? Are you a romantic—a person who believes that mankind can transform himself immediately and without hard work into a different form of consciousness? Or do you believe that the world can be changed to accord with our new possibilities and challenges only if we are willing to work hard and think creatively? (Obviously, given the pattern of this book it is inevitable that I shall disagree with much of the material in it. Inclusion here does not mean approval.)

Part one of the book suggests the various ways in which the future can be seen. The first section consists of three science-fiction stories which advance three views of the effect of time travel or knowledge of the past and future: one assumes that events are essentially determined, another that events are random, and a third assumes a complex interplay of forces. The second section reprints the views of various analysts of today about the future we can expect.

Part two collects a selection of the materials being printed about the future. These will permit you to begin to find for yourself in your own life other material which will aid you in looking at the future. Today, nearly everything you see and read is tinged with a view of the future.

Part three sets out a number of ways in which you can yourself participate in imagining the future. It is based on the reality that the future cannot be taught but can only be experienced. Part four provides tools and resources which will help you in your process of invention.

There are no slick answers in this book. The reader must participate: he cannot absorb knowledge like a sponge. If this work is used in class—whether as an introductory course to American history or American values or an advanced course on the future—the students must work together to draw out the meaning. Anybody reading it alone will not find ready-made analysis either. Often he will find it helpful to talk to others about the issues raised by the book.

This is not a propaganda book; it is an education book. Those who want to be told how to think and how to learn should not enter upon it. I have, of course, raised some of the questions which I see as significant in the material but each of you from your different perspectives will see others. This book is in a profound sense a Rorschach test, helping you to understand the principles on which you act today. It can also be a learning tool, permitting you to deepen your ideas about the way the future is created and the impact your own life can have on that future.

ROBERT THEOBALD
Wickenburg, Arizona
May 1971

PART ONE

how people think about the future

i
the nature
of
time

Science-fiction writers have always played with the nature of time and the degree of certainty of events. They have set out, in fictional form, some of the implications of various views about man's potential to change the past and the future.

Some stories have been written on the postulate that there can be no change in events, whatever happens. "What If—" suggests that if one chance event had not taken place it would have been replaced by other factors so that the end result would have been the same. Other stories have argued that even the elimination of key historical figures —such as Napoleon—would be compensated by other factors. Such stories take the point of view of the extrapolators: the future is determined by the past and man must live with it.

"The Sound of Thunder" goes to the other extreme. It is based on the postulate that history can be affected by the smallest chance event—that there is no order to history at all. The decision to turn in one direction rather than another, to see a movie rather than to stay home, alters one's life.

A third type of science-fiction story—"Life-Line" is the example chosen here—is built on the assumption that one's personal actions interact with existing trends to create new possibilities and that these possibilities are subject to understanding and prediction. There is system to the universe and the result of each individual's acts can be important.

As you read these stories, you should try to decide if there are illogicalities in each of the viewpoints expressed. For example, would not each premature killing of the Tyrannosaurus rex in "A Sound of Thunder" always have resulted in the destruction of other wild life? Why was the butterfly killed by Eckels so different? If the man with the frosted glass in "What If—" had met Norman and Livvy at any time before their train trip, would not the present have been different?

Another way to begin to understand your own views about whether events are fixed is to think about writing the same plot from another viewpoint. How would the stories have ended if the writers had held a different view of the nature of time and the potentials of man?

ISAAC ASIMOV

what
if—

Norman and Livvy were late, naturally, since catching a train is always a matter of last-minute delays, so they had to take the only available seat in the coach. It was the one toward the front; the one with nothing before it but the seat that faced wrong way, with its back hard against the front partition. While Norman heaved the suitcase onto the rack, Livvy found herself chafing a little.

If a couple took the wrong-way seat before them, they would be staring self-consciously into each others' faces all the hours it would take to reach New York; or else, which was scarcely better, they would have to erect synthetic barriers of newspaper. Still, there was no use in taking a chance on there being another unoccupied double seat elsewhere in the train.

Norman didn't seem to mind, and that was a little disappointing to Livvy. Usually they held their moods in common. That, Norman claimed, was why he remained sure that he had married the right girl.

He would say, "We fit each other, Livvy, and that's the key fact. When you're doing a jigsaw puzzle and one piece fits another, that's it. There are no other possibilities, and of course there are no other girls."

And she would laugh and say, "If you hadn't been on the

Reprinted from *Fantastic Stories* (Summer 1952) with the permission of Isaac Asimov.

streetcar that day, you would probably never have met me. What would you have done then?''

''Stayed a bachelor. Naturally. Besides, I would have met you through Georgette another day.''

''It wouldn't have been the same.''

''Sure it would.''

''No, it wouldn't. Besides, Georgette would never have introduced me. She was interested in you herself, and she's the type who knows better than to create a possible rival.''

''What nonsense.''

Livvy asked her favorite question: ''Norman, what if you had been one minute later at the streetcar corner and had taken the next car? What *do* you suppose would have happened?''

''And what if fish had wings and all of them flew to the top of the mountains? What would we have to eat on Fridays then?''

But they *had* caught the streetcar, and fish *didn't* have wings, so that now they had been married five years and ate fish on Fridays. And because they had been married five years, they were going to celebrate by spending a week in New York.

Then she remembered the present problem. ''I wish we could have found some other seat.''

Norman said, ''Sure. So do I. But no one has taken it yet, so we'll have relative privacy as far as Providence, anyway.''

Livvy was unconsoled, and felt herself justified when a plump little man walked down the central aisle of the coach. Now, where had he come from? The train was halfway between Boston and Providence, and if he had had a seat, why hadn't he kept it? She took out her vanity and considered her reflection. She had a theory that if she ignored the little man, he would pass by. So she concentrated on her light-brown hair which, in the rush of catching the train, had become disarranged just a little; at her blue eyes, and at her little mouth with the plump lips which Norman said looked like a permanent kiss.

Not bad, she thought.

Then she looked up, and the little man was in the seat opposite. He caught her eye and grinned widely. A series of lines curled about the edges of his smile. He lifted his hat hastily and put it down beside him on top of the little black box he had been carrying. A circle of white hair instantly sprang up stiffly about the large bald spot that made the center of his skull a desert.

She could not help smiling back a little, but then she caught sight of the black box again and the smile faded. She yanked at Norman's elbow.

Norman looked up from his newspaper. He had startlingly dark eyebrows that almost met above the bridge of his nose, giving him a formidable first appearance. But they and the dark eyes beneath bent upon her now with only the usual look of pleased and somewhat amused affection.

He said, "What's up?" He did not look at the plump little man opposite.

Livvy did her best to indicate what she saw by a little unobtrusive gesture of her hand and head. But the little man was watching and she felt a fool, since Norman simply stared at her blankly.

Finally she pulled him closer and whispered, "Don't you see what's printed on his box?"

She looked again as she said it, and there was no mistake. It was not very prominent, but the light caught it slantingly and it was a slightly more glistening area on a black background. In flowing script it said, "What If."

The little man was smiling again. He nodded his head rapidly and pointed to the words and then to himself several times over.

Norman said in an aside, "Must be his name."

Livvy replied, "Oh, how could that be anybody's name?"

Norman put his paper aside. "I'll show you." He leaned over and said, "Mr. If?"

The little man looked at him eagerly.

"Do you have the time, Mr. If?"

The little man took out a large watch from his vest pocket and displayed the dial.

"Thank you, Mr. If," said Norman. And again in a whisper, "See, Livvy."

He would have returned to his paper, but the little man

was opening his box and raising a finger periodically as he did so, to enforce their attention. It was just a slab of frosted glass that he removed—about six by nine inches in length and width and perhaps an inch thick. It had beveled edges, rounded corners, and was completely featureless. Then he took out a little wire stand on which the glass slab fitted comfortably. He rested the combination on his knees and looked proudly at them.

Livvy said, with sudden excitement, "Heavens, Norman, it's a picture of some sort."

Norman bent close. Then he looked at the little man. "What's this? A new kind of television?"

The little man shook his head, and Livvy said, "No, Norman, it's *us*."

"What?"

"Don't you see? That's the streetcar we met on. There you are in the back seat wearing that old fedora I threw away three years ago. And that's Georgette and myself getting on. The fat lady's in the way. Now! Can't you see us?"

He muttered, "It's some sort of illusion."

"But you see it too, don't you? That's why he calls this 'What If.' It will *show* us what if. What if the streetcar hadn't swerved . . ."

She was sure of it. She was very excited and very sure of it. As she looked at the picture in the glass slab, the late afternoon sunshine grew dimmer and the inchoate chatter of the passengers around and behind them began fading.

How she remembered that day. Norman knew Georgette and had been about to surrender his seat to her when the car swerved and threw Livvy into his lap. It was such a ridiculously corny situation, but it had worked. She had been so embarrassed that he was forced first into gallantry and then into conversation. An introduction from Georgette was not even necessary. By the time they got off the streetcar, he knew where she worked.

She could still remember Georgette glowering at her, sulkily forcing a smile when they themselves separated. Georgette said, "Norman seems to like you."

Livvy replied, "Oh, don't be silly! He was just being polite. But he is nice-looking, isn't he?"

It was only six months after that that they married.

And now here was that same streetcar again, with Norman and herself and Georgette. As she thought that, the smooth train noises, the rapid clack-clack of the wheels, vanished completely. Instead, she was in the swaying confines of the streetcar. She had just boarded it with Georgette at the previous stop.

Livvy shifted weight with the swaying of the streetcar, as did forty others, sitting and standing, all to the same monotonous and rather ridiculous rhythm. She said, "Somebody's motioning at you, Georgette. Do you know him?"

"At me?" Georgette directed a deliberately casual glance over her shoulder. Her artificially long eyelashes flickered. She said, "I know him a little. What do you suppose he wants?"

"Let's find out," said Livvy. She felt pleased and a little wicked.

Georgette had a well-known habit of hoarding her male acquaintances, and it was rather fun to annoy her this way. And besides, this one seemed quite . . . interesting.

She snaked past the line of standees, and Georgette followed without enthusiasm. It was just as Livvy arrived opposite the young man's seat that the streetcar lurched heavily as it rounded a curve. Livvy snatched desperately in the direction of the straps. Her fingertips caught and she held on. It was a long moment before she could breathe. For some reason, it had seemed that there were no straps close enough to be reached. Somehow, she felt that by all the laws of nature she should have fallen.

The young man did not look at her. He was smiling at Georgette and rising from his seat. He had astonishing eyebrows that gave him a rather competent and self-confident appearance. Livvy decided that she definitely liked him.

Georgette was saying, "Oh no, don't bother. We're getting off in about two stops."

They did. Livvy said, "I thought we were going to Sach's."

"We are. There's just something I remember having to attend to here. It won't take but a minute."

"Next stop, Providence!" the loud-speakers were blaring. The train was slowing and the world of the past had shrunk itself into the glass slab once more. The little man was still smiling at them.

Livvy turned to Norman. She felt a little frightened. "Were you through all that, too?"

He said, "What happened to the time? We *can't* be reaching Providence yet?" He looked at his watch. "I guess we are." Then, to Livvy, "You didn't fall that time."

"Then you *did* see it?" She frowned. "Now, that's like Georgette. I'm sure there was no reason to get off the streetcar except to prevent my meeting you. How long had you known Georgette before then, Norman?"

"Not very long. Just enough to be able to recognize her at sight and to feel that I ought to offer her my seat."

Livvy curled her lip.

Norman grinned, "You can't be jealous of a might-have-been, kid. Besides, what difference would it have made? I'd have been sufficiently interested in you to work out a way of meeting you."

"You didn't even look at me."

"I hardly had the chance."

"Then how would you have met me?"

"Some way. I don't know how. But you'll admit this is a rather foolish argument we're having."

They were leaving Providence. Livvy felt a trouble in her mind. The little man had been following their whispered conversation, with only the loss of his smile to show that he understood. She said to him, "Can you show us more?"

Norman interrupted, "Wait now, Livvy. What are you going to try to do?"

She said, "I want to see our wedding day. What it would have been if I had caught the strap."

Norman was visibly annoyed. "Now, that's not fair. We might not have been married on the same day, you know."

But she said, "Can you show it to me, Mr. If?" And the little man nodded.

The slab of glass was coming alive again, glowing a little. Then the light collected and condensed into figures. A tiny sound of organ music was in Livvy's ears without there actually being sound.

Norman said with relief, "Well, there I am. That's our wedding. Are you satisfied?"

The train sounds were disappearing again, and the last thing Livvy heard was her own voice saying, "Yes, there *you* are. But where am *I*?"

Livvy was well back in the pews. For a while she had not expected to attend at all. In the past months she had drifted further and further away from Georgette, without quite knowing why. She had heard of her engagement only through a mutual friend, and, of course, it was to Norman. She remembered very clearly that day, six months before, when she had first seen him on the streetcar. It was the time Georgette had so quickly snatched her out of sight. She had met him since on several occasions, but each time Georgette was with him, standing between.

Well, she had no cause for resentment; the man was certainly none of hers. Georgette, she thought, looked more beautiful than she really was. And *he* was very handsome indeed.

She felt sad and rather empty, as though something had gone wrong—something that she could not quite outline in her mind. Georgette had moved up the aisle without seeming to see her, but earlier she had caught *his* eyes and smiled at him. Livvy thought he had smiled in return.

She heard the words distantly as they drifted back to her, "I now pronounce you—"

The noise of the train was back. A woman swayed down the aisle, herding a little boy back to their seats. There were intermittent bursts of girlish laughter from a set of four teenage girls halfway down the coach. A conductor hurried past on some mysterious errand.

Livvy was frozenly aware of it all.

She sat there, staring straight ahead, while the trees outside blended into a fuzzy, furious green and the telephone poles galloped past.

She said, "It was *she* you married."

He stared at her for a moment and then one side of his mouth quirked a little. He said lightly, "I didn't really, Olivia. You're still my wife, you know. Just think about it for a few minutes."

She turned to him. "Yes, you married me—because I fell in your lap. If I hadn't, you would have married Georgette. If she hadn't wanted you, you would have married someone else. You would have married *anybody.* So much for your jigsaw-puzzle pieces."

Norman said very slowly, "Well—I'll—be—darned!" He put both hands to his head and smoothed down the straight hair over his ears where it had a tendency to tuft up. For the moment it gave him the appearance of trying to hold his head together. He said, "Now, look here, Livvy, you're making a silly fuss over a stupid magician's trick. You can't blame me for something I haven't done."

"You would have done it."

"How do you know?"

"You've seen it."

"I've seen a ridiculous piece of—of hypnotism, I suppose." His voice suddenly raised itself into anger. He turned to the little man opposite. "Off with you, Mr. If, or whatever your name is. Get out of here. We don't want you. Get out before I throw your little trick out the window and you after it."

Livvy yanked at his elbow. "Stop it. *Stop it!* You're in a crowded train."

The little man shrank back into the corner of the seat as far as he could go and held his little black bag behind him. Norman looked at him, then at Livvy, then at the elderly lady across the way who was regarding him with patent disapproval.

He turned pink and bit back a pungent remark. They rode in frozen silence to and through New London.

Fifteen minutes past New London, Norman said, "Livvy!"

She said nothing. She was looking out the window but saw nothing but the glass.

He said again, "Livvy! Livvy! Answer me!"

She said dully, "What do you want?"

He said, "Look, this is all nonsense. I don't know how the fellow does it, but even granting it's legitimate, you're not being fair. Why stop where you did? Suppose I *had* married Georgette, do you suppose *you* would have stayed single? For all I know, you were already married at the time of my supposed wedding. Maybe that's why I married Georgette."

"I wasn't married."

"How do you know?"

"I would have been able to tell. I knew what my own thoughts were."

"Then you would have been married within the next year."

Livvy grew angrier. The fact that a sane remnant within her clamored at the unreason of her anger did not soothe her. It irritated her further, instead. She said, "And if I did, it would be no business of yours, certainly."

"Of course it wouldn't. But it would make the point that in the world of reality we can't be held responsible for the 'what ifs.' "

Livvy's nostrils flared. She said nothing.

Norman said, "Look! You remember the big New Year's celebration at Winnie's place year before last?"

"I certainly do. You spilled a keg of alcohol all over me."

"That's beside the point, and besides, it was only a cocktail shaker's worth. What I'm trying to say is that Winnie is just about your best friend and had been long before you married me."

"What of it?"

"Georgette was a good friend of hers too, wasn't she?"

"Yes."

"All right, then. You and Georgette would have gone to the party regardless of which one of you I had married. I would have had nothing to do with it. Let him show us the party as it would have been if I had married Georgette, and I'll bet you'd be there with either your fiancé or your husband."

Livvy hesitated. She felt honestly afraid of just that.

He said, "Are you afraid to take the chance?"

And that, of course, decided her. She turned on him

furiously. "No, I'm not! And I hope I *am* married. There's no reason I should pine for you. What's more, I'd like to see what happens when you spill the shaker all over Georgette. She'll fill both your ears for you, and in public, too. I know *her.* Maybe you'll see a certain difference in the jigsaw pieces then." She faced forward and crossed her arms angrily and firmly across her chest.

Norman looked across at the little man, but there was no need to say anything. The glass slab was on his lap already. The sun slanted in from the west, and the white foam of hair that topped his head was edged with pink.

Norman said tensely, "Ready?"

Livvy nodded and let the noise of the train slide away again.

Livvy stood, a little flushed with recent cold, in the doorway. She had just removed her coat, with its sprinkling of snow, and her bare arms were still rebelling at the touch of open air.

She answered the shouts that greeted her with "Happy New Years" of her own, raising her voice to make herself heard over the squealing of the radio. Georgette's shrill tones were almost the first thing she heard upon entering, and now she steered toward her. She hadn't seen Georgette, or Norman, in weeks.

Georgette lifted an eyebrow, a mannerism she had lately cultivated, and said, "Isn't anyone with you, Olivia?" Her eyes swept the immediate surroundings and then returned to Livvy.

Livvy said indifferently, "I think Dick will be around later. There was something or other he had to do first." She felt as indifferent as she sounded.

Georgette smiled tightly. "Well, Norman's here. That ought to keep you from being lonely, dear. At least, it's turned out that way before."

And as she said so, Norman sauntered in from the kitchen. He had a cocktail shaker in his hand, and the rattling of ice cubes castanetted his words. "Line up, you rioting revelers, and get a mixture that will really revel your riots—Why, Livvy!"

He walked toward her, grinning his welcome, "Where've you been keeping yourself? I haven't seen you in twenty years, seems like. What's the matter? Doesn't Dick want anyone else to see you?"

"Fill my glass, Norman," said Georgette sharply.

"Right away," he said, not looking at her. "Do you want one too, Livvy? I'll get you a glass." He turned, and everything happened at once.

Livvy cried, "Watch out!" She saw it coming, even had a vague feeling that all this had happened before, but it played itself out inexorably. His heel caught the edge of the carpet; he lurched, tried to right himself, and lost the cocktail shaker. It seemed to jump out of his hands, and a pint of ice-cold liquor drenched Livvy from shoulder to hem.

She stood there, gasping. The noises muted about her, and for a few intolerable moments she made futile brushing gestures at her gown, while Norman kept repeating, "Damnation!" in rising tones.

Georgette said coolly, "It's too bad, Livvy. Just one of those things. I imagine the dress can't be very expensive."

Livvy turned and ran. She was in the bedroom, which was at least empty and relatively quiet. By the light of the fringe-shaded lamp on the dresser, she poked among the coats on the bed, looking for her own.

Norman had come in behind her. "Look, Livvy, don't pay any attention to what she said. I'm really devilishly sorry. I'll pay—"

"That's all right. It wasn't your fault." She blinked rapidly and didn't look at him. "I'll just go home and change."

"Are you coming back?"

"I don't know. I don't think so."

"Look, Livvy . . ." His warm fingers were on her shoulders—

Livvy felt a queer tearing sensation deep inside her, as though she were ripping away from clinging cobwebs and—

—and the train noises were back.

Something *did* go wrong with the time when she was in

there—in the slab. It was deep twilight now. The train lights were on. But it didn't matter. She seemed to be recovering from the wrench inside her.

Norman was rubbing his eyes with thumb and forefinger. "What happened?"

Livvy said, "It just ended. Suddenly."

Norman said uneasily, "You know, we'll be putting into New Haven soon." He looked at his watch and shook his head.

Livvy said wonderingly, "You spilled it on me."

"Well, so I did in real life."

"But in real life I was your wife. You ought to have spilled it on Georgette this time. Isn't that queer?" But she was thinking of Norman pursuing her; his hands on her shoulders. . . .

She looked up at him and said with warm satisfaction, "I wasn't married."

"No, you weren't. But was that Dick Reinhardt you were going around with?"

"Yes."

"You weren't planning to marry him, were you, Livvy?"

"Jealous, Norman?"

Norman looked confused. "Of that? Of a slab of glass? Of course not."

"I don't think I would have married him."

Norman said, "You know, I wish it hadn't ended when it did. There was something that was about to happen, I think." He stopped, then added slowly, "It was as though I would rather have done it to anybody else in the room."

"Even to Georgette."

"I wasn't giving two thoughts to Georgette. You don't believe me, I suppose."

"Maybe I do." She looked up at him. "I've been silly, Norman. Let's—let's live our real life. Let's not play with all the things that just might have been."

But he caught her hands. "No, Livvy. One last time. Let's see what we would have been doing right now, Livvy! This very minute! If I had married Georgette."

Livvy was a little frightened. "Let's not, Norman." She was thinking of his eyes, smiling hungrily at her as he held the shaker, while Georgette stood beside her, unregarded. She didn't *want* to know what happened afterward. She just wanted this life now, this *good* life.

New Haven came and went.

Norman said again, "I want to try, Livvy."

She said, "If you want to, Norman." She decided fiercely that it wouldn't matter. Nothing would matter. Her hands reached out and encircled his arm. She held it tightly, and while she held it she thought: "Nothing in the make-believe can take him from me."

Norman said to the little man, "Set 'em up again."

In the yellow light the process seemed to be slower. Gently the frosted slab cleared, like clouds being torn apart and dispersed by an unfelt wind.

Norman was saying, "There's something wrong. That's just the two of us, exactly as we are now."

He was right. Two little figures were sitting in a train on the seats which were farthest toward the front. The field was enlarging now—they were merging into it. Norman's voice was distant and fading.

"It's the same train," he was saying. "The window in back is cracked just as—"

Livvy was blindingly happy. She said, "I wish we were in New York."

He said, "It will be less than an hour, darling." Then he said, "I'm going to kiss you." He made a movement, as though he were about to begin.

"Not here! Oh, Norman, people are looking."

Norman drew back. He said, "We should have taken a taxi."

"From Boston to New York?"

"Sure. The privacy would have been worth it."

She laughed. "You're funny when you try to act ardent."

"It isn't an act." His voice was suddenly a little somber. "It's not just an hour, you know. I feel as though I've been waiting five years."

"I do, too."

"Why couldn't I have met you first? It was such a waste."

"Poor Georgette," Livvy sighed.

Norman moved impatiently. "Don't be sorry for her, Livvy. We never really made a go of it. She was glad to get rid of me."

"I know that. That's why I say 'Poor Georgette.' I'm just sorry for her for not being able to appreciate what she had."

"Well, see to it that *you* do," he said. "See to it that you're immensely appreciative, infinitely appreciative—or more than that, see that you're at least half as appreciative as I am of what *I've* got."

"Or else you'll divorce me, too?"

"Over my dead body," said Norman.

Livvy said, "It's all so strange. I keep thinking; 'What if you hadn't spilt the cocktails on me that time at the party?' You wouldn't have followed me out; you wouldn't have told me; I wouldn't have known. It would have been so different . . . everything."

"Nonsense. It would have been just the same. It would have all happened another time."

"I wonder," said Livvy softly.

Train noises merged into train noises. City lights flickered outside, and the atmosphere of New York was about them. The coach was astir with travelers dividing the baggage among themselves.

Livvy was an island in the turmoil until Norman shook her.

She looked at him and said, "The jigsaw pieces fit after all."

He said, "Yes."

She put a hand on his. "But it wasn't good, just the same. I was very wrong. I thought that because we had each other, we should have all the *possible* each others. But all the possibles are none of our business. The real is enough. Do you know what I mean?"

He nodded.

She said, "There are millions of other *what ifs.* I don't want to know what happened in any of them. I'll never say 'What if' again."

Norman said, "Relax, dear. Here's your coat." And he reached for the suitcases.

Livvy said with sudden sharpness, "Where's Mr. If?"

Norman turned slowly to the empty seat that faced them. Together they scanned the rest of the coach.

"Maybe," Norman said, "he went into the next coach."

"But why? Besides, he wouldn't leave his hat." And she bent to pick it up.

Norman said, "What hat?"

And Livvy stopped her fingers hovering over nothingness. She said, "It was here—I almost touched it." She straightened and said, "Oh, Norman, what if—"

Norman put a finger on her mouth. "Darling . . ."

She said, "I'm sorry. Here, let me help you with the suitcases."

The train dived into the tunnel beneath Park Avenue, and the noise of the wheels rose to a roar.

RAY BRADBURY

a sound
of
thunder

The sign on the wall seemed to quaver under a film of sliding warm water. Eckels felt his eyelids blink over his stare, and the sign burned in this momentary darkness:

TIME SAFARI, INC.
SAFARIS TO ANY YEAR IN THE PAST.
YOU NAME THE ANIMAL.
WE TAKE YOU THERE.
YOU SHOOT IT.

A warm phlegm gathered in Eckels' throat; he swallowed and pushed it down. The muscles around his mouth formed a smile as he put his hand slowly out upon the air, and in that hand waved a check for ten thousand dollars to the man behind the desk.

"Does this safari guarantee I come back alive?"

"We guarantee nothing," said the official, "except the dinosaurs." He turned. "This is Mr. Travis, your Safari Guide in the Past. He'll tell you what and where to shoot. If he says no shooting, no shooting. If you disobey instructions, there's a stiff penalty of another ten thousand dollars, plus possible government action, on your return."

Eckels glanced across the vast office at a mass and tangle, a snaking and humming of wires and steel boxes, at an aurora that flickered now orange, now silver, now blue. There was a sound like a gigantic bonfire burning all of Time, all the years and all the parchment calendars, all the hours piled high and set aflame.

A touch of the hand and this burning would, on the instant, beautifully reverse itself. Eckels remembered the wording in the advertisements to the letter. Out of chars and ashes, out of dust and coals, like golden salamanders, the old years, the green years, might leap; roses sweeten the air, white hair turn Irish-black, wrinkles vanish; all, everything fly back to seed, flee death, rush down to their beginnings, suns rise in western skies and set in glorious easts, moons eat themselves opposite to the custom, all and everything cupping one in another like Chinese boxes, rabbits in hats, all and everything returning to the fresh death, the seed death, the green death, to the time before the beginning. A touch of a hand might do it, the merest touch of a hand.

"Hell and damn," Eckels breathed, the light of the Machine on his thin face. "A real Time Machine." He shook his head. "Makes you think. If the election had gone badly yesterday, I might be here now running away from the results. Thank God Keith won. He'll make a fine President of the United States."

"Yes," said the man behind the desk: "We're lucky. If Deutscher had gotten in, we'd have the worst kind of dictatorship. There's an anti-everything man for you, a militarist, anti-Christ, anti-human, anti-intellectual. People called us up, you know, joking but not joking. Said if Deutscher became President they wanted to go live in 1492. Of course it's not our business to conduct Escapes, but to form Safaris. Anyway, Keith's President now. All you got to worry about is—"

"Shooting my dinosaur," Eckels finished it for him.

"A *Tyrannosaurus rex.* The Thunder Lizard, the damnedest monster in history. Sign this release. Anything happens to you, we're not responsible. Those dinosaurs are hungry."

Eckels flushed angrily. "Trying to scare me!"

"Frankly, yes. We don't want anyone going who'll panic at the first shot. Six Safari leaders were killed last year, and a dozen hunters. We're here to give you the damnedest thrill a *real* hunter ever asked for. Traveling you back sixty million years to bag the biggest damned game in all Time. Your personal check's still there. Tear it up.''

Mr. Eckels looked at the check for a long time. His fingers twitched.

"Good luck," said the man behind the desk. "Mr. Travis, he's all yours."

They moved silently across the room, taking their guns with them, toward the Machine, toward the silver metal and the roaring light.

First a day and then a night and then a day and then a night, then it was day-night-day-night-day. A week, a month, a year, a decade! A.D. 2055. A.D. 2019. 1999! 1957! Gone! The Machine roared.

They put on their oxygen helmets and tested the intercoms.

Eckels swayed on the padded seat, his face pale, his jaws stiff. He felt the trembling in his arms and he looked down and found his hands tight on the new rifle. There were four other men in the Machine. Travis, the Safari Leader, his assistant, Lesperance, and two other hunters, Billings and Kramer. They sat looking at each other, and the years blazed around them.

"Can these guns get a dinosaur cold?" Eckels felt his mouth saying.

"If you hit them right," said Travis on the helmet radio. "Some dinosaurs have two brains, one in the head, another far down the spinal column. We stay away from those. That's stretching luck. Put your first two shots into the eyes, if you can, blind them, and go back into the brain."

The Machine howled. Time was a film run backward. Suns fled and ten million moons fled after them. "Good God," said Eckels. "Every hunter that ever lived would envy us today. This makes Africa seem like Illinois."

The Machine slowed; its scream fell to a murmur. The Machine stopped.

The sun stopped in the sky.

The fog that had enveloped the Machine blew away and they were in an old time, a very old time indeed, three hunters and two Safari Heads with their blue metal guns across their knees.

"Christ isn't born yet," said Travis. "Moses has not gone to the mountain to talk with God. The Pyramids are still in the earth, waiting to be cut out and put up. *Remember* that, Alexander, Caesar, Napoleon, Hitler—none of them exists."

The men nodded.

"That"—Mr. Travis pointed—"is the jungle of sixty million two thousand and fifty-five years before President Keith."

He indicated a metal path that struck off into green wilderness, over steaming swamp, among giant ferns and palms.

"And that," he said, "is the Path, laid by Time Safari for your use. It floats six inches above the earth. Doesn't touch so much as one grass blade, flower, or tree. It's an antigravity metal. Its purpose is to keep you from touching this world of the past in any way. Stay on the Path. Don't go off it. I repeat. *Don't go off.* For *any* reason! If you fall off, there's a penalty. And don't shoot any animal we don't okay."

"Why?" asked Eckels.

They sat in the ancient wilderness. Far birds' cries blew on a wind, and the smell of tar and an old salt sea, moist grasses, and flowers the color of blood.

"We don't want to change the Future. We don't belong here in the Past. The government doesn't *like* us here. We have to pay big graft to keep our franchise. A Time Machine is damn finicky business. Not knowing it, we might kill an important animal, a small bird, a roach, a flower even, thus destroying an important link in a growing species."

"That's not clear," said Eckels.

"All right," Travis continued, "say we accidentally kill one mouse here. That means all the future families of this one particular mouse are destroyed, right?"

"Right."

"And all the families of the families of that one mouse! With a stamp of your foot, you annihilate first one, then a dozen, then a thousand, a million, a *billion* possible mice!"

"So they're dead," said Eckels. "So what?"

"So what?" Travis snorted quietly. "Well, what about the

foxes that'll need those mice to survive? For want of ten mice, a fox dies. For want of ten foxes, a lion starves. For want of a lion, all manner of insects, vultures, infinite billions of life forms are thrown into chaos and destruction. Eventually it all boils down to this: fifty-nine million years later, a cave man, one of a dozen on the *entire* world, goes hunting wild boar or saber-tooth tiger for food. But you, friend, have *stepped* on all the tigers in that region. By stepping on *one* single mouse. So the cave man starves. And the cave man, please note, is not just *any* expendable man, no! He is an *entire future nation.* From his loins would have sprung ten sons. From *their* loins one hundred sons, and thus onward to a civilization. Destroy this one man, and you destroy a race, a people, an entire history of life. It is comparable to slaying some of Adam's grandchildren. The stomp of your foot, on one mouse, could start an earthquake, the effects of which could shake our earth and destinies down through Time, to their very foundations. With the death of that one cave man, a billion others yet unborn are throttled in the womb. Perhaps Rome never rises on its seven hills. Perhaps Europe is forever a dark forest, and only Asia waxes healthy and teeming. Step on a mouse and you crush the Pyramids. Step on a mouse and you leave your print, like a Grand Canyon, across Eternity. Queen Elizabeth might never be born, Washington might not cross the Delaware, there might never be a United States at all. So be careful. Stay on the Path. *Never* step off!"

"I see," said Eckels. "Then it wouldn't pay for us even to touch the *grass?*"

"Correct. Crushing certain plants could add up infinitesimally. A little error here would multiply in sixty million years, all out of proportion. Of course maybe our theory is wrong. Maybe Time *can't* be changed by us. Or maybe it can be changed only in little subtle ways. A dead mouse here makes an insect imbalance there, a population disproportion later, a bad harvest further on, a depression, mass starvation, and, finally, a change in *social* temperament in far-flung countries. Something much more subtle, like that. Perhaps only a soft breath, a whisper, a hair, pollen on the air, such a slight, slight change that unless you looked close you wouldn't see it. Who knows? Who really can say he knows? We don't know. We're guessing. But until we do know for certain whether our messing around in Time *can* make a big roar or a little rustle in history, we're being damned careful. This Machine, this Path, your clothing and bodies, were sterilized, as you know, before the journey. We wear these oxygen helmets so we can't introduce our bacteria into an ancient atmosphere."

"How do we know which animals to shoot?"

"They're marked with red paint," said Travis. "Today, before our journey, we sent Lesperance here back with the Machine. He came to this particular era and followed certain animals."

"Studying them?"

"Right," said Lesperance. "I track them through their entire existence, noting which of them lives longest. Very few. How many times they mate. Not often. Life's short. When I find one that's going to die when a tree falls on him, or one that drowns in a tar pit, I note the exact hour, minute, and second. I shoot a paint bomb. It leaves a red patch on his hide. We can't miss it. Then I correlate our arrival in the Past so that we meet the Monster not more than two minutes before he would have died anyway. This way, we kill only animals with no future, that are never going to mate again. You see how *careful* we are?"

"But if you came back this morning in Time," said Eckels eagerly, "you must've bumped into *us,* our Safari! How did it turn out? Was it successful? Did all of us get through—alive?"

Travis and Lesperance gave each other a look.

"That'd be a paradox," said the latter. "Time doesn't permit that sort of mess—a man meeting himself. When such occasions threaten, Time steps aside. Like an airplane hitting an air pocket. You felt the Machine jump just before we stopped? That was us passing ourselves on the way back to the Future. We saw nothing. There's no way of telling *if* this expedition was a success, *if* we got our monster, or whether all of us—meaning *you,* Mr. Eckels—got out alive."

Eckels smiled palely.

"Cut that," said Travis sharply. "Everyone on his feet!"

They were ready to leave the Machine.

The jungle was high and the jungle was broad and the jungle was the entire world forever and forever. Sounds like music and sounds like flying tents filled the sky, and those were pterodactyls soaring with cavernous gray wings, gigantic bats out of a delirium and a night fever. Eckels, balanced on the narrow Path, aimed his rifle playfully.

"Stop that!" said Travis. "Don't even aim for fun, damn it! If your gun should go off—"

Eckels flushed. "Where's our *Tyrannosaurus?*"

Lesperance checked his wrist watch. "Up ahead. We'll bisect his trail in sixty seconds. Look for the red paint, for Christ's sake. Don't shoot till we give the word. Stay on the Path. *Stay on the Path!*"

They moved forward in the wind of morning.

"Strange," murmured Eckels. "Up ahead, sixty million years, Election Day over. Keith made President. Everyone celebrating. And here we are, a million years lost, and they don't exist. The things we worried about for months, a lifetime, not even born or thought about yet."

"Safety catches off, everyone!" ordered Travis. "You, first shot, Eckels. Second, Billings. Third, Kramer."

"I've hunted tiger, wild boar, buffalo, elephant, but Jesus, this is *it*," said Eckels. "I'm shaking like a kid."

"Ah," said Travis.

Everyone stopped.

Travis raised his hand. "Ahead," he whispered. "In the mist. There he is. There's His Royal Majesty now."

The jungle was wide and full of twitterings, rustlings, murmurs, and sighs.

Suddenly it all ceased, as if someone had shut a door.

Silence.

A sound of thunder.

Out of the mist, one hundred yards away, came *Tyrannosaurus rex.*

"Jesus God," whispered Eckels.

"Sh!"

It came on great oiled, resilient, striding legs. It towered thirty feet above half of the trees, a great evil god, folding its delicate watchmaker's claws close to its oily reptilian chest. Each lower leg was a piston, a thousand pounds of white bone, sunk in thick ropes of muscle, sheathed over in a gleam of pebbled skin like the mail of a terrible warrior. Each thigh was a ton of meat, ivory, and steel mesh. And from the great breathing cage of the upper body those two delicate arms dangled out front, arms with hands which might pick up and examine men like toys, while the snake neck coiled. And the head itself, a ton of sculptured stone, lifted easily upon the sky. Its mouth gaped, exposing a fence of teeth like daggers. Its eyes rolled, ostrich eggs, empty of all expression save hunger. It closed its mouth in a death grin. It ran, its pelvic bones crushing aside trees and bushes, its taloned feet clawing damp earth, leaving prints six inches deep wherever it settled its weight. It ran with a gliding ballet step, far too poised and balanced for its ten tons. It moved into a sunlit arena warily, its beautiful reptile hands feeling the air.

"My God!" Eckels twitched his mouth. "It could reach up and grab the moon."

"Sh!" Travis jerked angrily. "He hasn't seen us yet."

"It can't be killed." Eckels pronounced this verdict quietly, as if there could be no argument. He had weighed the evidence and this was his considered opinion. The rifle in his hands seemed a cap gun. "We were fools to come. This is impossible."

"Shut up!" hissed Travis.

"Nightmare."

"Turn around," commanded Travis. "Walk quietly to the Machine. We'll remit one-half your fee."

"I didn't realize it would be this *big*," said Eckels. "I miscalculated, that's all. And now I want out."

"It sees us!"

"There's the red paint on its chest!"

The Thunder Lizard raised itself. Its armored flesh glittered like a thousand green coins. The coins, crusted with slime, steamed. In the slime, tiny insects wriggled, so that the entire body seemed to twitch and undulate, even while the monster itself did not move. It exhaled. The stink of raw flesh blew down the wilderness.

"Get me out of here," said Eckels. "It was never like this

before. I was always sure I'd come through alive. I had good guides, good safaris, and safety. This time, I figured wrong. I've met my match and admit it. This is too much for me to get hold of."

"Don't run," said Lesperance. "Turn around. Hide in the Machine."

"Yes." Eckels seemed to be numb. He looked at his feet as if trying to make them move. He gave a grunt of helplessness.

"Eckels!"

He took a few steps, blinking, shuffling.

"Not *that* way!"

The Monster, at the first motion, lunged forward with a terrible scream. It covered one hundred yards in four seconds. The rifles jerked up and blazed fire. A windstorm from the beast's mouth engulfed them in the stench of slime and old blood. The Monster roared, teeth glittering with sun.

Eckels, not looking back, walked blindly to the edge of the Path, his gun limp in his arms, stepped off the Path, and walked, not knowing it, in the jungle. His feet sank into green moss. His legs moved him, and he felt alone and remote from the events behind.

The rifles cracked again. Their sound was lost in shriek and lizard thunder. The great lever of the reptile's tail swung up, lashed sideways. Trees exploded in clouds of leaf and branch. The Monster twitched its jeweler's hands down to fondle at the men, to twist them in half, to crush them like berries, to cram them into its teeth and its screaming throat. Its boulder-stone eyes leveled with the men. They saw themselves mirrored. They fired at the metallic eyelids and the blazing black iris.

Like a stone idol, like a mountain avalanche, *Tyrannosaurus* fell. Thundering, it clutched trees, pulled them with it. It wrenched and tore the metal Path. The men flung themselves back and away. The body hit, ten tons of cold flesh and stone. The guns fired. The Monster lashed its armored tail, twitched its snake jaws, and lay still. A fount of blood spurted from its throat. Somewhere inside, a sac of fluids burst. Sickening gushes drenched the hunters. They stood, red and glistening.

The thunder faded.

The jungle was silent. After the avalanche, a green peace. After the nightmare, morning.

Billings and Kramer sat on the pathway and threw up. Travis and Lesperance stood with smoking rifles, cursing steadily.

In the Time Machine, on his face, Eckels lay shivering. He had found his way back to the Path, climbed into the Machine.

Travis came walking, glanced at Eckels, took cotton gauze from a metal box, and returned to the others, who were sitting on the Path.

"Clean up."

They wiped the blood from their helmets. They began to curse too. The Monster lay, a hill of solid flesh. Within, you could hear the sighs and murmurs as the furthest chambers of it died, the organs malfunctioning, liquids running a final instant from pocket to sac to spleen, everything shutting off, closing up forever. It was like standing by a wrecked locomotive or a steam shovel at quitting time, all valves being released or levered tight. Bones cracked; the tonnage of its own flesh, off balance, dead weight, snapped the delicate forearms, caught underneath. The meat settled, quivering.

Another cracking sound. Overhead, a gigantic tree branch broke from its heavy mooring, fell. It crashed upon the dead beast with finality.

"There." Lesperance checked his watch. "Right on time. That's the giant tree that was scheduled to fall and kill this animal originally." He glanced at the two hunters. "You want the trophy picture?"

"What?"

"We can't take a trophy back to the Future. The body has to stay right here where it would have died originally, so the insects, birds, and bacteria can get at it, as they were intended to. Everything in balance. The body stays. But we *can* take a picture of you standing near it."

The two men tried to think, but gave up, shaking their heads.

They let themselves be led along the metal Path. They sank wearily into the Machine cushions. They gazed back at the ruined Monster, the stagnating mound, where already strange reptilian birds and golden insects were busy at the steaming armor.

A sound on the floor of the Time Machine stiffened them. Eckels sat there, shivering.

"I'm sorry," he said at last.

"Get up!" cried Travis.

Eckels got up.

"Go out on that Path alone," said Travis. He had his rifle pointed. "You're not coming back in the Machine. We're leaving you here!"

Lesperance seized Travis' arm. "Wait—"

"Stay out of this!" Travis shook his hand away. "This son of a bitch nearly killed us. But it isn't *that* so much. Hell, no. It's his *shoes!* Look at them! He ran off the Path. My God, that *ruins* us! Christ knows how much we'll forfeit. Tens of thousands of dollars of insurance! We guarantee no one leaves the Path. He left it. Oh, the damn fool! I'll have to report to the government. They might revoke our license to travel. God knows *what* he's done to Time, to History!"

"Take it easy, all he did was kick up some dirt."

"How do we *know?*" cried Travis. "We don't know anything! It's all a damn mystery! Get out there, Eckels!"

Eckels fumbled his shirt. "I'll pay anything. A hundred thousand dollars!"

Travis glared at Eckels' checkbook and spat. "Go out there. The Monster's next to the Path. Stick your arms up to your elbows in his mouth. Then you can come back with us."

"That's unreasonable!"

"The Monster's dead, you yellow bastard. The bullets! The bullets can't be left behind. They don't belong in the Past; they might change something. Here's my knife. Dig them out!"

The jungle was alive again, full of the old tremorings and bird cries. Eckels turned slowly to regard that primeval garbage dump, that hill of nightmares and terror. After a long time, like a sleepwalker, he shuffled out along the Path.

He returned, shuddering, five minutes later, his arms soaked and red to the elbows. He held out his hands. Each held a number of steel bullets. Then he fell. He lay where he fell, not moving.

"You didn't have to make him do that," said Lesperance.

"Didn't I? It's too early to tell." Travis nudged the still body. "He'll live. Next time he won't go hunting game like this. Okay." He jerked his thumb wearily at Lesperance. "Switch on. Let's go home."

1492.   1776.   1812.

They cleaned their hands and faces. They changed their caking shirts and pants. Eckels was up and around again, not speaking. Travis glared at him for a full ten minutes.

"Don't look at me," cried Eckels. "I haven't done anything."

"Who can tell?"

"Just ran off the Path, that's all, a little mud on my shoes—what do you want me to do—get down and pray?"

"We might need it. I'm warning you, Eckels, I might kill you yet. I've got my gun ready."

"I'm innocent. I've done nothing!"

1999.   2000.   2055.

The Machine stopped.

"Get out," said Travis.

The room was there as they had left it. But not the same as they had left it. The same man sat behind the same desk. But the same man did not quite sit behind the same desk.

Travis looked around swiftly. "Everything okay here?" he snapped.

"Fine. Welcome home!"

Travis did not relax. He seemed to be looking at the very atoms of the air itself, at the way the sun poured through the one high window.

"Okay, Eckels, get out. Don't ever come back."

Eckels could not move.

"You heard me," said Travis. "What're you *staring* at?"

Eckels stood smelling of the air, and there was a thing to the air, a chemical taint so subtle, so slight, that only a faint cry of his subliminal senses warned him it was there. The colors, white, gray, blue, orange, in the wall, in the furniture, in the sky beyond the window, were . . . were . . . And there was a *feel*. His flesh twitched. His hands twitched. He stood drinking the oddness with the pores of his body. Somewhere, someone must have been screaming one of those whistles that only a dog can hear. His body screamed silence in return. Beyond this room, beyond this wall, beyond this man who was not quite the same man seated at this desk that was not quite the same desk . . . lay an entire world of streets and people. What sort of world it was now, there was no telling. He could feel them moving there, beyond the walls, almost, like so many chess pieces blown in a dry wind. . . .

But the immediate thing was the sign painted on the office wall, the same sign he had read earlier today on first entering. Somehow, the sign had changed:

TYME SEFARI INC.
SEFARIS TU ANY YEER EN THE PAST.
YU NAIM THE ANIMALL.
WEE TAEK YOU THAIR.
YU SHOOT ITT.

Eckels felt himself fall into a chair. He fumbled crazily at the thick slime on his boots. He held up a clod of dirt trembling. "No, it *can't* be. Not a *little* thing like that. No!"

Embedded in the mud, glistening green and gold and black, was a butterfly, very beautiful, and very dead.

"Not a little thing like *that!* Not a butterfly!" cried Eckels.

It fell to the floor, an exquisite thing, a small thing that could upset balances and knock down a line of small dominoes and then big dominoes and then gigantic dominoes, all down the years across Time. Eckels' mind whirled. It *couldn't* change things. Killing one butterfly couldn't be *that* important! Could it?

His face was cold. His mouth trembled, asking: "Who— who won the presidential election yesterday?"

The man behind the desk laughed. "You joking? You know damn well. Deutscher, of course! Who else? Not that damn weakling Keith. We got an iron man now, a man with guts, by God!" The official stopped. "What's wrong?"

Eckels moaned. He dropped to his knees. He scrabbled at the golden butterfly with shaking fingers. "Can't we," he pleaded to the world, to himself, to the officials, to the Machine, "can't we take it *back,* can't we *make* it alive again? Can't we start over? Can't we—"

He did not move. Eyes shut, he waited, shivering. He heard Travis breathe loud in the room; he heard Travis shift his rifle, click the safety catch, and raise the weapon.

There was a sound of thunder.

ROBERT A. HEINLEIN

life-line

The chairman rapped loudly for order. Gradually the catcalls and boos died away as several self-appointed sergeants at arms persuaded a few hot-headed individuals to sit down. The speaker on the rostrum by the chairman seemed unaware of the disturbance. His bland, faintly insolent face was impassive. The chairman turned to the speaker and addressed him in a voice in which anger and annoyance were barely restrained.

"Dr. Pinero"—the "Doctor" was faintly stressed—"I must apologize to you for the unseemly outburst during your remarks. I am surprised that my colleagues should so far forget the dignity proper to men of science as to interrupt a speaker, no matter"—he paused and set his mouth—"no matter how great the provocation." Pinero smiled in his face, a smile that was in some way an open insult. The chairman visibly controlled his temper and continued: "I am anxious that the program be concluded decently and in order. I want you to finish your remarks. Nevertheless, I must ask you to refrain from affronting our intelligence with ideas that any educated man knows to be fallacious. Please confine yourself to your discovery—if you have made one."

Pinero spread his fat, white hands, palms down. "How can I possibly put a new idea into your heads, if I do not first remove your delusions?"

Reprinted from Robert A. Heinlein, *Astounding Science Fiction* (New York: Street & Smith, 1939) with the permission of the author's agent, Lurton Blassingame. Copyright © 1939 by Street & Smith Publications, Inc.

The audience stirred and muttered. Someone shouted from the rear of the hall: "Throw the charlatan out! We've had enough."

The chairman pounded his gavel.

"Gentlemen! Please!"

Then to Pinero, "Must I remind you that you are not a member of this body, and that we did not invite you?"

Pinero's eyebrows lifted. "So? I seem to remember an invitation on the letterhead of the Academy."

The chairman chewed his lower lip before replying. "True. I wrote that invitation myself. But it was at the request of one of the trustees—a fine, public-spirited gentleman, but not a scientist, not a member of the Academy."

Pinero smiled his irritating smile. "So? I should have guessed. Old Bidwell, not so, of Amalgamated Life Insurance? And he wanted his trained seals to expose me as a fraud, yes? For if I can tell a man the day of his own death, no one will buy his pretty policies. But how can you expose me, if you will not listen to me first? Even supposing you had the wit to understand me? Bah! He has sent jackals to tear down a lion." He deliberately turned his back on them.

The muttering of the crowd swelled and took on a vicious tone. The chairman cried vainly for order. There arose a figure in the front row.

"Mr. Chairman!"

The chairman grasped the opening and shouted: "Gentlemen! Dr. van Rhein Smitt has the floor." The commotion died away.

The doctor cleared his throat, smoothed the forelock of his beautiful white hair, and thrust one hand into a side pocket of his smartly tailored trousers. He assumed his women's-club manner.

"Mr. Chairman, fellow members of the Academy of Science, let us have tolerance. Even a murderer has the right to say his say before the State exacts its tribute. Shall we do less? Even though one may be intellectually certain of the verdict? I grant Dr. Pinero every consideration that should be given by this august body to any unaffiliated colleague, even though"—

he bowed slightly in Pinero's direction—"we may not be familiar with the university which bestowed his degree. If what he has to say is false, it cannot harm us. If what he has to say is true, we should know it." His mellow, cultivated voice rolled on, soothing and calming. "If the eminent doctor's manner appears a trifle inurbane of our tastes, we must bear in mind that the doctor may be from a place, or a stratum, not so meticulous in these matters. Now our good friend and benefactor has asked us to hear this person and carefully assess the merit of his claims. Let us do so with dignity and decorum."

He sat down to a rumble of applause, comfortably aware that he had enhanced his reputation as an intellectual leader. Tomorrow the papers would again mention the good sense and persuasive personality of "America's Handsomest University President." Who knows; maybe now old Bidwell would come through with that swimming-pool donation.

When the applause had ceased, the chairman turned to where the center of the disturbance sat, hands folded over his little round belly, face serene.

"Will you continue, Dr. Pinero?"

"Why should I?"

The chairman shrugged his shoulders. "You came for that purpose."

Pinero arose. "So true. So very true. But was I wise to come? Is there anyone here who has an open mind, who can stare a bare fact in the face without blushing? I think not. Even that so-beautiful gentleman who asked you to hear me out has already judged me and condemned me. He seeks order, not truth. Suppose truth defies order, will he accept it? Will you? I think not. Still, if I do not speak, you will win your point by default. The little man in the street will think that you little men have exposed me, Pinero, as a hoaxer, a pretender.

"I will repeat my discovery. In simple language, I have invented a technique to tell how long a man will live. I can give you advance billing of the Angel of Death. I can tell you when the Black Camel will kneel at your door. In five minutes' time, with my apparatus, I can tell any of you how many grains of sand are still left in your hour-glass." He paused and folded his arms across his chest. For a moment no one spoke. The audience grew restless.

Finally the chairman intervened, "You aren't finished, Dr. Pinero?"

"What more is there to say?"

"You haven't told us how your discovery works."

Pinero's eyebrows shot up. "You suggest that I should turn over the fruits of my work for children to play with? This is dangerous knowledge, my friend. I keep it for the man who understands it, myself." He tapped his chest.

"How are we to know that you have anything back of your wild claims?"

"So simple. You send a committee to watch me demonstrate. If it works, fine. You admit it and tell the world so. If it does not work, I am discredited, and will apologize. Even I, Pinero, will apologize."

A slender, stoop-shouldered man stood up in the back of the hall. The chair recognized him and he spoke.

"Mr. Chairman, how can the eminent doctor seriously propose such a course? Does he expect us to wait around for twenty or thirty years for someone to die and prove his claims?"

Pinero ignored the chair and answered directly.

"*Pfui!* Such nonsense! Are you so ignorant of statistics that you do not know that in any large group there is at least one who will die in the immediate future? I make you a proposition. Let me test each one of you in this room, and I will name the man who will die within the fortnight, yes, and the day and hour of his death." He glanced fiercely around the room. "Do you accept?"

Another figure got to his feet, a portly man who spoke in measured syllables. "I, for one, cannot countenance such an experiment. As a medical man, I have noted with sorrow the plain marks of serious heart trouble in many of our elder colleagues. If Dr. Pinero knows those symptoms, as he may, and were he to select as his victim one of their number, the man so selected would be likely to die on schedule, whether the distinguished speaker's mechanical egg timer works or not."

Another speaker backed him up at once. "Dr. Shepard is

right. Why should we waste time on voodoo tricks? It is my belief that this person who calls himself *Dr.* Pinero wants to use this body to give his statements authority. If we participate in this farce, we play into his hands. I don't know what his racket is, but you can bet that he has figured out some way to use us for advertising his schemes. I move, Mr. Chairman, that we proceed with our regular business."

The motion carried by acclamation, but Pinero did not sit down. Amidst cries of "Order! Order!" he shook his untidy head at them, and had his say.

"Barbarians! Imbeciles! Stupid dolts! Your kind have blocked the recognition of every great discovery since time began. Such ignorant canaille are enough to start Galileo spinning in his grave. That fat fool down there twiddling his elk's tooth calls himself a medical man. Witch doctor would be a better term! That little bald-headed runt over there—You! You style yourself a philosopher, and prate about life and time in your neat categories. What do you know of either one? How can you ever learn when you won't examine the truth when you have a chance? Bah!" He spat upon the stage. "You call this an Academy of Science. I call it an undertakers' convention, interested only in embalming the ideas of your red-blooded predecessors."

He paused for breath and was grasped on each side by two members of the platform committee and rushed out the wings. Several reporters arose hastily from the press table and followed him. The chairman declared the meeting adjourned.

The newspapermen caught up with Pinero as he was going out by the stage door. He walked with a light, springy step, and whistled a little tune. There was no trace of the belligerence he had shown a moment before. They crowded about him. "How about an interview, doc?" "What d'yuh think of modern education?" "You certainly told 'em. What are your views on life after death?" "Take off your hat, doc, and look at the birdie."

He grinned at them all. "One at a time, boys, and not so fast. I used to be a newspaperman myself. How about coming up to my place?"

A few minutes later they were trying to find places to sit

down in Pinero's messy bed-living room, and lighting his cigars. Pinero looked around and beamed. "What'll it be, boys? Scotch or Bourbon?" When that was taken care of he got down to business. "Now, boys, what do you want to know?"

"Lay it on the line, doc. Have you got something, or haven't you?"

"Most assuredly I have something, my young friend."

"Then tell us how it works. That guff you handed the profs won't get you anywhere now."

"Please, my dear fellow. It is my invention. I expect to make some money with it. Would you have me give it away to the first person who asks for it?"

"See here, doc, you've got to give us something if you expect to get a break in the morning papers. What do you use? A crystal ball?"

"No, not quite. Would you like to see my apparatus?"

"Sure. Now we're getting somewhere."

He ushered them into an adjoining room, and waved his hand. "There it is, boys." The mass of equipment that met their eyes vaguely resembled a medico's office X-ray gear. Beyond the obvious fact that it used electrical power, and that some of the dials were calibrated in familiar terms, a casual inspection gave no clue to its actual use.

"What's the principle, doc?"

Pinero pursed his lips and considered. "No doubt you are all familiar with the truism that life is electrical in nature. Well, that truism isn't worth a damn, but it will help to give you an idea of the principle. You have also been told that time is a fourth dimension. Maybe you believe it, perhaps not. It has been said so many times that it has ceased to have any meaning. It is simply a cliché that windbags use to impress fools. But I want you to try to visualize it now, and try to feel it emotionally."

He stepped up to one of the reporters. "Suppose we take you as an example. Your name is Rogers, is it not? Very well, Rogers, you are a space-time event having duration four ways. You are not quite six feet tall, you are about twenty inches wide and perhaps ten inches thick. In time, there stretches behind you more of this space-time event, reaching to, perhaps, 1905, of which we see a cross section here at right angles to the time axis, and as thick as the present. At the far end is a baby, smelling of sour milk and drooling its breakfast on its bib. At the other end lies, perhaps, an old man some place in the 1980s. Imagine this space-time event, which we call Rogers, as a long pink worm, continuous through the years. It stretches past us here in 1939, and the cross section we see appears as a single, discreet body. But that is illusion. There is physical continuity to this pink worm, enduring through the years. As a matter of fact, there is physical continuity in this concept to the entire race, for these pink worms branch off from other pink worms. In this fashion the race is like a vine whose branches intertwine and send out shoots. Only by taking a cross section of the vine would we fall into the error of believing that the shootlets were discreet individuals."

He paused and looked around at their faces. One of them, a dour, hard-bitten chap, put in a word.

"That's all very pretty, Pinero, if true, but where does that get you?"

Pinero favored him with an unresentful smile. "Patience, my friend. I asked you to think of life as electrical. Now think of our long, pink worm as a conductor of electricity. You have heard, perhaps, of the fact that electrical engineers can, by certain measurements, predict the exact location of a break in a transatlantic cable without ever leaving the shore. I do the same with our pink worms. By applying my instruments to the cross section here in this room I can tell where the break occurs; that is to say, where death takes place. Or, if you like, I can reverse the connections and tell you the date of your birth. But that is uninteresting; you already know it."

The dour individual sneered. "I've caught you, doc. If what you say about the race being like a vine of pink worms is true, you can't tell birthdays, because the connection with the race is continuous at birth. Your electrical conductor reaches on back through the mother into a man's remotest ancestors."

Pinero beamed. "True, and clever, my friend. But you have pushed the analogy too far. It is not done in the precise manner in which one measures the length of an electrical conductor. In some ways it is more like measuring the length of a long corridor by bouncing an echo off the far end. At birth there is a sort of twist in the corridor, and, by proper calibration, I can detect the echo from that twist."

"Let's see you prove it."

"Certainly, my dear friend. Will you be a subject?"

One of the others spoke up. "He's called your bluff, Luke. Put up or shut up."

"I'm game. What do I do?"

"First write the date of your birth on a sheet of paper, and hand it to one of your colleagues."

Luke complied. "Now what?"

"Remove your outer clothing and step upon these scales. Now tell me, were you ever very much thinner, or very much fatter, than you are now? No? What did you weigh at birth? Ten pounds? A fine bouncing baby boy. They don't come so big any more."

"What is all this flubdubbery?"

"I am trying to approximate the average cross section of our long pink conductor, my dear Luke. Now will you seat yourself here? Then place this electrode in your mouth. No, it will not hurt you; the voltage is quite low, less than one micro-volt, but I must have a good connection." The doctor left him and went behind his apparatus, where he lowered a hood over his head before touching his controls. Some of the exposed dials came to life and a low humming came from the machine. It stopped and the doctor popped out of his little hide-away.

"I get sometime in February, 1902. Who has the piece of paper with the date?"

It was produced and unfolded. The custodian read, "February 22, 1902."

The stillness that followed was broken by a voice from the edge of the little group. "Doc, can I have another drink?"

The tension relaxed, and several spoke at once: "Try it on me, doc." "Me first, doc; I'm an orphan and really want to know." "How about it, doc? Give us all a little loose play."

He smilingly complied, ducking in and out of the hood like a gopher from its hole. When they all had twin slips of paper to prove the doctor's skill, Luke broke a long silence.

"How about showing how you predict death, Pinero?"

"If you wish. Who will try it?"

No one answered. Several of them nudged Luke forward. "Go ahead, smart guy. You asked for it." He allowed himself to be seated in the chair. Pinero changed some of the switches, then entered the hood. When the humming ceased he came out, rubbing his hands briskly together.

"Well, that's all there is to see, boys. Got enough for a story?"

"Hey, what about the prediction? When does Luke get his 'thirty'?"

Luke faced him. "Yes, how about it?"

Pinero looked pained. "Gentlemen, I am surprised at you. I give that information for a fee. Besides, it is a professional confidence. I never tell anyone but the client who consults me."

"I don't mind. Go ahead and tell them."

"I am very sorry, I really must refuse. I only agreed to show you how; not to give the results."

Luke ground the butt of his cigarette into the floor. "It's a hoax, boys. He probably looked up the age of every reporter in town just to be ready to pull this. It won't wash, Pinero."

Pinero gazed at him sadly. "Are you married, my friend?"

"No."

"Do you have anyone dependent on you? Any close relatives?"

"No. Why? Do you want to adopt me?"

Pinero shook his head. "I am very sorry for you, my dear Luke. You will die before tomorrow."

DEATH PUNCHES TIME CLOCK

. . . within twenty minutes of Pinero's strange prediction, Timons was struck by a falling sign while walking down Broadway toward the offices of the *Daily Herald* where he was employed.

Dr. Pinero declined to comment but confirmed the story that he had predicted Timons' death by means of his so-called chronovitameter. Chief of Police Roy. . . .

LEGAL NOTICE

To whom it may concern, greetings; I, John Cabot Winthrop III, of the firm of Winthrop, Winthrop, Ditmars and Winthrop, Attorneys-at-law, do affirm that Hugo Pinero of this city did hand to me ten thousand dollars in lawful money of the United States, and did instruct me to place it in escrow with a chartered bank of my selection with escrow instructions as follows:

The entire bond shall be forfeit, and shall forthwith be paid to the first client of Hugo Pinero and/or Sands of Time, Inc. who shall exceed his life tenure as predicted by Hugo Pinero by one per centum, or to the estate of the first client who shall fail of such predicted tenure in a like amount, whichever occurs first in point of time.

Subscribed and sworn,
John Cabot Winthrop III.

Subscribed and sworn to before
me this 2nd day of April, 1939.
Albert M. Swanson
Notary Public in and for this
county and State. My commission
expires June 17, 1939.

"Good evening, Mr. and Mrs. Radio Audience, let's go to press! Flash! Hugo Pinero, the Miracle Man from Nowhere, has made his thousandth death prediction without anyone claiming the reward he offered to the first person who catches him failing to call the turn. With thirteen of his clients already dead, it is mathematically certain that he has a private line to the office of the Old Man with the Scythe. That is one piece of news I don't want to know about before it happens. Your coast-to-coast correspondent will *not* be a client of Prophet Pinero—"

The judge's watery baritone cut through the stale air of the courtroom. "Please, Mr. Weems, let us return to our subject. This court granted your prayer for a temporary restraining order, and now you ask that it be made permanent. In rebuttal, Dr. Pinero claims that you have presented no cause and asks that the injunction be lifted, and that I order your client to cease from attempts to interfere with what Pinero describes as a simple, lawful business. As you are not addressing a jury, please omit the rhetoric and tell me in plain language why I should not grant his prayer."

Mr. Weems jerked his chin nervously, making his flabby gray dewlap drag across his high stiff collar, and resumed:

"May it please the honorable court, I represent the public—"

"Just a moment. I thought you were appearing for Amalgamated Life Insurance."

"I am, your honor, in a formal sense. In a wider sense I represent several other of the major assurance, fiduciary and financial institutions, their stockholders and policy holders, who constitute a majority of the citizenry. In addition we feel that we protect the interests of the entire population, unorganized, inarticulate and otherwise unprotected."

"I thought that I represented the public," observed the judge dryly, "I am afraid I must regard you as appearing for your client of record. But continue. What is your thesis?"

The elderly barrister attempted to swallow his Adam's apple, then began again: "Your honor, we contend that there are two separate reasons why this injunction should be made permanent, and, further, that each reason is sufficient alone.

"In the first place, this person is engaged in the practice of soothsaying, an occupation proscribed both in common law and statute. He is a common fortuneteller, a vagabond charlatan who preys on the gullibility of the public. He is cleverer than the ordinary gypsy palm reader, astrologer or table tipper, and to the same extent more dangerous. He makes false claims of modern scientific methods to give a spurious dignity to the thaumaturgy. We have here in court leading representatives of the Academy of Science to give expert witness as to the absurdity of his claims.

"In the second place, even if this person's claims were true —granting for the sake of argument such an absurdity"—Mr. Weems permitted himself a thin-lipped smile—"we contend that his activities are contrary to the public interest in general, and unlawfully injurious to the interests of my client in particular. We are prepared to produce numerous exhibits with the legal custodians to prove that this person did publish, or cause to have published, utterances urging the public to dispense with the priceless boon of life insurance to the great detriment of their welfare and to the financial damage of my client."

Pinero arose in his place. "Your honor, may I say a few words?"

"What is it?"

"I believe I can simplify the situation if permitted to make a brief analysis."

"Your honor," put in Weems, "this is most irregular."

"Patience, Mr. Weems. Your interests will be protected. It seems to me that we need more light and less noise in this matter. If Dr. Pinero can shorten the proceedings by speaking at this time, I am inclined to let him. Proceed, Dr. Pinero."

"Thank you, your honor. Taking the last of Mr. Weems' points first, I am prepared to stipulate that I published the utterances he speaks of—"

"One moment, doctor. You have chosen to act as your own attorney. Are you sure you are competent to protect your own interests?"

"I am prepared to chance it, your honor. Our friends here can easily prove what I stipulate."

"Very well. You may proceed."

"I will stipulate that many persons have canceled life insurance policies as a result thereof, but I challenge them to show that anyone so doing has suffered any loss or damage therefrom. It is true that the Amalgamated has lost business through my activities, but that is the natural result of my discovery, which has made their policies as obsolete as the bow and arrow. If an injunction is granted on that ground, I shall set up a coal-oil lamp factory, and then ask for an injunction against the Edison and General Electric companies to forbid them to manufacture incandescent bulbs.

"I will stipulate that I am engaged in the business of making predictions of death, but I deny that I am practicing magic, black, white or rainbow-colored. If to make predictions by methods of scientific accuracy is illegal, then the actuaries of the Amalgamated have been guilty for years, in that they predict the exact percentage that will die each year in any given large group. I predict death retail; the Amalgamated predicts it wholesale. If their actions are legal, how can mine be illegal?

"I admit that it makes a difference whether I can do what I claim, or not; and I will stipulate that the so-called expert witnesses from the Academy of Science will testify that I cannot. But they know nothing of my method and cannot give truly expert testimony on it—"

"Just a moment, doctor. Mr. Weems, is it true that your expert witnesses are not conversant with Dr. Pinero's theory and methods?"

Mr. Weems looked worried. He drummed on the table top, then answered, "Will the court grant me a few moments' indulgence?"

"Certainly."

Mr. Weems held a hurried whispered consultation with his cohorts, then faced the bench. "We have a procedure to suggest, your honor. If Dr. Pinero will take the stand and explain the theory and practice of his alleged method, then these distinguished scientists will be able to advise the court as to the validity of his claims."

The judge looked inquiringly at Pinero, who responded: "I will not willingly agree to that. Whether my process is true or false, it would be dangerous to let it fall into the hands of fools and quacks"—he waved his hand at the group of professors seated in the front row, paused and smiled maliciously—"as these gentlemen know quite well. Furthermore, it is not necessary to know the process in order to prove that it will work. Is it necessary to understand the complex miracle of biological reproduction in order to observe that a hen lays eggs? Is it necessary for me to re-educate this entire body of self-appointed custodians of wisdom—cure them of their ingrown superstitions—in order to prove that my predictions are correct?

"There are but two ways of forming an opinion in science. One is the scientific method; the other, the scholastic. One can judge from experiment, or one can blindly accept authority. To the scientific mind, experimental proof is all-important, and theory is merely a convenience in description, to be junked when it no longer fits. To the academic mind, authority is everything, and facts are junked when they do not fit theory laid down by authority.

"It is this point of view—academic minds clinging like oysters to disproved theories—that has blocked every advance of knowledge in history. I am prepared to prove my method by experiment, and, like Galileo in another court, I insist, 'It still moves!'

"Once before I offered such proof to this same body of self-styled experts, and they rejected it. I renew my offer; let me measure the life length of the members of the Academy of Science. Let them appoint a committee to judge the results. I will seal my findings in two sets of envelopes; on the outside of each envelope in one set will appear the name of a member; on the inside, the date of his death. In the other envelopes I will place names; on the outside I will place dates. Let the committee place the envelopes in a vault, then meet from time to time to open the appropriate envelopes. In such a large body of men some deaths may be expected, if Amalgamated actuaries can be trusted, every week or two. In such a fashion they will accumulate data very rapidly to prove that Pinero is a liar, or no."

He stopped, and thrust out his chest until it almost caught up with his little round belly. He glared at the sweating savants. "Well?"

The judge raised his eyebrows, and caught Mr. Weems' eye. "Do you accept?"

"Your honor, I think the proposal highly improper—"

The judge cut him short. "I warn you that I shall rule

against you if you do not accept, or propose an equally reasonable method of arriving at the truth."

Weems opened his mouth, changed his mind, looked up and down the faces of the learned witnesses, and faced the bench. "We accept, your honor."

"Very well. Arrange the details between you. The temporary injunction is lifted, and Dr. Pinero must not be molested in the pursuit of his business. Decision on the petition for permanent injunction is reserved without prejudice pending the accumulation of evidence. Before we leave this matter I wish to comment on the theory implied by you, Mr. Weems, when you claimed damage to your client. There has grown up in the minds of certain groups in this country the notion that because a man or corporation has made a profit out of the public for a number of years, the government and the courts are charged with the duty of guaranteeing such profit in the future, even in the face of changing circumstances and contrary to public interest. This strange doctrine is not supported by statute nor common law. Neither individuals nor corporations have any right to come into court and ask that the clock of history be stopped, or turned back."

Bidwell grunted in annoyance. "Weems, if you can't think up anything better than that, Amalgamated is going to need a new chief attorney. It's been ten weeks since you lost the injunction, and that little wart is coining money hand over fist. Meantime, every insurance firm in the country's going broke. Hoskins, what's our loss ratio?"

"It's hard to say, Mr. Bidwell. It gets worse every day. We've paid off thirteen big policies this week; all of them taken out since Pinero started operations."

A spare little man spoke up. "I say, Bidwell, we aren't accepting any new applicants for United, until we have time to check and be sure that they have not consulted Pinero. Can't we afford to wait until the scientists show him up?"

Bidwell snorted. "You blasted optimist! They won't show him up. Aldrich, can't you face a fact? The fat little pest has something; how, I don't know. This is a fight to the finish. If we wait, we're licked." He threw his cigar into a cuspidor, and bit savagely into a fresh one. "Clear out of here, all of you! I'll handle this my own way. You, too, Aldrich. United may wait, but Amalgamated won't."

Weems cleared his throat apprehensively. "Mr. Bidwell, I trust you will consult me before embarking on any major change in policy?"

Bidwell grunted. They filed out. When they were all gone and the door closed, Bidwell snapped the switch of the interoffice announcer. "O.K.; send him in."

The outer door opened. A slight, dapper figure stood for a moment at the threshold. His small, dark eyes glanced quickly about the room before he entered, then he moved up to Bidwell with a quick, soft tread. He spoke to Bidwell in a flat, emotionless voice. His face remained impassive except for the live, animal eyes. "You wanted to talk to me?"

"Yes."

"What's the proposition?"

"Sit down, and we'll talk."

Pinero met the young couple at the door of his inner office.

"Come in, my dears, come in. Sit down. Make yourselves at home. Now tell me, what do you want of Pinero? Surely such young people are not anxious about the final roll call?"

The boy's pleasant young face showed slight confusion. "Well, you see, Dr. Pinero, I'm Ed Hartley and this is my wife, Betty. We're going to have . . . that is, Betty is expecting a baby and, well—"

Pinero smiled benignly. "I understand. You want to know how long you will live in order to make the best possible provision for the youngster. Quite wise. Do you both want readings, or just yourself?"

The girl answered, "Both of us, we think."

Pinero beamed at her. "Quite so. I agree. Your reading presents certain technical difficulties at this time, but I can give you some information now. Now come into my laboratory, my dears, and we'll commence."

He rang for their case histories, then showed them into his workshop. "Mrs. Hartley first, please. If you will go behind that screen and remove your shoes and your outer clothing, please."

He turned away and made some minor adjustments of his apparatus. Ed nodded to his wife, who slipped behind the screen and reappeared almost at once, dressed in a slip. Pinero glanced up.

"This way, my dear. First we must weigh you. There. Now take your place on the stand. This electrode in your mouth. No, Ed, you mustn't touch her while she is in the circuit. It won't take a minute. Remain quiet."

He dove under the machine's hood and the dials sprang into life. Very shortly he came out, with a perturbed look on his face. "Ed, did you touch her?"

"No, doctor." Pinero ducked back again and remained a little longer. When he came out this time, he told the girl to get down and dress. He turned to her husband.

"Ed, make yourself ready."

"What's Betty's reading, doctor?"

"There is a little difficulty. I want to test you first."

When he came out from taking the youth's reading, his face was more troubled than ever. Ed inquired as to his trouble. Pinero shrugged his shoulders and brought a smile to his lips.

"Nothing to concern you, my boy. A little mechanical misadjustment, I think. But I shan't be able to give you two your readings today. I shall need to overhaul my machine. Can you come back tomorrow?"

"Why, I think so. Say, I'm sorry about your machine. I hope it isn't serious."

"It isn't, I'm sure. Will you come back into my office and visit for a bit?"

"Thank you, doctor. You are very kind."

"But, Ed, I've got to meet Ellen."

Pinero turned the full force of his personality on her. "Won't you grant me a few moments, my dear young lady? I am old, and like the sparkle of young folks' company. I get very little of it. Please." He nudged them gently into his office and seated them. Then he ordered lemonade and cookies sent in, offered them cigarettes and lit a cigar.

Forty minutes later Ed listened entranced, while Betty was quite evidently acutely nervous and anxious to leave, as the doctor spun out a story concerning his adventures as a young man in Terra del Fuego. When the doctor stopped to relight his cigar, she stood up.

"Doctor, we really must leave. Couldn't we hear the rest tomorrow?"

"Tomorrow? There will not be time tomorrow."

"But you haven't time today, either. Your secretary has rung five times."

"Couldn't you spare me just a few more minutes?"

"I really can't today, doctor. I have an appointment. There is someone waiting for me."

"There is no way to induce you?"

"I'm afraid not. Come, Ed."

After they had gone, the doctor stepped to the window and stared out over the city. Presently, he picked out two tiny figures as they left the office building. He watched them hurry to the corner, wait for the lights to change, then start across the street. When they were part way across, there came the scream of a siren. The two little figures hesitated, started back, stopped and turned. Then the car was upon them. As the car slammed to a stop, they showed up from beneath it, no longer two figures, but simply a limp, unorganized heap of clothing.

Presently the doctor turned away from the window. Then he picked up his phone and spoke to his secretary.

"Cancel my appointments for the rest of the day. . . . No. . . . No one. . . . I don't care; cancel them."

Then he sat down in his chair. His cigar went out. Long after dark he held it, still unlighted.

Pinero sat down at his dining table and contemplated the gourmet's luncheon spread before him. He had ordered this meal with particular care, and had come home a little early in order to enjoy it fully.

Somewhat later he let a few drops of fiori d'Alpini roll around his tongue and trickle down his throat. The heavy, fragrant sirup warmed his mouth and reminded him of the little mountain flowers for which it was named. He sighed. It had been a good meal, an exquisite meal and had justified the exotic liqueur.

His musing was interrupted by a disturbance at the front door. The voice of his elderly maidservant was raised in remonstrance. A heavy male voice interrupted her. The commotion moved down the hall and the dining-room door was pushed open.

"Mia Madonna! Non si puo entrare! The Master is eating!"

"Never mind, Angela. I have time to see these gentlemen. You may go."

Pinero faced the surly-faced spokesman of the intruders. "You have business with me; yes?"

"You bet we have. Decent people have had enough of your damned nonsense."

"And so?"

The caller did not answer at once. A smaller, dapper individual moved out from behind him and faced Pinero.

"We might as well begin." The chairman of the committee placed a key in the lock box and opened it. "Wenzell, will you help me pick out today's envelopes?" He was interrupted by a touch on his arm.

"Dr. Baird, you are wanted on the telephone."

"Very well. Bring the instrument here."

When it was fetched he placed the receiver to his ear. "Hello. . . . Yes; speaking. . . . What? . . . No, we have heard nothing. . . . Destroyed the machine, you say. . . . Dead! How? . . . No! No statement. None at all. . . . Call me later."

He slammed the instrument down and pushed it from him.

"What's up?"

"Who's dead now?"

Baird held up one hand. "Quiet, gentlemen, please! Pinero was murdered a few moments ago at his home."

"Murdered!"

"That isn't all. About the same time vandals broke into his office and smashed his apparatus."

No one spoke at first. The committee members glanced

around at each other. No one seemed anxious to be the first to comment.

Finally one spoke up. "Get it out."

"Get what out?"

"Pinero's envelope. It's in there, too. I've seen it."

Baird located it, and slowly tore it open. He unfolded the single sheet of paper and scanned it.

"Well? Out with it!"

"One thirteen p.m. . . . today."

They took this in silence.

Their dynamic calm was broken by a member across the table from Baird reaching for the lock box. Baird interposed a hand.

"What do you want?"

"My prediction. It's in there—we're all in there."

"Yes, yes."

"We're all in there."

"Let's have them."

Baird placed both hands over the box. He held the eye of the man opposite him, but did not speak. He licked his lips. The corner of his mouth twitched. His hands shook. Still he did not speak. The man opposite relaxed back into his chair.

"You're right, of course," he said.

"Bring me that wastebasket." Baird's voice was low and strained, but steady.

He accepted it and dumped the litter on the rug. He placed the tin basket on the table before him. He tore half a dozen envelopes across, set a match to them, and dropped them in the basket. Then he started tearing a double handful at a time, and fed the fire steadily. The smoke made him cough, and tears ran out of his smarting eyes. Someone got up and opened a window. When Baird was through, he pushed the basket away from him, looked down and spoke.

"I'm afraid I've ruined this table top."

ii
world views
of
futurists

We can see the future in various ways: inflexible and determined, unordered and chaotic, open to intelligent direction. This section of the book will provide examples of the various points of view.

The extrapolators believe that man's ideas and beliefs will remain the same—and so will the trends we confront. Even though individuals may change their own life-styles, these changes are seen as ripples on the surface of an unchanging current.

There are two types of extrapolators: optimists and pessimists. The best-known futurists are optimistic. They claim that the inevitable future is essentially desirable. Herman Kahn and Anthony Wiener state this point of view in the first piece.

Mark Rudd states the viewpoint of the pessimistic extrapolators in the second piece. He sees no possibility of changing the future but he finds present trends so undesirable that he feels he has the right to stop the system in any way he can. He argues that the system is so evil it must be destroyed. These people state—without much real hope—that a new system might grow out of the ruins of the old.

HERMAN KAHN
ANTHONY J. WIENER

faustian powers
and
human choices

SOME TWENTY-FIRST CENTURY
TECHNOLOGICAL AND ECONOMIC
ISSUES

introduction

Among the important respects in which industrial society differs
from all the societies that went before, perhaps the most significant is that it has institutionalized secular, manipulative ration-

We are grateful to Gail Albert, Raymond D. Gastil, and William Pfaff for
their suggestions and assistance. The authors bear sole responsibility for the
views expressed. This article is one of a series from a continuing project at the
Hudson Institute. Other publications in the series include Herman Kahn and
Anthony J. Wiener, *The Year 2000: A Framework for Speculation on the Next
Thirty-Three Years* (New York: Macmillan, 1967), © 1967, The Hudson Insti-
tute; Anthony J. Wiener, "Faustian Progress," in Richard Kostelanetz, ed.,
Beyond Left and Right: Radical Thought for Our Time (New York: William
Morrow and Co., 1968); Anthony J. Wiener and Herman Kahn, "On 'Studying'
the Future Social Effects of Science," in *Encyclopedia Britannica Yearbook
of Science;* and Herman Kahn, "On Alternative World Futures," in Morton A.
Kaplan, ed., *New Approaches to International Relations* (New York: St. Martin's
Press.)

ality, and thus both economic and technological development. The basic trends of Western society, most of which can be traced back as far as the twelfth or eleventh centuries, can be seen as part of a common, complex trend of interacting elements. For analytic purposes, we have separated them into thirteen rubrics, as shown here.

There is a basic, long-term, multifold trend toward:

1. Increasingly sensate[1] (empirical, this-worldly, secular, humanistic, pragmatic, utilitarian, contractual, epicurean or hedonistic, etc.) cultures,
2. Bourgeois, bureaucratic, "meritocratic," democratic (and nationalistic?) elites,
3. Accumulation of scientific and technological knowledge,
4. Institutionalization of change, especially research, development, innovation and diffusion,
5. Worldwide industrialization and modernization,
6. Increasing affluence and (recently) leisure,
7. Population growth,
8. Urbanization and (soon) the growth of megalopolises,
9. Decreasing importance of primary (and recently) secondary occupations,
10. Literacy and education,
11. Increasing capability for mass destruction,
12. Increasing tempo of change, and
13. Increasing universality of the multifold trend.

These processes of change, each facilitating the other, have become routinely—one might even say inexorably—cumulative. It is well known that, as a result, the rate of change of many aspects of social life has become exponential, nor is it likely that many of the changes that are in process will begin to decelerate during the next fifty years. Some of these trends present serious issues that are beyond the scope of this paper. (Population growth and urbanization deserve special men-

1. We have discussed this terminology (sensate, bourgeois) and the elements of the trend in *The Year 2000,* pp. 39–65. There also we discussed some of the methodological problems of projecting "trends," including the role of "surprises" and the possibility of cyclical forces.

tion. . . .) Here, however, we wish to focus on some of the new problems created by our successes in achieving unprecedented kinds of economic and technological powers.

To speak, to use tools, to pass learning on to children; to put fire, domestic animals, wind, falling water, and other energy sources to human use; to gather food, fuel, clothing, and seeds for winter; to save, invest, plan, build, and innovate in order to decrease dangers and insecurities and to increase the power to change natural things to suit one's purposes; in sum, to subdue Nature, and render her subject to human will—such have been the results, if not always the conscious goals, of eons of striving. Success would seem to be at hand; as we approach the beginning of the twenty-first century, our capacities for and commitment to economic development and technological control over our external and internal environment, as well as the concomitant systematic innovation, application, and diffusion of these capacities, seem to be increasing, and without foreseeable limit.

Clearly it is worthwhile to overcome both the deprivations caused by economic scarcity and the dangers and frustrations caused by impotence before the forces of nature. To increase economic development is to increase the availability of at least some of the things that people need and want. To develop technologically is to increase the capacity to achieve at least some human purposes that are widespread and legitimate. These Promethean accomplishments, though they are mixed blessings, are the results of persistent and concerted effort and intelligence, and on the whole they are occasions for satisfaction.

In this case, as in others, it has been desirable to solve old problems in spite of the new problems created by the solutions themselves. The purpose of this paper, however, is to focus attention on some of the new problems created by technological and economic progress. Through such progress such issues arise as the accumulation, augmentation, and proliferation of weapons of mass destruction; the loss of privacy and solitude; the increase of governmental and/or private power over individuals; the loss of human scale and perspective and the dehumanization of social life or even of the psychobiological self;

the growth of dangerously vulnerable, deceptive or degradable centralization of administrative or technological systems; the creation of other new capabilities so inherently dangerous as seriously to risk disastrous abuse; and the acceleration of changes that are too rapid or cataclysmic to permit successful adjustment. Perhaps most crucial, choices are posed that are too large, complex, important, uncertain, or comprehensive to be safely left to fallible humans, whether they are acting privately or publicly, individually or in organizations—choices, however, that become inescapable once these new capabilities have been gained.

The capacities of our culture and institutions to adapt to so much change in so comparatively short a time may be a major question; the stresses in domestic societies and in the international system may not be managed sufficiently by meliorist policies. Since the underdeveloped countries are even further removed in industrial and social life from these new technologies than we are, the cultural shock of their partial adaptation to the new technologies may even be greater for them. The possibility must be faced that man's unremitting, Faustian striving may ultimately remake his natural conditions—environmental, social, and psychobiological—so far as to begin to dehumanize man or to degrade his political or ecological situation in very costly or even irrevocable ways.

We would not wish to arrest this process, perhaps not even to slow it down; on balance, it is too valuable. There is a widespread though simplistic, Luddite response to problems of technology, in which the artifacts themselves become the targets of hostility; surely it would be generally more useful to criticize specific human choices, in which technology plays but a passive, instrumental role. Nor do we find plausible the prevalent rhetoric to the effect that technology is about to open gates either to Heaven or to Hell, that technology now presents man with some simple and decisive choice between immolation and utopia. Choices on earth seem likely to remain more confusing; utopias may sometimes be hard to tell from Brave New Worlds; evils may be not stark and obvious, but subtle, slow-acting, uncertain, and well distributed among all the available options.

Our purpose in this paper, then, is not to view the technological and economic prospects of the next fifty years with alarm, to try to arouse a humanistic (or romantic) reaction against the forces of change, or to argue for a pessimistic assessment of the prospects for human values. We are on the whole optimistic; but we wish to survey the range of problems that are already becoming discernible and that could—if social responses are not adequate—lead to very unhappy results.

While few would now believe that the mere multiplication of productive powers is likely to bring mankind into utopia, or into anything resembling it, it would be ironic (but not unprecedented) if this multiplication of resources were to create problems too serious for the solutions that those very resources should make feasible. Efforts will doubtlessly be needed to invent and implement ways of coping with the new and unfamiliar problems that will certainly arise. (What these will and should be is beyond the scope of this paper, which is intended, of course, to raise such issues rather than to evaluate and settle them.) Yet, despite best efforts, social policies frequently go wrong.[2]

economic change

In trying to get a large view of man's prospects, as seems to be appropriate for this consultation, we might for purposes of discussion consider five past and future economic stages, as listed in the table below. The first of these we would call "pre-agricultural"; almost every society remained in this level until about 8000 B.C. At about that time "permanent" (i.e., systematic and sustained) agriculture is supposed to have started in the "fertile crescent" of the Middle East. We can think of this as the beginning of the "agricultural" or "pre-industrial" stage. One way to characterize this stage is to note that the annual per capita product of a society was very likely to fall between 50 and 200

2. In *The Year 2000,* we explore some of the ways this can happen and some of the things that might permit anticipation of difficulties early enough to cope with them; see especially chapter ten.

(1965) U.S. dollars. The level was not very much above the pre-agricultural—but many more people were supported at this level. Given this base, it became possible to divert about 5 or 10 percent of the agricultural product to build and maintain cities, and thus to create a "civic" culture and "civilizations."

stages of economic change[3]

ECONOMIC SYSTEM	ANNUAL PER CAPITA PRODUCT IN (1965) DOLS.	LEADING SECTORS APPEARED
1. Pre-agricultural		1st 500,000 to 1,000,000 years
2. Pre-industrial (or agricultural)	50–200	
		8th Millenium B.C.
(Industrial revolution)	(Transitional)	(Eighteenth century)
3. Industrial	500–2,000	Nineteenth century
(mass consumption)	(Transitional)	(Twentieth century)
4. Post-industrial	5,000–20,000	Twenty-first century
5. Almost post-economic	50,000–200,000	Twenty-second century

It has been argued that until the industrial revolution no society ever produced much more or less than $50 to $200 per capita per year for any extended period. During the late eighteenth century, the industrial revolution, which in some ways had begun much earlier, became an obvious facet of English society. Industrialization then spread rapidly in the West, more slowly elsewhere, and, of course, has yet to reach many societies. (We can think of an "industrial society" as having a per capita product of about ten times that of a pre-industrial, i.e., between $500 and $2,000.)

Today in the U.S., Western Europe, and Japan, industrial society has been gradually transformed into what sometimes is called a mass consumption society. We think of mass consumption as a transitional stage to what we will call the "post-industrial" society—much as the industrial revolution can be thought of as a transitional stage between pre-industrial and industrial stages.

3. In *The Year 2000,* we drew these lines somewhat differently—more empirically, in a way that is more influenced by current conditions, issues, and emphases (see pp. 58–60). For this paper, considering the possible effects of adding another twenty years of changes in price structures and other important factors, we "rounded off" our categories.

This post-industrial stage can be characterized in many ways.[4] We will define it here by the achievement of another increase of a factor of 10 or so over the industrial society in per capita product (to perhaps $5,000 to $20,000 per capita). By the year 2020, about 20 percent of the world's population should be living in such societies. We can of course expect many important qualitative changes to occur in these societies, in addition to those associated with the simple and direct effects of being richer. We can also envisage that if anything like current growth rates continue, at some point between the end of the twenty-first and the early twenty-second century we should see the beginnings of what might be thought of as the "almost post-economic" society, in which annual gross product per capita ranges from $50,000 to $200,000. By "almost post-economic" we mean that at this level of affluence a great many traditional economic issues will disappear or become minor, though, of course, others will remain and there will be some new ones.[5]

Our task here is to project fifty years ahead. If current trends continue[6] the world's nations might be distributed about as follows. Perhaps 5 percent—perhaps less—of the world's population should live in nations that might roughly (and in many ways inaccurately, by then) be termed pre-industrial. At the other extreme, 5 percent or so might be living in nations that are either beginning to show "post-economic" features, or are manifesting them clearly. In between, about 20 percent of the world's population might live in states that are clearly post-industrial, some even approaching or entering the "post-eco-

4. See, for example, Daniel Bell's "Notes on the Post-Industrial Society," in *The Public Interest,* Nos. 6 and 7, Winter and Spring, 1967; and *The Year 2000,* especially pp. 25, 185–220.

5. Of course, it is difficult to say precisely what the meaning of gross national product would be in an "almost post-economic" society; even a post-industrial economy is different enough from current models to make comparisons very slippery; see *The Year 2000,* pp. 130–133, 210.

6. A very bad assumption for projection, though for this purpose better than any *single* alternative assumption. See *The Year 2000,* pp. 7–8, 34–39. Chapter III gives GNP, population, and GNP per capita projections to the year 2020 for 29 countries; these projections supersede our draft projections distributed last winter by the chairman to participants in this conference.

nomic" stage; about 10 percent might live in states which one could think of as mass-consumption societies (that is, in transition between industrial and post-industrial); another 10 percent of the world might live in what we might think of as mature industrial societies; and more than half the world might live in nations which we can regard as partially industrialized.[7] Of this last group more than 90 percent (or about half the world's population) is likely to live in six large nations: China, India, Brazil, Pakistan, Indonesia, and Nigeria. Whether or not one or more of these six nations passes our rather arbitrary lower bound of "industrial" status, at $500 per capita, they will all have large cities and other enclaves which will certainly be at least industrial and parts of which might even be post-industrial. On the other hand, there will be many areas in these "large and partially industrialized" countries, particularly some or most rural areas, that for the most part will be in a pre-industrial, usually sixteenth or seventeenth century, condition, modified, however, by the addition of such industrial products as the electric light, transistorized radio and television, bulldozers, and even crop dusters and fertilizers. Such disparities of income and level of modernization may create very important stresses within as well as between countries.

We would expect to find almost all of Europe, including the Soviet Union, but possibly excluding some eastern European countries and some countries on the southern and eastern rim of Europe, such as Portugal, Spain and Ireland, in the post-industrial, and to some extent in the almost post-economic categories. However the excluded countries would presumably have reached at least the "mass-consumption" level. They would probably be joined by such Latin American nations as Argentina, Venezuela, Mexico, Colombia, etc.; a good deal of the Sinic culture area, outside China, such as Taiwan, South Korea, Philippines, Malaysia, etc., the Union of South Africa and possibly some of the Arab countries and Turkey (assuming there are no disruptive changes in these states). Much of Africa and

7. By 2020 the term "industrial revolution," with its connotations of eighteenth-century England, will seem unlikely to fit this status as well as the term "partially industrialized."

some of China and Latin America might still be only partially industrialized—even if economic growth rates become quite high and population growth rates eventually decrease, but assuming both of these still stay within reasonable current expectations. In such a world there will be opportunities for creative and exciting lives for many; and orderly, decent, and remarkably full lives for the mass of people in the unprecedentedly affluent societies.

MARK RUDD

the future
of
the movement

[The Columbia Faculty] had another basic liberal conception of themselves and of the university, namely that they needed peace and quiet to continue their weapons research, conflict resolution, politics or government or whatever lies they happened to be teaching. They wanted peace and quiet and they didn't want kids coming and bringing the outside world into the university. Although they were politically adept and their fields may very well have been government or sociology, they didn't understand what we were really out for—that we were really concerned with imperialism and racism.

They didn't understand that at times we'd be impolite about this or "intolerant" of the other side's rights (like the right of the university to keep expanding and keep throwing people out of their homes or their right to keep developing weapons for the Pentagon). They didn't understand that what we did had to be done. We tried to convince them, but they sided with the administration. Since they didn't side with *us,* they were on the other side. It was just that clear—they said that they were in the middle but politically they had to choose a side. If they didn't, they were on the side of the *status quo.* They were naïve in thinking that they could be in the middle and they were naïve in some of the things they did. For example, they put up a blockade around

From Mark Rudd, "Events and Issues of the Columbia Revolt," in *The University and Revolution* © 1969 edited by Gary R. Weaver and James H. Weaver. Reprinted with the permission of Prentice-Hall, Englewood Cliffs, N.J.

Low Library before the jocks [i.e., athletes] did it. They were the cops before the jocks were there. In addition, they were the people we had to fight the most. They would come round to the buildings, trying to scare people, saying the bust was coming, the jocks were coming, beware of the right-wing reaction, time is of the essence, all of these phrases. Although they said they supported us, they weren't out for the same goals we were. [Mark Rudd is drawing his examples from the events at Columbia in 1968—ed.]

There were a lot of reasons for this. One is that the faculty is engaged in the process of transmitting lies from one group to another and the lies they tell, especially in the social sciences, are lies that help to perpetuate the *status quo*. Lies like pluralism and what economics is about in this country. Or else they teach the wrong stuff. If you're in economics, they don't teach you critical economics, they teach you how to do statistics so you can work for the Pentagon or for GM. Or, if you're in sociology you don't learn how to criticize the society: you don't learn about the roots of the society although you might learn about doing research into people's attitudes. It's complete ideology we get from our professors. And they're so committed to this garbage that they're not about to join a movement to overthrow the ruling class in this society because they believe in the things that they're teaching. They have to be committed to those lies or they'd have tremendous identity problems. That's why so few professors side with us. This is not "free speech," these are not "liberal" issues. We are involved in getting down to the roots of things.

mark rudd:
a personal vision

I could stand here and recite a whole list of ills in this society. I could also give you some ideas I have about what a nice society would look like. I think it would be very abstract, but you can see already that some of the things that we're opposed to have to do with exploitation of people and that behind all of this we see, in this society, a ruling class. That's what the whole trustee bit at Columbia was about. We talked about how the ruling class uses Columbia.

People have written books on ideology and I can't give it a name, "socialism," "communism"—I really would rather not. Listen to what I say and maybe some of the things that I believe will come through. Living in this society, seeing how it's run, opposition to it, and opposition to racism, imperialism, and repression is very positive. If you're against repression, you're for freedom; if you're against racism, you're for a society in which people treat each other as human beings. I have certain ideas about the way society could be, and I know that our goals at the moment are developing a mass democratic socialist movement.

I know that any blueprint I wrote for the institutions in a so-cialist society would either be unworkable, utopian, or else I'd become a Stalinist, to force people into the blueprint. So, I think that the democratic institutions will be determined by how we make the revolution. The thing we're looking for now is the development of a mass democratic, political socialist move-ment. The movement can be defined in terms of being against racism, being for national liberation in the third world, being against the system of capital and private profit. To the people fighting for their freedom in the third world, it doesn't matter if the president of the United States is Eisenhower, John Kennedy (who was responsible for the Bay of Pigs), Johnson, or even McCarthy (who said he would stand up to communism in Thai-land). Liberal policies are as bad as the conservative policies.

the function of
the university:
enlightenment or expediency?

I think you're making a fundamental error when you define the interests of those who rule the University in terms of their economic profit. You're a vulgar Marxist if you do that because some of these guys are not making strict economic profit off the University. Just getting people socialized to take a role, filling a slot in the society, even that serves the interests of the ruling class. And that's very different from direct economic profit. We don't want to be vulgar Marxists about it. The way that the University is set up with a professor who stands giving you the line, orienting you toward a hierarchical relationship, is itself very helpful to the ruling class. Also, the ideas that are taught are extremely important. The lie about the governmental process, about pluralism, groups working out their interests being represented in the final decisions, is not the way the government works. That's the theory of pluralism and that's not the way things go.

The functions of the University are very intricate: they turn out personnel. IBM puts a million and a half into Columbia School of Business; it gets out of it a program in international marketing. The State Department or the CIA gives x amount of money to Columbia School of International Affairs and they get out of it a piece of data about the national income of Czechoslovakia.

Now let's try to look at the University for enlightenment. Columbia students re-evaluated their lives. They re-evaluated what we have been saying about imperialism and racism. They identified with the oppressed of this world, the Vietnamese and the blacks, and they joined the movement. Their lives were changed. I would like to see us develop a university that has a critical function. Except for the radical students, universities don't promote real change.

the system: possibility of change from within

Even if we were assured that one can change the foreign policy of the United States from the inside and that one can actually learn about the foreign policy of the United States at a university, foreign-service schools train people who don't want to change foreign policy. These institutions are even more dangerous because, as in the case of the Russian Institute at Columbia, rationalizations are developed for things like the Cold War. Moreover, people have been trained there for use in Cold War institutions like the Free Europe Committee, the State Department, and the CIA and Radio Free Europe. I also know that the ideas there are used by people predominantly to perpetuate this system. They develop more and more sophisticated means of controlling the people of Peru at the Latin American Institute at Columbia. Knowledge, however, can be used on both sides. We had Anthropology Department people, radicals, who decided they wanted to help the liberation movement in Peru. They did research into the social structure of Peru, but they realized that their findings could be used equally well by the State Department and by the military for repression of the liberation movement in Peru.

I don't agree with the assumption that one can change the system from the inside. To think that you're going to change a foreign policy that's based on the interests of the ruling class in the society by working for the State Department, and to think that these foreign policies don't have a political basis as well as an economic or class basis, is crazy. I think the way that we've got to change foreign policy is through a mass movement of people re-evaluating this country and its goals, as well as their own goals. The masses would then oppose the war in Vietnam not because it was an accident, and not because the United States is getting whipped, but because it's imperialist and it doesn't serve their interest at all. It hurts their interests. We're doing our own analysis of this country, and we have to go outside of the institutions of repression which exist in order to do it. Now if you're interested in changing the foreign policy, why don't you join us? You can work through research; you can work with other committed people who are studying problems; you can also work to develop a mass movement of people committed to changing the foreign policy of the country. That's the only alternative I can see. I want us to develop a university that has a critical function.

the future
of the
movement

The issues we raise are not predominantly student-oriented. They have to do with the relations of the university to the rest of the world. Our question now is how to broaden out the student movement and to bring more working-class people, people in the community, and black people to that same kind of radical understanding of the society that we have. Basically, the campus is highly politicized and people are at the point where they understand the issues in general. We're now going to talk in specific terms about these different things, these viewpoints that we've raised. The student movement must now relate these specific tactics and viewpoints to the world. It must become an agent for change in a worldwide arena.

I believe that the views of the positive and negative extrapolators make sense if, and only if, you believe that there cannot be fundamental change in patterns and trends. An increasing number of thinkers are convinced that it is neither possible nor desirable for present trends to continue for an indefinite period. The simplest reason for this conclusion is that unlimited economic growth will certainly destroy the environment and the ecological balance so seriously that man can no longer live on the earth.

Early in the sixties, Dennis Gabor, professor at the Imperial College of Science and Technology in London, stated: ". . . exponential curves grow to infinity only in mathematics. In the physical world they either turn round and saturate, or they break down catastrophically. It is our duty as thinking men to do our best toward a gentle saturation, instead of sustaining the exponential growth, though this faces us with very unfamiliar and distasteful problems."

The next piece by Joseph Wood Krutch, who was one of the great naturalists, enlarges on the reasons why we cannot expect the continuation of present trends.

JOSEPH WOOD KRUTCH

what the year 2000 won't be like

The end of a millennium doesn't come around very often. When the last one approached, many people are said to have believed that the world would come to an end in the year 1000. It didn't. But now that 2000 is only thirty-two years away, prophecy is again an active business—and it is upsetting to realize that had these prophecies been made in 1900 rather than in 1967, they would have been far less disturbed by problems then undreamed of. Neither World War I—in 1900 only fourteen, not thirty-two years away—nor World War II would have been anticipated, much less their consequences. Those of us who were alive then did not realize that we were living in a brief Indian summer, and this fact does not encourage confidence in the prophecies now being made.

Unless some of the more extravagant predictions concerning the near-abolition of death are fulfilled, I personally have no stake in any world even thirty-two years away. If, therefore, I have spent two or three weeks examining and comparing a number of serious prophecies, it is only out of curiosity—reinforced by such concern as one can have for that posterity which, as a cynic once remarked, "never did anything for me."

The prophecies are surprisingly numerous and elaborate,

some from interdisciplinary teams, some from one or two bold individuals. Among the first are the ambitious symposium published in the Spring 1966 issue of *American Scholar* and the even more ambitious one reported in the 300 pages of the Summer 1967 issue of *Daedalus,* the journal of the American Academy of Arts and Sciences. Also known to me, though only in summary, are contributions from the American Institute of Planners. Notable among individual pronouncements are those by Buckminster Fuller in both the *American Scholar* and the *Saturday Review;* by René Dubos of the Rockefeller Institute; by Robert Sinsheiner, professor of biophysics at California Institute of Technology; by Vladimir Engelhardt, director of the biology section of the Russian Academy of Sciences; and a substantial volume by Anthony J. Wiener and Herman Kahn.

At a less sophisticated level there are the perennial articles in the women's magazines promising such contributions to the good life as cooking by electronic ovens and telephones with TV attachments. There is also the assurance given by an avant-garde magazine that we won't have to wait until the year 2000 for "festivals of pornographic films at Lincoln Center"—which the magazine promises to achieve by 1970. Nevertheless, I had best say right here that, having listened to the confident voices of at least a score of intelligent and informed men, I am no more sure than I was before what the future has in store for us. There are so many conflicting forces making for so many possibilities that there are a dozen possible futures, no one of which seems certain enough to justify saying, "This is what it is going to be like."

Almost without exception, these prophecies depend upon projections or extrapolations which consist essentially of prolonging the curve with a dotted line on some chart. And though each prophet tends to concern himself almost exclusively with trends observable in his own field of study—with very little attention to the possibility that they will be increasingly influenced by other trends in other fields—I suppose that the majority would accept the list of those tendencies expected to continue as it was drawn up by a contributor to *Daedalus.* It includes the following: "an increasingly sensate (empirical, this-worldly, secular-humanistic, pragmatic, utilitarian, hedonistic) culture; world-wide industrialization and modernization; increasing affluence and (recently) leisure; population growth; urbanization and (soon) the growth of megalopolises; increased literacy and education; increased capacity for mass destruction."

Undoubtedly, these are, at the moment, trends which nearly anybody could have listed. But as soon as one begins to consider them critically, it becomes apparent that they are far from a reliable basis for predicting the future. The method itself disregards the fact that—fortunately—trends do not always continue. If they did, we would be justified in concluding, for instance, that smog and water pollution have obviously been increasing at a rate which makes it inevitable that we will either suffocate or die of intestinal disorders by the year so-and-so. Maybe we will, but possibly we won't. Conscious determination to resist the trend can be effective, though most of the prophets leave that out of consideration. In the second place, even if some of these trends continue to follow the curve drawn by the past and even if no new ones develop, the fact still remains that one trend may collide so disruptively with another that both cannot possibly continue. Surely, the consequences of "increased capacity for mass destruction" might reverse several of the other trends—including that toward population growth. And if certain other prophets are right in assuming that we will not use our increased capacity for mass destruction, then population growth might reverse other trends—for instance, the trend toward affluence.

Consider for a moment the contradictory estimates to the extent to which population pressures are a dominating factor. Secretary of the Interior Stewart Udall, in the article "Our Perilous Population Implosion," protested eloquently against the fatalism which considers only how an overpopulated earth might be fed and housed, rather than how it might be controlled. Paul Sears pointed out several years ago that the most important problem in connection with space is not how to get to the moon but how to avoid running out of it here on earth, and he warned that "no known form of life has been observed to multiply without bumping up against limitations imposed by the space it occupies." Then he added that those who brush the problem aside by assuring us that technology will solve it forget that "the limitations involve not only quantity but quality."

All the projections of the population curve give us stupefying numbers expected to be reached even before the year 2000. A recent study of animal behavior proved that overcrowding produces psychotic behavior and certainly suggests that the reaction of human beings is probably similar—even that the crime explosion may be the result of the overcrowding to which we are already subject. René Dubos, microbiologist and experimental psychologist, warns us that survival depends not so much on our ability to avoid famine and sustain a minimal standard of living as on the quality and diversity of our urban environment. "Just as important [as physical requirements] for maintaining human life is an environment in which it is possible to satisfy the longing for quiet, privacy, independence, initiative, and open space. These are not luxuries but constitute real biological necessities." Yet not a single prophet that I have heard predicts that there will be any successful effort to contain population growth in the near future.

Just to add to our worries, Jean Bourgeis-Pichat, director of the French National Institute of Demographic Studies, declares that medical science will certainly raise problems other than increasing population pressures:

> We are on the eve of an era in which society will have to decide who will survive and who will die. The new medical techniques are becoming so expensive that it soon will be impossible to give the benefit of them to everybody, and society will certainly not let money decide the issue. We will soon be confronted with a problem of choice, and when we say choice we mean a moral problem. Is our cultural state ready for that? I think this is open to doubt.

Compare these thoughts with Bernard Shaw's *Doctor's Dilemma*. On the other hand, all this is waved aside by one of the contributors to the *American Scholar's* symposium with the casual pronouncement that "in hedonic potential, megalopolis is no more and no less a natural environment for man than Athens or a peasant village," and in the same issue of the magazine an assistant dean at Carnegie Tech assures us that the abundance produced by the "productivity revolution" is an assurance that the prospect for world-wide abundance and leisure "will not be delayed by more than a few generations by the population explosion." Buckminster Fuller makes this even simpler by assuring us that "the only real world problem is that of the performance per pound of the world's metals and other resources."

The probable incompatibility of the recognized trends is enough to make them a very shaky basis for predictions that claim to be more than a guess, but there is another reason why existing trends do not necessarily—in fact, very often do not—define the future. How safe is it to assume that something totally unexpected will not create some trend of the times more important than any now recognized? Would anyone have predicted Pasteur's great discovery thirty years before he made it —or insulin, or penicillin? Very few physicists would have predicted thirty-two years before Pearl Harbor that atomic fission would be achieved so soon. Yet this last development was probably the most fateful of all the events of the twentieth century— as well as, perhaps, one of the most horrible of all of the possible solutions of the population problem.

And what of the so-called conquest of space? To some, including educator and writer Willy Ley, it promises the solution of most of our problems. Others may be more inclined to agree with Loren Eiseley that the wealth and creative intelligence being invested in it may constitute a public sacrifice equal to the building of the pyramids. They may then remember that the pyramids were responsible for the otherwise incomprehensible fact that, though what we would now call the national income of Egypt was very great, the majority of its people lived in abject poverty. On the other hand, it is perhaps equally probable that the recognition of the economic burden, or even simple disillusion with the results, may, even before the year 2000, make the obsession with outer space remembered only as a temporary folly.

For all I or anybody else can know, the increasing taste for violence, both public and private—both for gain and for fun—

may tell us more about the future than any of the other trends, though I do not remember that it was ever cited as being significant by any of the prophets I read. What of LSD as an invention possibly as important as Pasteur's discovery or penicillin or insulin? The prophets, moreover, for the most part take no account of those intangibles—mental, moral, or emotional—which some are probably quite apt to dismiss as mere by-products of economic and social conditions. Are McLuhanism and the hippie philosophies only, as I assume, fleeting phenomena? If they are not, who can measure the possible effect of the hippies' rejection of society or the McLuhanites' scorn for the word?

Based on most of the prophecies I have consulted, one would hardly suspect the existence of such phenomena as the existentialist's denial of meaning in the universe and of external sanctions for any moral code. Neither, to descend to a lower level, would one meet with any recognition of the possible significance and consequences of that enormous appetite for pornography, the mere existence of which seems to me to be more important than the question of whether it should or should not be regulated by law. Nevertheless, the quality of life in the year 2000 may depend as much upon such beliefs, attitudes, and faiths as it does upon the trends recognized by most of the prophets.

The quality of life—that is precisely what seems to be almost entirely left out of consideration in many prophecies. In many of them, the nearest that one comes to even a reference to the concept of a good life is that declaration previously quoted concerning the "hedonic potential of megalopolis," and, even in this case, the acceptance of such a term as more meaningful than, say, either "the prospect for happiness" or "the possibility of a good life" seems to me in itself likely to have an influence upon the kind of life we are preparing for the future.

So, too, I suspect, might be the persistence of two trends which I have observed in the majority of the prophets which are often characteristic of those who are afraid of being accused of unscientific attitudes unless they assume: (1) that the past not only suggests but actually determines the future; and (2) that, although one may attempt to describe that future, one should avoid judging it. These two assumptions lead, sometimes unintentionally, to a sort of fatalism. Since the future is going to be determined by certain known factors, one is compelled to say simply that what will be will be.

Many of those who use the method of projection talk about planning for the future. Probably at least some of them would reject rigid determinism. Yet planning does not mean planning a main outline for the future, but merely planning ways of meeting and perhaps alleviating what cannot be avoided. So far as I can recall, the only direct and adequate recognition of this necessary result of the method of projection was by two of the participants in the *Daedalus* symposium. The first, Lawrence Frank, social psychologist and retired foundation official, remarked that whereas our ancestors often accepted a theological fatalism, "today we seem to be relinquishing this theological conception as we accept a new kind of fatalism expressed in a series of trends." The second, Matthew Meselson, professor of biology at Harvard, suggested that he would prefer "normative forecasting" to the kind which most of his fellow members of the *Daedalus* symposium seemed to practice. The last session reported is, therefore, headed: "The Need for Normative Studies." But the speeches seem for the most part to suggest postponing that for a future meeting.

Normative is a word which many—perhaps most—scientists are more than merely suspicious of, for it implies a rejection of complete relativism and it accepts the distinction they refuse to make between the normal and the average, between what is and what ought to be. But there seems little reason for wanting to know what the future threatens to be like unless there is some possibility of changing it and some willingness to assume that some futures would be better than others.

If sociology seems somewhat too completely content to describe and predict without attempting either to judge or control, that is certainly not a charge which can be leveled against some of the biologists, who also have been inspired to prophecy by the approaching end of a millennium. The Russian biochemist, Vladimir Engelhardt, is relatively unsensational compared to at least some of his American colleagues. He assures us only that science, having moved on from its concern with the management of the inanimate, has now learned how to apply the same successful methods to living creatures, including man. By the year 2000, he says, we will have pep pills which have no after-effects and which banish fatigue entirely; cancer will be no more serious than a nose cold; and defective organs will be replaced by spare parts as routinely as is now the case with other machines.

Perhaps even Dr. Engelhardt is somewhat guilty of that hubris to which many scientists are prone, but he is humility itself compared to Robert Sinsheiner, professor of biophysics at Cal Tech, who declared before his institution's 75th anniversary conference that the scientist has now in effect become both Nature with a capital N and God with a capital G. Until today, he stated, prophecy has been a very chancy business, but now that science has become "the prime mover of change," it is not unreasonable to hope that the race of prophets employing its method may have become reliable. Science has now proved beyond question that there is no qualitative difference between the animate and the inanimate, and though we don't yet know exactly how the inanimate becomes conscious, there is every reason to believe that we will soon be rid of that bothersome mystery also. "It has become increasingly clear," Professor Sinsheiner said, "that all the properties of life can be understood to be simply inherent in the material properties of the complex molecule which comprises the cell." Already we make proteins; soon we will make viruses, and then living cells—which will be, as he calls it, "the second Genesis."

In their new book, *The Year 2000,* Anthony J. Wiener (formerly of the Massachusetts Institute of Technology) and Herman Kahn (formerly of the RAND Corporation) issue a solemn warning against just such unlimited confidence in the benefits of mankind's increasing power and such blindness to the threat inherent in its lagging wisdom:

> Practically all of the major technological changes since the beginning of industrialization have resulted in unforeseen consequences. . . . Our very power over nature threatens to become itself a source of power that is out of control. . . . Choices are

posed that are too large, too complex, important, uncertain, or comprehensive to be safely left to fallible humans.

Sinsheiner, on the other hand, had no such doubts. He is willing to entrust "fallible human beings" with powers, not only over man's physical and social environment, but over his physiology and his personality. Now that we are beginning to understand the role of DNA, he says, we are masters not only of the human body, but also of the future human being. "Would you like to control the sex of your offspring? Would you like your son to be six feet tall? Seven feet? . . . We know of no intrinsic limits to the lifespan. How long would you like to live?"

How would *you* like to be able to determine this or that? To me, it seems that a more pertinent question would be: "How would you like *someone else* to answer these questions for you?" And it most certainly would be *someone else*. Is there—will there ever be—a someone who should be entrusted with that ultimate power which Sinsheiner then goes on to describe as follows?

> Essentially we will surely come to the time when man will have the power to alter, specifically and consciously, his very genes. This will be a new event in the universe. No longer need nature wait for the chance to be patient and the slow process of selection. Intelligence can be applied to evolution.

Does the use made by man of the powers he has achieved suggest that he is ready to merit another such stupendous development? Should we not wait until he has become a little wiser before he holds the whole future of mankind in his hands? Not long ago I was told that the October 1967 issue of the British journal *Science* predicts that within half a century we will be breeding unusually intelligent animals for low grade labor. Wouldn't unusually stupid human beings prove more useful and easier to create?

An increasing number of people agree with Krutch that if present trends should continue for even a limited period of time, mankind will not survive. The conclusions of the pessimistic extrapolators are widely shared—but their proposals for action are not.

The fact that people agree on the seriousness of the crisis that America—and the world—now faces does not mean that there is agreement on the approaches which should be used. A large group of people believe that a new world view, or mind-set or consciousness is automatically coming into existence which will lead to the automatic solution of present problems. The Greening of America *by Charles Reich states this thesis. The first chapter is reprinted here.*

CHARLES A. REICH

the coming american revolution

America is dealing death, not only to people in other lands, but to its own people. So say the most thoughtful and passionate of our youth, from California to Connecticut. This realization is not limited to the new generation. Talk to a retired school teacher in Mendocino, a judge in Washington, D.C., a housewife in Belmont, Massachusetts, a dude rancher in the Washington Cascades. We think of ourselves as an incredibly rich country, but we are beginning to realize that we are also a desperately poor country—poor in most of the things that throughout the history of mankind have been cherished as riches.

There is a revolution coming. It will not be like revolutions of the past. It will originate with the individual and with culture, and it will change the political structure only as its final act. It will not require violence to succeed, and it cannot be successfully resisted by violence. It is now spreading with amazing rapidity, and already our laws, institutions and social structure are changing in consequence. It promises a higher reason, a more human community, and a new and liberated individual. Its ultimate creation will be a new and enduring wholeness and beauty—a renewed relationship of man to himself, to other men, to society, to nature, and to the land.

This is the revolution of the new generation. Their protest and rebellion, their culture, clothes, music, drugs, ways of thought, and liberated life-style are not a passing fad or a form of dissent and refusal, nor are they in any sense irrational. The whole emerging pattern, from ideals to campus demonstrations to beads and bell bottoms to the Woodstock Festival, makes sense and is part of a consistent philosophy. It is both necessary and inevitable, and in time it will include not only youth, but all people in America.

The logic and necessity of the new generation—and what they are so furiously opposed to—must be seen against a background of what has gone wrong in America. It must be understood in light of the betrayal and loss of the American dream, the rise of the Corporate State of the 1960's, and the way in which that State dominates, exploits, and ultimately destroys both nature and man. Its rationality must be measured against the insanity of existing "reason"—reason that makes impoverishment, dehumanization, and even war appear to be logical and necessary. Its logic must be read from the fact that the Americans have lost control of the machinery of their society, and only new values and a new culture can restore control. Its emotions and spirit can be comprehended only by seeing contemporary America through the eyes of the new generation.

The meaning and the future of the revolution must emerge from a truer perspective. The revolution is a movement to bring man's thinking, his society, and his life to terms with the revolution of technology and science that has already taken place. Technology demands of man a new mind—a higher, transcendent reason—if it is to be controlled and guided rather than to become an unthinking monster. It demands a new individual responsibility for values, or it will dictate all values. And it promises a life that is more liberated and more beautiful than any man has known, if man has the courage and the imagination to seize that life.

The transformation that is coming invites us to reexamine our own lives. It confronts us with a personal and individual choice: are we satisfied with how we have lived; how would we live differently. It offers us a recovery of self. It faces us with the fact that this choice cannot be evaded, for as the freedom is already there, so must the responsibility be there.

At the heart of everything is what we shall call a change of consciousness. This means a "new head"—a new way of living —a new man. This is what the new generation has been searching for, and what it has started achieving. Industrialism produced a new man, too—one adapted to the demands of the machine. In contrast, today's emerging consciousness seeks a new knowledge of what it means to be human, in order that the machine, having been built, may now be turned to human ends; in order that man once more can become a creative force, renewing and creating his own life and thus giving life back to his society.

It is essential to place the American crisis and this change within individuals in a philosophic perspective, showing how we got to where we are, and where we are going. Current events are so overwhelming that we only see from day to day, merely responding to each crisis as it comes, seeing only immediate evils, and seeking inadequate solutions such as merely ending the war, or merely changing our domestic priorities. A longer-range view is necessary.

What is the nature of the present American crisis? Most of us see it as a collection of problems, not necessarily related to each other, and, although profoundly troubling, nevertheless within the reach of reason and reform. But if we list these problems, not according to topic, but as elements of larger issues concerning the structure of our society itself, we can see that the present crisis is an organic one, that it arises out of the basic premises by which we live and that no mere reform can touch it.

1. *Disorder, corruption, hypocrisy, war.* The front pages of newspapers tell of the disintegration of the social fabric, and the resulting atmosphere of anxiety and terror in which we all live. Lawlessness is most often associated with crime and riots, but there is lawlessness and corruption in all the major institutions of our society—

matched by an indifference to responsibility and consequences, and a pervasive hypocrisy that refuses to acknowledge the facts that are everywhere visible. Both lawlessness and evasion found expression in the Vietnam War, with its unprincipled destruction of everything human, and its random, indifferent, technological cruelty.

2. *Poverty, distorted priorities, and law-making by private power.* America presents a picture of drastic poverty amid affluence, an extremity of contrast unknown in other industrial nations. Likewise there is a superabundance of some goods, services, and activities such as defense manufacture, while other needs, such as education and medical care, are at a starvation level for many. These closely related kinds of inequality are not the accidents of a free economy, they are intentionally and rigidly built into the laws of our society by those with powerful influence; an example is the tax structure which subsidizes private wealth and production of luxuries and weapons at the direct expense of impoverished people and impoverished services. The nation has a planned economy, and the planning is done by the exercise of private power without concern for the general good.

3. *Uncontrolled technology and the destruction of environment.* Technology and production can be great benefactors of man, but they are mindless instruments; if undirected they careen along with a momentum of their own. In our country they pulverize everything in their path: the landscape, the natural environment, history and tradition, the amenities and civilities, the privacy and spaciousness of life, beauty, and the fragile, slow-growing social structures which bind us together. Organization and bureaucracy, which are applications of technology to social institutions, increasingly dictate how we shall live our lives, with the logic of organization taking precedence over any other values.

4. *Decline of democracy and liberty; powerlessness.* The

Constitution and Bill of Rights have been weakened, imperceptibly but steadily. The nation has gradually become a rigid managerial hierarchy, with a small elite and a great mass of the disenfranchised. Democracy has rapidly lost ground as power is increasingly captured by giant managerial institutions and corporations, and decisions are made by experts, specialists, and professionals safely insulated from the feelings of the people. Most governmental power has shifted from Congress to administrative agencies, and corporate power is free to ignore both stockholders and consumers. As regulation and administration have grown, liberty has been eroded and bureaucratic discretion has taken the place of the rule of law. Today both dissent and efforts at change are dealt with by repression. The pervasiveness of police, security men, and military, and compulsory military service show the changed character of American liberty.

5. *The artificiality of work and culture.* Work and living have become more and more pointless and empty. There is no lack of meaningful projects that cry out to be done, but our working days are used up in work that lacks meaning: making useless or harmful products, or servicing the bureaucratic structures. For most Americans, work is mindless, exhausting, boring, servile, and hateful, something to be endured while "life" is confined to "time off." At the same time our culture has been reduced to the grossly commercial; all cultural values are for sale, and those that fail to make a profit are not preserved. Our life activities have become plastic, vicarious, and false to our genuine needs, activities fabricated by others and forced upon us.

6. *Absence of community.* America is one vast, terrifying anti-community. The great organizations to which most people give their working day, and the apartments and suburbs to which they return at night, are equally places of loneliness and alienation. Modern living has obliterated place, locality, and neighborhood, and given us

the anonymous separateness of our existence. The family, the most basic social system, has been ruthlessly stripped to its functional essentials. Friendship has been coated over with a layer of impenetrable artificiality as men strive to live roles designed for them. Protocol, competition, hostility, and fear have replaced the warmth of the circle of affection which might sustain man against a hostile universe.

7. *Loss of self.* Of all of the forms of impoverishment that can be seen or felt in America, loss of self, or death in life, is surely the most devastating. It is, even more than the draft and the Vietnam War, the source of discontent and rage in the new generation. Beginning with school, if not before, an individual is systematically stripped of his imagination, his creativity, his heritage, his dreams, and his personal uniqueness, in order to style him into a productive unit for a mass, technological society. Instinct, feeling, and spontaneity are repressed by overwhelming forces. As the individual is drawn into the meritocracy, his working life is split from his home life, and both suffer from a lack of wholeness. Eventually, people virtually become their professions, roles, or occupations, and are thenceforth strangers to themselves. Blacks long ago felt their deprivation of identity and potential for life. But white "soul" and blues are just beginning. Only a segment of youth is articulately aware that they too suffer an enforced loss of self—they too are losing the lives that could be theirs.

What has caused the American system to go wrong in such an organic way? The first crucial fact is the existence of a universal sense of powerlessness. We seem to be living in a society that no one created and that no one wants. The feeling of powerlessness extends even to the inhabitants of executive offices. Yet, paradoxically, it is also a fact that we have available to us the means to begin coping with virtually all of the problems that beset us. Most people would initially deny this, but reflection shows how true it is. We know what causes crime and social disorder, and what can be done to eliminate those causes. We know the steps that can be taken to create greater economic quality. We are in possession of techniques to fashion and preserve more livable cities and environments. Our problems are vast, but so is our store of techniques; it is simply not being put to use.

Urban riots offer a well-documented case in point for the late 1960's. They were predictable and they were predicted. Their causes and the appropriate remedies (which include education, housing, and jobs) have been known and described for many years by students of social problems. After the riots took place, a presidential commission reviewed the events, and their findings gave wide publicity to the same knowledge; the commission's recommendations were not acted upon, just as the preexisting knowledge had not been acted upon. Response was either nonexistent, absurdly inadequate, or childishly irrational (such as the proposal to deprive looters of jobs with public agencies).

The American crisis, then, seems clearly to be related to an inability to act. But what is the cause of this paralysis? Why, in the face of every warning, have we been unable to act? Why have we not used our resources more wisely and justly? We tell ourselves that social failure comes down to an individual moral failure: we must have the will to act; we must first find concern and compassion in our hearts. The theme is deep in America, from Hawthorne to E. B. White, from the Puritans to Richard Nixon, from *Time* to *The New York Times.* But this diagnosis is not good enough. It is contradicted by the *experience* of powerlessness that is encountered by so many people today. In 1968 a majority of the people certainly wanted peace, but they could not turn their individual wills into action by society. It is not that we do not will action, but that we are unable to act, unable to put existing knowledge to use. Is something wrong with the machinery of society? It apparently no longer works, or we no longer know how to make it work.

What is the machinery that we rely upon to turn our wishes into realities? In the private sphere, the market system. In the public sphere, the public version of the market system: voter democracy, or democratic pluralism. In both spheres, a system of administration and law, resting ultimately on the Constitution. Could it be that the American crisis results from a structure that is obsolete? All of the other machinery we use becomes obsolete in a short time. A social institution, which is, after all, only another type of machinery, is not necessarily immune from the same laws of obsolescence. The ideals or principles of a society might remain valid, but the means for applying the principles could lose their effectiveness.

If we seek to explain the American crisis in terms of obsolete structure, we might find an illustration in the ideal and the machinery of free speech. The ideal or principle is that every opinion must be expressed freely in order that truth be arrived at. But the machinery for carrying out this ideal was designed for a very different society than ours, a society of small villages, town meetings, and face-to-face discussions. The First Amendment furnishes no workable means for the public to be adequately informed about complex issues. News is cut down into a commodity by the mass media, a staccato piece of show business, and no one who only watches television and reads a typical newspaper could possibly know enough to be an intelligent voter. The vital decisions of the private sector of the economy receive even less adequate coverage and reporting. Moreover, the media systematically deny any fundamentally different or dissenting point of view a chance to be heard at all—it is simply kept off the air and out of the newspapers. The opinion that does get on television is commercially sponsored and thus heavily subsidized by government tax policies; the opinion that is not allowed is sometimes heavily penalized by the same tax laws (thus: the Georgia-Pacific Lumber Company's advertising is tax deductible; conservation advertising may not be). In short, our machinery for free speech is hopelessly ineffectual in the light of the way society is organized today, and this illustrates the plight of most of our democratic machinery which has not adapted to changing realities.

To explain the American crisis only in the above terms is, however, far from adequate. For one thing, it fails to take account of the whole Marxist analysis of capitalism. Those who analyze society in terms of class interests point out that there are powerful and privileged groups that profit greatly by the status quo. This power elite, and the monopolistic corporations it represents, has long exploited both people and environment. It profits from poverty, inequality, and war; it has a well-founded fear of democracy, liberty, and communal solidarity. The Marxists would argue that our government machinery is not naïvely obsolete; it has been captured by class interests. The same free speech illustration we used above would also illustrate a Marxist analysis; the media only disseminate the opinions that serve the interests of monopoly capital.

The Marxist analysis of the American crisis seems convincing. But is it a satisfactory explanation? The difficulty is that in focusing so strongly on economic interest, it does not take into account the vital factors of bureaucracy, organization, and technology which do dominate America today. These factors have a powerful momentum of their own that may not be inconsistent with class interests, but may well be indifferent to them. Thus we may be in the grip, not of capitalist exploiters, but of mindless, impersonal forces that pursue their own, non-human logic. A great deal of evidence supports this view.

Can the American crisis be defined, then, in terms of obsolete structure, monopoly capitalism, mindless technology, or perhaps some combination of the three? The question that we started with still remains: why are we unable to do anything to solve our problems? Government machinery can be overhauled; monopoly capitalism may be subjected to social regulation, as it has been in not only the communist countries but in the moderate-socialist countries; and technology is, after all, only a tool. There is something even deeper behind the crisis of structure and the crisis of inaction.

Whenever any attempt is made to begin confronting America's problems, we encounter a profound lack of understanding. This lack of understanding is not merely a phenomenon of the masses, for it extends to the powerful, the well educated, and the elite; it is not simply a lack of knowledge, for it includes many people who possess more than enough information. Its basis is a pervasive unreality. Our picture of our economy, of how we are governed, of how our culture is made, of how we may be threatened at home or abroad, is fantastically out of keeping with contemporary realities. Indeed, the central fact about America in 1970 is the discrepancy between the realities of our society and our beliefs about them. The gap is even greater in terms of our failure to understand the possibilities and potential of American life.

Unreality is the true source of powerlessness. What we do not understand, we cannot control. And when we cannot comprehend the major forces, structures, and values that pervade our existence, they must inevitably come to dominate us. Thus a true definition of the American crisis would say this: we no longer understand the system under which we live, hence the structure has become obsolete and we have become powerless; in turn, the system has been permitted to assume unchallenged power to dominate our lives, and now rumbles along, unguided and therefore indifferent to human ends.

What is this "understanding" that holds such a key place in our contemporary situation? Clearly the word "understanding" is inadequate, for we are talking about something much broader and deeper than "understanding" usually connotes. To describe what we are talking about, we propose to use the term "consciousness." It is a term that already has several meanings, including an important one in Marx, a medical one, a psychoanalytic one, a literary or artistic one, and one given us by users of hallucinogenic drugs. Our use of the term "consciousness" will not be exactly like any of these, but it gains meaning from all of them, and is consistent with all of them.

Consciousness, as we are using the term, is not a set of opinions, information, or values, but a total configuration in any given individual, which makes up his whole perception of reality, his whole world view. It is a common observation that once one has ascertained a man's beliefs on one subject, one is likely to be able to predict a whole range of views and reactions. Ask a stranger on a bus or airplane about psychiatry or redwoods or police or taxes or morals or war, and you can guess with fair accuracy his views on all the rest of these topics and many others besides, even though they are seemingly unrelated. If he thinks wilderness areas should be "developed" he is quite likely to favor punitive treatment for campus disruptions. If he is enthusiastic about hunting wild animals, he probably believes that the American economic system rests on individual business activity, and has an aversion to people with long hair.

It is apparent that the particular views we have mentioned really are related, and that an individual's opinions, understanding, and values are all part of some invisible whole. It is also apparent that consciousness is in substantial degree (but not necessarily entirely) socially determined. One evidence of this is the fact that many people have consciousnesses that are roughly similar, especially members of the same generation with the same social backgrounds. Also, when one hears a person's views and opinions, one can often tell something about his background, experience, and social role. The unity of consciousness in any individual is also revealed by the way in which it resists change, even in the smallest detail, and maintains a remarkable cohesion. Quite evidently the individual cannot allow any part of his consciousness to be challenged without feeling that the whole configuration is threatened. Thus a person who believes in "free enterprise" as part of his total perception of reality may resist, despite an overwhelming showing, the conclusion that "free enterprise" no longer serves to produce the same social consequences that it used to. Such a conclusion might undermine all of the assumptions under which this person has lived. Similarly, the violent reaction of some older people to long hair on boys shows that the adults feel a threat to the whole reality that they have constructed and lived by. An argument between people who are on different levels of consciousness often goes nowhere; there is no common ground on which they can meet.

Included within the idea of consciousness is a person's background, education, politics, insight, values, emotions, and philosophy, but consciousness is more than these or even the sum of them. It is the whole man; his "head"; his way of life. It is that by which he creates his own life and thus creates the society in which he lives.

As a mass phenomenon, consciousness is formed by the underlying economic and social conditions. There was a consciousness that went with peasant life in the Middle Ages, and a consciousness that went with small town, preindustrial life in America. Culture and government interact with consciousness; they are its products but they also help to form it. While consciousness is the creator of any social system, it can lag behind a system, once created, and even be manipulated by that system. Lag and manipulation are the factors that produce a consciousness characterized by unreality. If we believe in free enterprise, but the nation has become an interlocking corporate system, we are living in unreality as the victims of lag, and we are powerless to cope with the existing corporate system.

To show how this has worked out in America, and to show the true meaning of the new generation, we have attempted to classify three general types of consciousness. These three types predominate in America today. One was formed in the nineteenth century, the second in the first half of this century, the third is just emerging. Consciousness I is the traditional outlook of the American farmer, small businessman, and worker who is trying to get ahead. Consciousness II represents the values of an organizational society. Consciousness III is the new generation. The three categories are, of course, highly impressionistic and arbitrary; they make no pretense to be scientific. And, since each type of consciousness is a construct, we would not expect any real individual to exhibit in symmetrical perfection all the characteristics of one type of consciousness.

The concept of consciousness gives us the elements from which we can fashion an argument about what has happened and what is happening to America. For the chaos we have just described is not chaos at all, but part of a coherent pattern of history, values, and thought. In the paragraphs that follow, we set forth the logic that emerges from behind the crisis of our contemporary life.

The great question of these times is how to live in and with a technological society; what mind and what way of life can preserve man's humanity and his very existence against the domination of the forces he has created. This question is at the root of the American crisis, beneath all the immediate issues of lawlessness, poverty, meaninglessness, and war. It is this question to which America's new generation is beginning to discover an answer, an answer based on a renewal of life that carries the hope of restoring us to our sources and ourselves.

At the opening of the industrial era, Western society underwent a major change of values in which scientific technique, materialism, and the market system became ascendant over other, more humanistic values. Although the contradiction was not recognized at the time, these industrial values were inconsistent with the democratic and spiritual ideals of the new American nation, and they soon began to undermine these American ideals.

Every stage of human civilization is accompanied by, and also influenced by, a consciousness. When civilization changes slowly, the existing consciousness is likely to be in substantial accord with underlying material realities. But industrialism brought sudden uprooting and a rapidly accelerating rate of change. Consciousness then began to lag increasingly far behind reality, or to lose touch with a portion of reality altogether. Today a large segment of the American people still have a consciousness which was appropriate to the nineteenth-century society of small towns, face-to-face relationships, and individual economic enterprise. Another large segment of the people have a consciousness formed by organized technological and corporate society, but far removed from the realities of human needs.

In the second half of the twentieth century, this combination of an anachronistic consciousness characterized by myth, and an inhuman consciousness dominated by the machine-rationality of the Corporate State, have, between them, proved utterly unable to manage, guide, or control the immense apparatus of technology and organization that America has built. In consequence, this apparatus of power has become a mindless juggernaut, destroying the environment, obliterating human values, and assuming domination over the lives and minds of its subjects. To the injustices and exploitation of the nineteenth century, the Corporate State has added depersonalization, meaninglessness, and repression, until it has threatened to destroy all meaning and all life.

Faced with this threat to their very existence, the inhabitants of America have begun, as a matter of urgent biological necessity, to develop a new consciousness appropriate to today's realities and therefore capable of mastering the apparatus of power and bringing it under human control. This new consciousness is based on the present state of technology, and could not have arisen without it. And it represents a higher, transcendent form of reason: no lesser consciousness could permit us to exist, given the present state of our technology.

This transcendent reason has made its first appearance among the youth of America. It is the product of the contradictions, failures, and exigencies of the Corporate State itself, not of any force external to the State. It is now in the process of rapidly spreading to wider and wider segments of youth, and by degrees to older people, as they experience the recovery of self that marks conversion to a different consciousness. The new consciousness is also in the process of revolutionizing the structure of our society. It does not accomplish this by direct political means, but by changing culture and the quality of individual lives, which in turn change politics and, ultimately, structure.

When the new consciousness has achieved its revolution and rescued us from destruction, it must go about the task of learning how to live in a new way. This new way of life presupposes all that modern science can offer. It tells us how to make technology and science work for, and not against, the interests of man. The new way of life proposes a concept of work in which quality, dedication, and excellence are preserved, but work is nonalienated, is the free choice of each person, integrated into a full and satisfying life, and expresses and affirms each individual being. The new way of life makes both possible and necessary a culture that is nonartificial and nonalienated, a form of community in which love, respect, and a mutual search for wisdom replace the competition and separation of the past, and a liberation of each individual in which he is enabled to grow toward the highest possibilities of the human spirit.

The task of learning how to live in this way represents the chief philosophic undertaking for man after he saves himself from his present danger. It requires man to create a reality—a fiction based on what can offer men the best hope of a life that is both satisfying and beautiful. The process of that creation, which has already been started by our youth in this moment of utmost sterility, darkest night, and extremest peril, is what we have undertaken to describe in this book.

The thesis of Charles Reich is summarized in the following paragraph which is printed on the jacket cover of the volume: "There is a revolution coming. It will not be like the revolutions of the past. It will originate with the individual and with culture, and it will change the political structure only as its final act. It will not require violence to succeed, and it cannot be successfully resisted by violence. This is the revolution of the new generation."

There are many who accept the thesis that a revolution in consciousness is taking place. But there is one over-whelming reaction to Reich: if we are to change the society through changing the individual, how are the obvious crises of today to be handled while the revolution in con-sciousness is going on? What are the mechanisms which can be used to change the society before the process of dissolution so obviously under way makes it impossible to live hopeful lives?

The amount of poverty in the United States increased in 1970, the situation of the poor areas of the world worsened, those who have been "educated" find themselves increas-ingly in a world which has no need of their skills. How are we to deal with these and the other multi-faceted crises taking place today?

The speech by the Honorable Allan J. MacEachen, presi-dent of the Canadian Privy Council, which follows explores some of the potential for citizen-government communica-tion.

ALLAN J. MacEACHEN

it is time to humanize technology

We will examine the present state of North American society, where quite clearly something has gone awry with many relationships. Then we will look to the future, asking these questions: "Are there other ways of seeing reality—nature, society, ourselves? Can we agree on a new order of values and devise new policies which will better serve human well-being?"

I wish to share with you some social analyses which point beyond the present gloom to a better tomorrow. They do not offer immediate answers to the complex problems which now confound us. However these analyses indicate the direction we should travel. They show the way to new horizons of understanding which may well reveal the viable policies for which we are searching.

inventory: "something has gone wrong"

GLOBAL TIME OF TROUBLES

The 1970s are turning out to be the "time of troubles" some observers predicted. Every sector of the globe is experiencing so-

From a speech given at the University of North Carolina, Greensboro, February 15, 1971. Reprinted courtesy of Allan J. MacEachen.

cial turmoil. Human affairs are in a state of transition; a massive shift in mentalities and structures is underway. So there is confusion everywhere. Only on the moon is there a Sea of Serenity.

NORTH AMERICAN MALAISE

In North America—so recently considered immune from upheaval—"something has gone wrong" with the brave new technological society our generation confidently set out to build after the Second World War. We have developed unequalled technical capacities. We also have unequalled public problems and private anxieties. Americans and Canadians alike are experiencing a deepening malaise of the spirit, which pervades every age and income group.

SIGNS OF THE CRISIS STATE

The litany of our public problems is getting longer: wars that do not end, and an arms race which is not slackening. The income gap between the rich and the poor man, between depressed and growth regions in each nation, and between rich countries and poor countries. Pollution of air, water, soil and life cycles. Population pressures. Urban swarm and rural decline. Outbreaks of violence and terrorism. Unemployment and inflation. Widening health and welfare needs. Budget problems and tax loads. Housing shortages and school dropouts. The gradual breakdown of transportation and communications in an age of instant electronics and jet travel.

Governments and other institutions are trying to cope with this lengthening inventory of public woes. Each problem is vast and complex. And these problems are not isolated from one another. They are interrelated; they are "megaproblems." Seen all together they tend to baffle the mind and freeze the will. Policy makers wonder, "are we powerless to resolve them?"

Add the not-so-private anxieties of citizens. This malaise is not confined to deprived minorities. Nor to dissenting youth. Now middle-aged, middle-income voices are also asking troubled questions, articulating their loneliness, alienation, fears.

These personal apprehensions are also interrelated, and they reach beyond North America. The Black power advocate, the rebelling white student, the demonstrator for women's liberation, the petitioner for segregation, the kid on drugs and the parent on alcohol, the urban guerrilla . . . and, yes, the rioting worker in Poland, the suicide team in Japan, and the Red Guard extremist in Peking; all are linked together. Each in his or her own way feels desperate, up against the wall.

MORE OF THE SAME
WILL NOT SUFFICE

There is a dawning realization that more of the same policies, more patchwork, more tinkering will not bring us out of our present crisis state. All of us—public leaders as well as private citizens—are coming up against the wall. Can we get over the wall? Can we tunnel through? Can we go around it? Rather than panic, it would be wise to stand back and size up our predicament.

analysis: why our
present predicament?

DEEPER QUESTIONS ABOUT ROOT CAUSES

This is happening. An increasing number of public leaders and private citizens—to borrow an old phrase—are making an "agonizing reappraisal" of the present predicament. They are asking deeper questions, probing for root causes. The questions David Riesman has heard Americans asking are also being put by many Canadians: "What can we believe? Who will lead us? Where are we going?"

A Canadian colleague, the Minister of National Health and Welfare, raised related questions during a recent address. Mr. Munro noted: "In our era of history, the post-industrial society, our values are being questioned. . . ."

One Canadian sampling of the public mood turned up some

revealing answers from citizens, which no doubt are echoed in the U.S. A young mother said, "Social problems come about because of the way we live." A worker's views: "We are so busy 'making it' we have no time for people." An older woman: "It is very hard to be a person in today's society. You feel lost." And a high school student: "School has nothing to do with being a person." A social activist put it this way: "I'm defined by what I produce, not by the fact that I love my wife and can make my children laugh." And a community developer said, "Each of us lives in a mechanical envelope. We are lonely for friends."

A weekly editor in Western Canada has offered further insights: "The major local problem is one that bedevils the whole country. It is the false message that salvation lies in material things, quantity first. This breaks rich and poor alike . . ."

QUESTIONING THE VALUES
OF THE MEGAMACHINE

Many are questioning the values which undergird this clockwork system. People are beginning to suspect that the megamachine has an impoverishing social ethic; that it fashions technical giants and spiritual pygmies.

Question: Is the Gross National Product (the GNP) an adequate measure of society's activity? What about its disproducts, such as waste? What of those values in life which cannot be measured quantitatively? Perhaps the GNP is more misleading than informative. If taken alone as a measure of progress, it may reveal only that we are a "gross national people."

Question: "Why do many public policies focus on the efficient functioning of systems (business, labor, education) rather than the well-being of persons?

Another consideration: In serving the insatiable appetites of the productive system, many forms of work are geared at a feverish pace. Often the drain leaves little reserve for other activities. What is happening to interpersonal relations as a result? In the family, for instance? What happens to friendships, privacy, love, laughter, imagination? Why the seeming scarcity of these qualities?

The megamachine operates on the assumption that material goods are always in short supply. "More for you" is supposed to mean "less for me." And what happens? Does this norm perpetuate material wealth for some, material poverty for others, and—so it seems—an inner emptiness for most? So some "win" and many "lose." Or maybe we're all becoming losers this way? The existing social environment was shaped by forebears who competed for material goods. . . . Is the traditional assumption that "more for you" necessarily means "less for me" valid today? Perhaps this approach is outdated, even perilously inadequate, especially when we take into account the wide range of human values—including the interpersonal relationships so necessary to life. Shouldn't we take a hard, critical look at the practicality of competitive self-interest in a world in which we are increasingly interdependent, in which our mutuality of interests is growing in every sphere of activity, cultural, social, political and economic?

What is "development" anyway? Obviously, any adequate development policy should encompass more than economic well-being, basic as this is. It should also take into account and foster if it can those other values which make life human—family relationships, friendships, civic participation and the like. Furthermore, it is becoming clear that well-being in this fuller sense can never be achieved so long as we spend so much time and energy producing and consuming material goods in a competitive rat race. Many signs indicate that this preoccupation is yielding diminishing human returns. We have need of a new order of values in order to humanize technical society. We are rather like the Tin Woodman in search of a heart . . . so we can love, so we can live.

Some religious leaders in Canada are making the same point. Before retiring as moderator of the United Church, Dr. Robert McClure said that poverty and affluence are reverse sides of the same problem: "Poverty brings misery . . . [and yet] any moderately great degree of affluence almost seems to preclude happiness."

THE PATTERN OF THESE CRITICISMS

Notice that these analyses all point to the technical-economic system which dominates North American culture: the clockwork world for which all of us labor to produce and consume, the megamachine which imposes its methods and values on every institution—government, school, and church as well as the industrial complex.

This clockwork system—followed in varied ways by capitalist, socialist, and communist states alike—regards goods, events, and people as time-space units, as measurable quantities to be managed and controlled in the common service of ever more production, more consumption, and, it turns out, more pollution. Now, in its own way, each critical voice is asking, "Economic growth, yes, but for what? And at what human cost? Is giving material output the first place really the key to human well-being?"

QUESTIONING THE MENTAL FRAMEWORK

In turn, these value judgments raise other, even more fundamental questions. Questions about the prevailing mentality or world view behind the clockwork society. If this mindset has given rise to our megaproblems and malaise, then it must take too limited a view of reality, and especially of man. We need to reexamine our root assumptions and premises, the way we see and understand nature, social organization, ourselves.

Reality is never fixed, nor is it completely knowable. No single culture, however sophisticated, sees reality in its entirety. In the industrialized society to which we belong the predominant view of reality was shaped by cultural forces reaching back to Southern and Northern Europe. This prevailing world view is characterized by abstract reasoning, by technique, and by moral concepts (such as the work ethic) which together produced the scientific method, modern technology, and our major political-social structures.

No need to proclaim the many benefits our technical world view has yielded. Today we are concerned with its shortcomings. This once-unquestioned mental framework is showing signs of bankruptcy; it seems unable to reveal a viable way out of our present time of troubles. Why? Some inadequacies and limitations are becoming apparent:

This mentality has taught us to think too much in terms of opposites—in either/or, good/bad terms.

The clockwork mind-set views reality in lineal, sequential fashion. It sees reality in bits and pieces, as parts separated from one another rather than interrelated. Time is seen in segments, not as continuous flow. Space is conceived as boundaries, not as horizons.

This understanding of reality also sees men as parts of economic systems and political ideologies. But man is more comprehensive than the systems he creates. Persons stand above and beyond any conceptualized system.

The bits-and-pieces closed-in mind-set is found in a popular approach to problem solving and decision making. In response to specific problems, policies tend to be devised piecemeal. Moreover, such policies sometimes end up in contradiction with one another because their individual focus is too narrow; they do not take adequate account of human needs in related fields. In such cases, a comprehensive view of human well-being is lacking.

A related inadequacy: The prevailing technological outlook is rooted in a rationality which virtually excludes all feelings. So it loses close touch with emotions and imagination, which have their own cogent reasons. This learned capacity to focus on some aspects of reality to the exclusion of others is seen in the popular overemphasis on economic output which neglects other human capacities and needs. Technically minded man can become so adept at this kind of closed-in thinking that after a while he no longer sees what he excludes; it has become unreal. But, of course, what is left out is very real and vital to adequate understanding.

If, in decision making, vital human data is excluded it is impossible to make an adequate diagnosis of the question at hand. From this initial inadequacy a chain reaction will follow: inadequate process, inadequate or even damaging outcomes. In these and related ways, the prevailing North American view —the one which still dominates much problem solving and decision making—is diminishing us, rather than enriching our lives.

alternative approaches: stepping through the looking glass

WHAT KIND OF SOCIAL CHANGE?

Often in life we know what we do not like about a given situation, while we are still somewhat vague about better alternatives. That is the stage many of us are at now. We are deeply troubled, but we are not yet sure which way we want to go. We do know, like it or not, that social change is here to stay. Can we take charge of this change? And if we can, what kind of social change do we want? In what direction do we want to move?

Do we want more of the same Gross National Product next year and next decade? Is this calculable future—based on statistical projections—all we can foresee? If so, our prospects seem decidedly dismal. Even if we were to try to build a Fortress North America to lock out the rest of humanity (while locking in ourselves), we probably couldn't avoid internal collapse.

Are there "alternative futures?" Is a better quality of life possible? Is a humanized technology foreseeable? Can we begin to visualize a social order which fulfills more human aspirations?

AN ALTERNATIVE WAY OF SEEING REALITY: IS IT FANCIFUL?

We have to find some way of putting industrialized man back together again—reuniting mind and body, reason and feelings, and his public and private lives. If we are hard pressed enough (and it's coming to that), if we want to badly enough, we'll find a way. We'll find a way to step from our present mentality "through the looking glass" into a mindscape with broader horizons. Within this new framework of understanding "man and his world" we will work out a revised order of values (a blend of old and new norms), we will decide on new public policies, and we will find new methods of pursuing them.

This is not fanciful daydreaming. The genesis of a new consciousness is already in process. It is coming to birth. Some prototypes are among us, even part of our own life experiences, if we recognize them for what they are.

REFLECTING ON SOME CLUES

Consider these clues:

Some other world views have been in our midst for generations. Only in recent years has the white majority deigned to pay much attention to these minority cultures in North America: those of the black man, the Mexican-American, the red man. In many respects these minority cultures see reality differently and live by another scale of values. Once it was widely supposed that we had nothing to learn from these fellow citizens. But if we are discerning enough, we could learn a good deal.

The Canadian Indian, to cite one example, communes as much by silence as by word; he reaches out to the whole person. For him property is communal rather than private. Sharing is part of everyday living. Nature is respected, not exploited. He is in tune with the rhythms of life, not with abstract concepts of life. Is it so surprising that the typical Indian is not much interested in adopting our individualistic, acquisitive, work-oriented mentality and ways of living?

Another clue is closer to home, even on our doorstep. Consider the counterculture of youth: those called "hippie," those immersed in the drug scene, and yes, also many sons and daughters who are not impressed by our vaunted standard of living. Let us be cool enough to ask why. Why their long hair, the bizarre dress, the conspicuous symbols of peace and poverty? Why the drugs? Why the disregard for property? Why the occasional violence?

If we look beyond the excesses, the mere fads and fancies, what may we learn? Positively, what are dissenting youth trying to tell us? Especially in the folk songs and spirit rock which appear to embody much of their testament? Are they trying to show us that the person, not property, is central; that friendship is more important than profit; that work has to be meaningful; that creative leisure—including reflection and festivals—is more enriching than feverish buying and selling?

This countering world view is present in every neighborhood. To varying degrees, it is shared by most young people, including many who appear "straight" to us. And coming on strong is the generation of the very young. They are growing up —as if it were in their genes—with new ways of perceiving, evaluating, behaving.

Yet another clue is to be found in our own experiences. Consider the difference between the style of our public or work life and that of our more private life at home and with friends.

Even though the family is much influenced by technical-commerce pressures, at home most of us still try to live according to another set of norms, by a more human world view. Each family member is valued for his or her worth as an unique person, without much regard to "productivity" or "success." Love-making is not time-tabled (or hardly ever). Work and leisure patterns are more geared to life rhythms. There is time—if not enough—for quiet conversation, for noisy fun. And when there is a family crisis, usually an effort is made to see the problem in its full human context—whether it is a son's lagging studies, or a daughter's involvement, or a spouse's emotional upset. In the family, there is a conscious effort to live together as persons in community, with mutual interests not self-interests usually given first place.

In North America's minority cultures, in the counter-culture of youth, in the more private segment of our lives with family and friends . . . in all these we see other world views, and other value systems. However crowded by the dominating mentality of business and work, these old/new perceptions and value systems persevere. Indeed, they are spreading, they are catching on. In them we are seeing the outlines of a more livable future, the first green shoots of a new spring.

future hopes: some indications of a "new history" in the making

OVERVIEW

We may even say a "new history" is already in the making. Poets and philosophers, social scientists, political and religious leaders alike recognize this. Prime Minister Trudeau has said that Canadians are seeking "a new set of values to recreate us." Vatican II discerned "the birth of a new humanism in which man is defined first of all by his responsibility to his brothers and to history." The World Council of Churches sees humanity struggling towards what it calls "The Responsible Society."

Offsetting our deepening malaise, then, there are these growing hopes that technical man is beginning to fashion a more human future. Some indications of this "new history" are to be glimpsed in certain perceptions, questions, and value orientations which are coming to the fore. They are a mix of old and new. They provoke thought, even if they do not necessarily evoke consent.

SOME PERCEPTIONS

Consider these propositions:

We begin to see that public problems bedevilling us are rooted in our inadequate world view and impoverished social ethic. They are related parts of the social fallout from technical excess.

Rationality is not enough. Individualism is not enough.

Production-consumption is not enough. If we expect to devise policies which serve men adequately, we need to break through to a broader, deeper, more nearly complete concept of what it means to be human. (Here we may learn from our neighbors in the Third World. In Latin America especially an "awakening of consciousness" is underway among the masses. Bold innovators are testing new approaches to social animation and participation.)

Once man—the human person in community with others—is given first place in our perceptions, we begin to reassess economic systems and political ideologies in this light. We try to think through how systems can be changed to fit and serve people, not the other way round.

Can North American technology be reconstructed to fit and serve people? What kind of social environment should we try to create? What is required, first of all, is a wider and deeper understanding of human well-being. Even though competitive habits persist, we are beginning to appreciate that our mutual interests really outweigh self-interests. There is more to be gained by collaboration in pursuit of common goals, more to be lost by competition at cross-purposes. This is obviously so in family life, in other interpersonal relations, and yes, also, in public affairs. There is much more to be gained than lost by working together to reduce pollution, control inflation, foster employment, reduce welfare dependency. So we are coming to see that the well-being of all—including economic well-being—will be best served in the context of mutual enterprise. What has always been recognized as the more moral way is now coming to be recognized as also the more practical way. Indeed, it is one key to our common survival.

We also begin to see that the policy choices before us may transcend apparent dichotomies. Familiar either/or options—such as security or risk, public sphere or private sector, inflation or unemployment—may not be the opposites we have thought them to be. The most promising options may be in the direction of "both/and." Given a heightened understanding of our mutuality of interests, we should be able, for instance, to devise public policies which ensure relatively full employment *and* relative price stability at the same time. (As one observer puts it, if we probe the hyphenated spaces between our popular either/or concepts we may come upon a "third philosophy," a "third ethic," and a "third politics.")

SOME QUESTIONS

Provocative questions which raise new alternatives:

> If family living patterns reflect a more human world view, can ways be found to bring this value system into the public sphere of business and politics?

> Can we glimpse the man of tomorrow in the youth of today? How may the new generation contribute effectively to policy making? How may minority groups enter the mainstream of decision making? How may self-help groups among the deprived have an impact on the public policy?

> What is a satisfactory "standard of living?" What constitutes well-being in a fully human sense? Can this well-being be achieved if we are mainly preoccupied with satisfying material needs? If we endlessly want more and more things, does this not lead necessarily to the neglect of other basic needs—social, cultural, spiritual wants?

INDICATIONS OF A NEW ORDER OF VALUES

Bring together these perceptions and questions. They reveal that a revised scale of social values is taking shape. Some evident priorities, again old and yet new:

> The human person has first and centre place in social order.

> And not the individual in isolation. Only by relating with

one another do we become persons in any satisfying sense.

Social organization should be restructured so as to enhance rather than hinder human relationships. Structures should enable persons to develop together— each in his own way and at his own pace. Mutuality of interest, not self-interest, should be fostered. Economic activity, which now dominates other relationships, should be contained within the larger context of social development.

Leadership should be more horizontal (a gathering-in kind) and less vertical (the imposing kind).

AN OPEN APPROACH TO POLICY MAKING

How do we move into this more human future? By research. By reflecting on our own experiences. By brainstorming together, seeking breakthroughs to new perspectives. Not that the future can be precisely planned and carefully programmed; that is the clockwork approach. At every stage in building the "new history," we will have to learn to keep all the options open—if possible avoiding rigid either/or choices, always allowing for new contingencies. Policy makers and citizens will have to live with more uncertainties, fewer rules. It will be more frustrating but ultimately it should be more rewarding for all.

Our thesis is that new perceptions can transform persons, who together can transform society through public policies better attuned to human well-being.

Learning to see reality in a new way takes time. Restructuring our common habitation will take still more time. We may take heart in the fact that this great enterprise is already underway. We need not expect Utopia, of course, but we can hope with some confidence for a better tomorrow. We have to hope. In the words of one of your countrymen:

Since Hiroshima we have known that the old man must die. The man of devouring ambition, the consuming man must give way to the new man, the man of understanding, the servant of life.

> The future depends upon our opening of ourselves to the emergence of the servant.
>
> (Kelly, *Sat. Review,* March 7, 1970)

Wider participation is key. No leadership, no matter how enlightened, can adequately interpret the complex, shifting aspirations of people without continuous communication with the grassroots.

By way of summing up, consider the "both/and" approach to development policies advocated at the 1970 World Conference on Religion and Peace. Delegates of many persuasions and from every continent agreed as follows:

> There is no universal model of development. Each country must establish and be free to establish its own model. . . . We must encourage a pluralistic strategy of change and liberation. Some may choose the Marxist model, or a mixed one. Or they might, to the benefit of all, creatively evolve another model, the goal of which is not ever increasing . . . consumption and mere economic growth, but decent subsistence, social justice, and liberation from the forces which dehumanize man. . . ."
>
> (Workshop II on Development, Oct. 1970)

Can we state a world view from which we can work which combines a belief in man's potential with a realistic statement of the urgency of our situation? A Call to Celebration which follows represents the attempts of many people to state the world view of the era we are so rapidly entering.

a call to
celebration

I
and many others
known
and unknown to me
call you:

> to celebrate our joint power to provide all human beings with the food, clothing, and shelter they need to delight in living.

> to discover, together with us, what we must do to use mankind's unlimited power to create the humanity, the dignity and the joyfulness of each one of us. ,

> to be responsibly aware of your personal ability to express your true feelings and to gather us together in their expression.

We can only live these changes: we cannot think our way to humanity. Every one of us, and every group with which we live and work, must become the model of the era which we desire to create. The many models which will develop should give each one of us an environment in which we can celebrate our potential: and discover the way into a more humane world.

We are challenged to break the obsolete social and economic systems which divide our world between the overprivileged and the underprivileged. All of us, whether governmental leader or protestor, businessman or worker, professor or student share a common guilt. We have failed to discover how the necessary changes in our ideals and our social structures can be made. Each of us, therefore, through our ineffectiveness and our lack of responsible awareness, causes the suffering around the world.

All of us are cripples—some physically, some mentally, some emotionally. We must, therefore, strive cooperatively to create the new world. There is no time left for destruction, for hatred, for anger. We must build, in hope and joy and celebration. Let us cease to fight the structures of the industrial age. Let us rather seek the new era of abundance with self-chosen work and freedom to follow the drum of one's own heart. Let us recognize that a striving for self-realization, for poetry and play, is basic to man once his needs for food, clothing, and shelter have been met that we will choose those areas of activity which will contribute to our own development and will be meaningful to our society.

the destructiveness of industrial-age values

But we must also recognize that our thrust toward self-realization is profoundly hampered by outmoded, industrial-age structures. We are presently constrained and driven by the impact of man's ever-growing powers. Our existing systems force us to develop and accept any weaponry system which may be technologically possible; our present systems force us to develop and accept any improvement in machinery, equipment, materials and supplies which will increase production and lower costs; our present systems force us to develop and accept advertising and consumer seduction.

In order to convince the citizen that he controls his destiny, that morality informs decisions, and that technology is the servant rather than the driving force, it is necessary to distort information. The ideal of informing the public has given way to trying to convince the public that forced actions are actually desirable actions.

Miscalculations in these increasingly complex relationalizations and consequent scandal, account for the increasing preoccupation with the honesty of both private and public decision makers. It is, therefore, tempting to attack those holding roles as national leader, professor, student. But such attacks on individuals often disguise the real nature of the crisis we confront:

the demonic nature of present systems which force man to consent to his own deepening self-destruction.

the way ahead

We can escape from these dehumanizing systems. The way ahead will be found by those who are unwilling to be constrained by the apparently all-determining forces and structures of the industrial age. Our freedom and power are determined by our willingness to accept responsibility for the future.

Indeed the future has already broken into the present. We each live in many times. The present of one is the past of another, and the future of yet another. We are called to live knowing and showing that the future exists, and that each one of us can call it in, when we are willing, to redress the balance of the past.

In the future we must end the use of coercive power and authority; the ability to demand action on the basis of one's hierarchical position. If any one phrase can sum up the nature of the new era, it is *the end of privilege and license.* Authority should emerge through a particular ability to advance a specific shared purpose. We must abandon our attempt to solve our problems through shifting power balances or attempting to create more efficient bureaucratic machines.

We call you to join man's race to maturity and to work with us in inventing the future. We believe that a human adventure is just beginning: that mankind has so far been restricted in developing its innovative and creative powers because it was overwhelmed by toil. Now we are free to be as human as we wish.

The celebration of man's humanity through joining together in the healing expression of one's relationships with others and one's growing acceptance of one's own nature and needs will clearly create major confrontations with existing values and systems. The expanding dignity of each man and each human relationship must necessarily challenge existing systems.

The call is to live the future: let us join together joyfully to celebrate our awareness that we can make our life today the shape of tomorrow's future.

PART TWO

choosing
your view
of
the future

The material in this section of the book should be seen as a basis for your own collection which you can make from reading newspapers and magazines, listening to radio, watching television, seeing films, looking at advertisements, etc. Today you will find all around you indications of future trends. Some of them are specific and easy to identify (they have not been included in this part of the book to any great extent): the possibility of living for 100 years on the average, instead of 70, and even the chance of immortality, the development of the techniques required for genetic manipulation, the creation of the skills required for underwater living, etc. Other materials, such as those gathered here, merely imply a view of the future—they are based on one of the three sets of assumptions discussed in Part One of the book.

If you are to gain a real sense of the future—and your view of it—you will need to collect your own material which reflects and deepens your understanding of what is going to happen. The material here can never be more than an inadequate substitute for your own effort.

This section has been arranged so as to juxtapose different views of the same subject. The unexpected relationships may help you to perceive ideas which otherwise would not have emerged.

How should you use this material? There is no single answer to this question: each person will, and should, use it in his own way. One pattern which may, however, be useful for you would be to try to discover the world view of the writer of each piece: is he an extrapolator, either positive or negative; a romantic who believes that there are no limitations on man's actions; or a system thinker who believes that man is constrained by his past but is nevertheless able to create a different future based on his imagined dreams of a better world?

Once you have done this, you may want to ask whether it would be possible to use the same technique if one holds a different world view. For example, can cartoonists really be anything else than pessimistic extrapolators? Are poets, most naturally, romantics? To extend this line of thought, what styles are best suited to the various world views: how will a positive extrapolator normally convey his message, what will a negative extrapolator do, how can a romantic communicate, and what is natural to a system thinker?

Do you feel that the various items in this part of the book could have been more effectively communicated using different styles: poetry instead of prose, prose instead of poetry, words instead of pictures, pictures instead of words? Can you transform any of the messages into different styles and make them more effective?

How are you to identify the world views of those who produced the various styles of communication in this part of the book? There are no easy, trick methods. Some people indeed may hold noncompatible views and their pieces may be internally inconsistent. There are, however, some clues:

Extrapolators believe that the future is determined and that it cannot be affected by man's efforts—he is caught up in forces which are out of his control. They talk about more, bigger, larger, etc.

Positive extrapolators *see the developments in store for man as generally valuable although they admit that there are some disadvantages to the developments that can be foreseen. They chronicle the probable developments by writing in academic styles and they are hostile to popularizations, to movement of communication outside professional structures. They see the expert as critical to the future and worry about how sufficient experts are to be created to meet the needs of the culture.*

Negative extrapolators *believe that the developments which are inevitable are intolerable. They believe that they therefore have a right to do anything they can to disrupt these developments and to prevent them from occurring. They do not believe that the developments can be stopped unless there is a total breakdown in the culture. They hope that such a breakdown will lead to the creation of a new culture although the means by which this new culture will come about are not specified. Negative extrapolators see their main hope in terms of publicity. They act in ways which attract the media—street demonstrations, violence, etc. The media, which also act on an extrapolator model, are attracted to the negative extrapolators and give them far more coverage than their numbers would justify.*

Romantics *believe that change will take place regardless of the actions of individuals and that a new world view or consciousness is coming into existence. They concentrate on creating new life-styles and believe that the creation of these life-styles will change the system. They see no reason to engage in political activity for the system will be changed without actions specifically designed for this purpose. It is sufficient to act humanely—the rest will follow automatically.*

System thinkers *agree that a new world view is necessary*

for the survival of the world and they too believe that it is in the process of coming into existence. They are primarily interested in helping people to understand the new consciousness they are developing and also in discovering how to manage a highly complex technological society when the bureaucratic patterns now being used cease to operate effectively.

There is no easy way to capsule the basic views of this last group except to state that they are interested in the ability to communicate rather than the power to command. They recognize that constrained obedience is rarely useful and often disastrous. They are interested in creating a world in which each individual makes his own decisions about his own future and the communications facilities are available to mesh individuals' disparate goals into an overall pattern for "spaceship earth."

We are still trying to find out what it means to be a system thinker. Little of the material here represents this view.

Reprinted from *The Herblock Gallery* (New York: Simon & Schuster, 1968).
Used with permission.

In 1970, Hawaii held a Governor's Conference on the Year 2000. The Conference was concerned with the kind of Hawaii desired for the future and what could be done to move the state in the desired directions.

One of the preparatory reports was on the role of Science and Technology in Hawaii in the Year 2000. It was written by a task force chaired by Dr. Terrence A. Rogers, director of the Pacific Biomedical Research Center at the University of Hawaii. The summary of the report used here was published in the Honolulu Advertiser as one method of bringing the conclusions of the task force to the attention of the general public.

What methods should your state and city be using to inform people of the changes which may occur between now and the year 2000? Are your schools teaching children about the reality of the future world or are they teaching about a past which has already vanished?

WILLIAM HELTON

science and
technology
in hawaii 2000

The year is 2000 and you have to get from the airport to down-town Honolulu in five minutes. How do you do it?

Simple. You step into a small, automatically controlled capsule which takes you on your way at a rate of 15 miles per hour on tracks high above the streets.

Once downtown, you step out of the capsule, take a device out of your pocket and unlock one of the many public vehicles available and drive to your destination, leaving the vehicle be-hind for use by someone else.

For by 2000, downtown Honolulu—like cities on the Main-land—will be off-limits to private automobiles. Other modes of transportation will have taken their place.

Such is one of the many visions of the Task Force on Sci-ence and Technology in the Year 2000.

Through its chairman, Dr. Terence A. Rogers, director of the Pacific Biomedical Research Center at the University of Hawaii, the task force paints an exciting picture of Island life 30 years hence.

But it also is careful to point out the hazards that lie along the way.

On the positive side, the report notes such possibilities as

Review article from the Honolulu *Advertiser*, July 27, 1970. Reprinted courtesy of the Honolulu *Advertiser*.

plastic heart valves, deep freeze organ banks, gas-turbine passenger cars, a thriving micro-miniaturized electronics industry in the Islands and new teaching techniques enabling a student to learn a foreign language in a few days.

Along with these, however, mankind also faces the ominous possibilities of armies of asexually produced identical soldiers, the potential of controlling thoughts of individuals by electrodes and the behavior of societies by drugs, gross invasions of privacy, and other dangers.

The 80-page preliminary report investigates the pros and cons of possible changes in electronics, transportation, energy sources, materials, food and applied behavior sciences.

The methods by which a traveler will make his way downtown in 2000 reflect the guidelines used by the committee in probing the future—a consideration of what is technically possible and a deep concern for preserving the environment.

"Cities in the next 30 years will experience a transportation revolution," the task force writes.

"Gaping needs will need to be met in health, education, job opportunities, and housing, but not a single one of these needs can be fully met without drastic development of our transportation systems."

Thus, the 21st century traveler will move by electric vehicles (instead of internal combustion-powered vehicles) along electronic highways, which will move more cars per lane per hour and be safer than present highways.

To get between urban centers, a traveler also will have a computer controlled Dial-a-Bus, a hybrid between an ordinary bus and a taxi. It would pick up our traveler at his door, or a nearby station.

The computer would keep tabs on all buses, select the nearest vehicle to our caller, and dispatch it through a pre-set optimal routing program.

Downtown, the traveler also may use elevated, covered moving sidewalks, or express tubes for "people capsules."

What about air travel?

"In the air the tendency will be towards specialization in

certain types of traffic—hypersonic and supersonic transports for well-off travelers in a hurry, subsonic jumbo jets for families with plenty of luggage or for freight and general aviation."

micro-miniaturization

In the field of electronics, the most important development foreseen, and one that could play an important role in the Islands, is the micro-miniaturization of integrated circuits.

"The importance of this can hardly be over-estimated. Complex circuits need now occupy only one-1,000th of the volume of the 'conventional' transistorized circuits which were considered advanced a decade ago," the task force suggests.

Micro-electronics also will lead to extremely flexible personal communications, such as pocket radio-telephones linked to the regular telephone system, or pocket-sized computers giving individual citizens access to the whole Library of Congress or to all securities transactions.

One drawback, however, is that with the advent of such devices, it will be possible "to bug anyone, almost anywhere."

"New generations of electronic eavesdropping devices could be developed at any time by a paternalistic government or secret agency . . .

"Accordingly, it would seem that the individual privacy can best be preserved by constant vigilance regarding the rules of evidence and by-laws through which the private citizen could more readily get restitution from snoopers than by attempting to control the technological developments . . ."

On the positive side, however, the task force writes that the surgical implantation of a brain stimulator could potentially help the "violent schizophrenic, the autistic child, or the mentally defective."

But herewith arise other ethical problems. "Who is to bear the God-like responsibility and power (through a switch, no less), to control the mind of another?" the report asks.

"Starting from the excellent intent of modifying criminal or sociopathic behavior, the authorities might easily decide to modify the behavior of any persistently thorny character, making him tractable and cooperative.

But while Rogers and his colleagues recognized the danger of "thought control" they also note that similar processes can be put to positive use in developing new teaching techniques, permitting, for example, a student to progress at his own rate.

And through the use of "saturation" approaches (the kind used to sell political candidates to the American public), reinforced by hypnosis and drug-preparation of the student's mind, it may be possible to teach a foreign language in a matter of days.

progress and problems

In the field of medical science, the march of progress also could run into ethical problems.

For example, in genetics it will be possible "to alter human makeup and perhaps even change the course of human evolution.

"Possible misuses of this scientific potential would include the development of an army made up of identical soldiers . . . or we could conceive of a work force of nearly mindless slaves."

Still, in terms of what is technically possible, Islanders can expect to have better health care in 2000.

For example, there would be a series of mechanical hearts, kidneys and other "organs," surgically implanted "receivers" and "amplifiers" for the deaf and partially blind; and micro-surgery with laser-type devices.

Moreover, virtually all diseases known now will have been under "nominal control" by 2000, and others will have been eradicated. However, new mutant forms will appear, and there will be a fight to control these.

Medical scientists also will try altering the environment as a means of disease prevention.

"For example, fuel, food, social poisons such as tobacco, etc.—all will be engineered to remove factors causative or contributory to disease patterns," the report said.

On the subject of euphoric drugs, the report notes that throughout human history, drugs, including alcohol, have been used to make life more bearable. This will still be with us in 2000.

"Probably the thing that we can most optimistically predict is that the new drugs will have fewer destructive side effects, and yet still be highly efficacious in doing whatever we need to have done to our view of reality."

While there will be a shortage of some materials in 2000, the task force does not see any problem of food shortages (discounting the problem of distribution).

Enough to feed a world population of some 6 billion in 2000 will be "easily within the grasp of mankind as far as science and technology are concerned," the task force says.

"The number of persons supportable on earth is ultimately limited by the amount of space a person needs to work and live in reasonable comfort, and not by production of food.

"At the present projection, over-population is our major problem—not starvation."

The report predicted that there would be a severe shortage of silver, lead, zinc, mercury and large diamonds by 2000. There will be definite shortages of gold and platinum and possible shortages of magnesium, tungsten and tin.

While it may be possible to extract some of these materials from the sea or get them from other sources, the task force suggests that society should work to "stretch" the available supply, even if it means changing some values.

"One should encourage the public to reject design obsolescence (a new model car every year, etc.). Some of these measures can be handled via the tax structure or similar means.

reconsider value systems

"However, the really important change is much harder to handle. That is the re-orientation of the whole value system of the public (not just of the engineer).

"In that connection one might make the generally unpopular observation that in the long run we are not helping anybody by exporting our value system to less 'developed' countries.

"The contrary may well be true. Present day college students will be the 'establishment' of the year 2000.

"It is hard to visualize that any major change in the public value system will happen in so short a time, unless severe shortages or other events force us."

While the futurists saw innovations in some fields and possible "surprises" in electronics, they looked at the construction industry as likely to remain basically conservative because of the building code.

On the subject of energy supply, the report discusses the possibilities of several systems to provide the 6,500 megawatts Hawaii will need in 30 years.

Among these are solar collectors on Haleakala and Mauna Kea, ocean-wave generators at storm-surf coastal zones, a geothermal installation drawing energy from Kilauea volcano and a massive nuclear fission plant on Molokai.

Because of the relatively small projected power need and because the State cannot tie into adjoining power grids, the task force predicts that Hawaii will lag behind other states in converting to nuclear power plants.

That is, unless "public concern and support for the preservation of the quality of the environment" accelerates "the introduction of nuclear power to Hawaii well ahead of the rate at which it would be justified on economic considerations alone," the report says.

the certainty
of
surprises

At the May 1971 meeting of the World Future Society W. D. Rowe of the Mitre Corporation said: "We don't live in a surprise-free environment."

He illustrated his point in the following way. Suppose everybody in the room were polled on where they would be in ten minutes. One person answers: "We'll all be dead." Since that answer is a minority of one, it would be eliminated from further consideration. "But that's the guy who's got the bomb in his suitcase," said Mr. Rowe, "and he's the guy I'm looking for."

When you examine the future are you interested in what "most everybody" thinks or are you looking for the maverick who may have new knowledge not yet known to the culture?

It has often been assumed that the new technologies could lead directly to a police state. Although there have been attempts to use the technologies for this purpose, they have been largely unsuccessful. It appears at this point as though there is a greater risk of breakdown and chaos than of dictatorship and fascism.

The next piece explains this paradox. It is of critical importance as one tries to plan for the future. If the new technologies make possible a police state and a controlled world, one set of reactions are appropriate. If the greatest danger is a breakdown of any form of system because the available power cannot be used, then we must imagine new methods of action.

Written in the context of the Arab high-jackings of late 1970, it is already out of date. The issues it raises have not changed, however.

JAMES RESTON

the impotence of power

NEW YORK—The supreme irony of this age of power is its impotence to deal with determined or fanatical minorities. Mr. Jefferson, who had very little military power, could deal effectively with the Barbary pirates early in the 19th century, but Mr. Nixon, who has apocalyptic power, cannot handle the Arab pirates without risking the lives of the Americans he wants to rescue.

You can almost put it down as a rule that the more complicated a society is the more vulnerable it is to sabotage. It is not only the great jet airliners that can be disrupted at the whim of a few desperate men, but even vast modern cities like New York are at the mercy of any fanatics who know how to get at the critical centers of electrical power.

The violent events of the last few years illustrate the point. We have not yet had to face organized guerrilla war in the urban centers of America, but the skyjackers, the wreckers in the universities, and even the unorganized hoodlums have given us some idea of what can be done by tyrannical minorities.

danger of infection

Each of these problems, of course, is different, but in all of them only a very few men were able to bring the operations of vast enterprises to a halt. Probably the most spectacular example of the power of the weak over the strong has been the operation of the Communist guerrillas in Southeast Asia, first against the organized power of France, and then even against an American expeditionary force of over half a million men. . . .

The danger in the present wave of skyjacking is that it can easily spread into an infectious disorder, and not only in the Middle East. It is a quick and comparatively easy way to dramatize any cause, and it seems to have a compelling appeal for deranged minds.

Even the risks involved in highjacking a jet or going down the right manholes to sabotage the power of a city are scarcely as great today as robbing a bank. Nixon, for all his power, cannot even perform the first duty of government, which is to protect its own citizens, not because he is weak, but because his strength is so great that he dare not use it. . . .

He has 1,800 marines with the U.S. Sixth Fleet in the Mediterranean and a 1,500-man airborne brigade in Germany. It is within his power to parachute them in the night into the Jordanian desert and overwhelm the Arab pirates, but he might easily lose the lives of the trapped Americans in the process.

So we are left with the problem of dealing with anarchy. Putting a military guard on planes in international traffic is not a solution, though the armed guards on the El Al planes have complicated the problem and raised the risks for the skyjackers.

effective sanction

Probably the most effective sanction would be to isolate any country whose citizens engage in international piracy. This would mean an agreement by all the major airlines not to fly into any country harboring the pirates, and not allowing that country's planes to use the airfields of the major nations of the world.

The objection to this, of course, is that the sanction is not precise, and in the case of Jordan would actually punish the government that is fighting the guerrillas. Nevertheless, such an arrangement might encourage the Arab governments to take more vigorous action against the pirates than they have been willing to take in the past.

There is, however, no foolproof way to deal with the problem. Closer inspection of baggage would help. So would very strict limitations on hand-baggage that could be carried into the cabin, but short of turning international flights into nudist parties, which might be a little awkward or even embarrassing, there would still be the danger of concealing weapons even from a vigilant frisker.

Accordingly, President Nixon has undoubtedly been right to hold his temper and hope that the Arabs have hurt their cause so severely by these adventures that they will stop the nonsense on their own.

This, however, is far from a sure thing. All you have to do is take a long walk through almost any American city these days to realize how many angry and demented people there are wandering around loose—many of them willing to risk their lives to remove some real or imagined grievance.

Once the normal restraints of interdependent cities or systems are broken, the anarchy tends to feed on itself, and this is now the danger in a world with so many frustrated and even demented people.

EWAN MacCOLL

five
fingers

Five fingers has the hand,
five fingers, five fingers.
Four fingers and a thumb, say it either way.
Four and one add up to five,
that number helped us stay alive,
helped the human race survive
up until the present day.

Five fingers and the brain,
five fingers, five fingers.
Five fingers and the brain
made a pact one day.
The brain it said, "We'll make a team,
the best the world has ever seen;
we'll pool resources, work and scheme
and that without delay."

Five fingers and the brain,
five fingers, five fingers.
Five fingers and the brain
went to work one day,
made a spear and made a bow,
laid the mighty jungle low,

learned to hunt and make things grow
and mould things out of clay.

Five fingers and the brain,
five fingers, five fingers.
Five fingers and the brain
busy at work and play,
making music, carving bone,
painting pictures, working stone,
learning all that can be known
and growing every day.

Five fingers and the brain,
five fingers, five fingers.
Five fingers and the brain
working night and day
built the world and then got smart,
opened up the atom's heart.
The fingers said, "It's time to part
and go our separate ways."

Five fingers and the brain,
five fingers, five fingers.
Five fingers and the brain,
quarreling night and day,
they've got the know-how and the skill
to make and build, destroy and kill.
The choice is theirs for good or ill,
to find a human way.

PEGGY SEEGER

there's better
things

Kind friends I want to warn you
Because I love us all,
No doubt you read your papers,
But the half can never be told.
Politicians will try and fool you, and get you to agree
To blow this world to glory and end humanity.

But there's better things to do—than blow this world in two
You could live into your old age, and your kids be normal too.
There's better things for you—That all on earth must do
Gotta pledge your feet on the road to peace and
see your journey through.
Now some folks think that danger
Can't reach this peaceful shore
They must see planes and soldiers
Before they call it war.
Kind friends I will remind you
The atom's very small
It can blow you all to glory
And you can't see it at all.

CHORUS:
Now some folks they are holy
In the Bible it is told

That judgment comes tomorrow
So today pray for your soul.
But that is not sufficient
Tomorrow is today
They'll blow you all to glory
While you just sit and pray.

"As Nearly As We Can Translate, It Says: 'We Are Agreed In Principle On Preventing The Spread Of Nuclear Weapons; However...'"

"As Nearly as We Can Translate, It Says: 'We are Agreed in Principle On Preventing the Spread of Nuclear Weapons; However . . .'" Reprinted from *The Herblock Gallery* (New York: Simon & Schuster, 1968). Used with permission.

What does the future hold? What are the options? John W. Gardner explores the past and the future and suggests that there may still be time to change our course.

Does the style that he used for making his point increase, or decrease, the chance that we will act to change our society in time?

JOHN W. GARDNER

uncritical lovers, unloving critics

In the seventeenth and eighteenth centuries, increasing numbers of people began to believe that men could determine their own fate, shape their own institutions, and gain command of the social forces that buffeted them. Before then, from the beginning, men had believed that all the major features of their life were determined by immemorial custom or fate or the will of God. It was one of the Copernican turns of history that brought man gradually over two or three centuries to the firm conviction that he could have a hand in shaping his institutions.

No one really knows all the ingredients that went into the change, but we can identify some major elements. One was the emergence with the scientific revolution of a way of thinking that sought objectively identifiable cause-and-effect relationships. People trained in that way of thinking about the physical world were bound to note that the social world, too, had its causes and effects. And with that discovery came, inevitably, the idea that one might manipulate the cause to alter the effect.

At the same time people became less and less inclined to explain their daily lives and institutions in terms of God's will. And that trend has continued to this day. Less and less do men suppose, even those who believe devoutly in a Supreme Being, that God busies himself with the day-to-day microadministration of the world.

From a speech given at the University of North Carolina, Greensboro, February 15, 1971. Reprinted courtesy of John W. Gardner.

While all of this was happening, new modes of transportation and communication were breaking down parochial attitudes all over the world. As men discovered that human institutions and customs varied enormously from one society to the next, it became increasingly difficult to think of one's own institutions as unalterable and increasingly easy to conceive of a society in which men consciously shaped their institutions and customs.

The result is that today any bright high school student can discourse on social forces and institutional change. A few centuries ago, even for learned men, such matters were "given," ordained, not subject to analysis, fixed in the great design of things.

Up to a point the new views were immensely exhilarating. In the writings of our founding fathers, for example, one encounters a mood approaching exaltation as they proceeded to shape a new nation. But more recently another consequence has become apparent: the new views place an enormous—in some instances, an unbearable—burden on the social structures that man has evolved over the centuries. Those structures have become the sole target and receptacle for all man's hope and hostility. He has replaced his fervent prayer to God with a shrill cry of anger against his own institutions. I claim no special insight into the unknowable Deity, but He must be chuckling.

Men can tolerate extraordinary hardship if they think it is an unalterable part of life's travail. But an administered frustration—unsanctioned by religion or custom or deeply rooted values—is more than the spirit can bear. So increasingly men rage at their institutions. All kinds of men rage at all kinds of institutions, here and around the world. Most of them have no clear vision of the kind of world they want to build; they only know they don't want the kind of world they have.

So much for the past and present.

I told you I would take you three centuries into the future. I am able to do this thanks to a Cornell scientist who recently discovered how man may step off the time dimension and visit the past or future at will. You may be surprised you haven't heard about this, but he's finding his capacity to know the future rather profitable. He doesn't want to publicize his findings until he has won a few more horse races.

At any rate he gave me a few pills, and since I'm not interested in horse races, I decided to find out what the future holds in the struggle between man and his institutions. I cannot guarantee the results. I do not offer what follows as a prediction. Perhaps the pill just gave me bad dreams.

The first thing I learned is that in the last third of the twentieth century the rage to demolish succeeded beyond the fondest dreams of the dismantlers. They brought everything tumbling down. Since the hostility to institutions was a product of modern minds, the demolition was most thorough in the most advanced nations.

You will be pleased to know that unlike the fall of Rome, this decline was not followed by hundreds of years of darkness. In fact, there followed less than a century of chaos and disorder. In the latter part of the twenty-first century the rebuilding began. Since chaos is always followed by authoritarianism, this was a period of iron rule, worldwide—a world society rigidly organized and controlled. I don't think I shall tell you what language was spoken.

But tyrannies tend to grow lax, even under futuristic methods of thought control. By the end of the twenty-second century, the sternly disciplined institutions of the world society had grown relatively tolerant, and the old human impulse to be free had begun to reassert itself.

In the new, more permissive atmosphere, men were again allowed to study history, which had been under a ban for two centuries. The effect was electric. To those austere and antiseptic minds, conditioned to the requirements of a technically advanced authoritarianism, the rediscovery of man's history was intoxicating. It generated an intellectual excitement that dominated the whole twenty-third century. Scholars were entranced by the variety of human experience, shocked by the violence and barbarism, saddened by the stupidities, and exalted by the achievements of their forebears. And as they searched that history, excitedly, sadly, lovingly, they returned increasingly to the twentieth century as a moment of curious and critical importance in the long pageant.

All the evidence available to them indicated that the preceding centuries had seen a vast and impressive movement in the direction of institutions that were responsive to the will of men. There were setbacks, to be sure, and trouble and hypocrisy and failures, but over the years the trend was unmistakable. Why then in the late twentieth century did men turn on their institutions and destroy them in a fit of impatience? As one twenty-third-century scholar put it, "Until we answer that question we shall never be sure that we are not preparing the same fate for ourselves."

As they studied the history of the twentieth century, they discovered that human expectations had risen sharply in the middle years of the century. They observed that men came to demand more and more of their institutions and to demand it with greater intransigence. And they noted that the demands for instant performance led to instant disillusionment, for while aspirations leapt ahead, human institutions remained sluggish —less sluggish, to be sure, than at any previous time in history, but still inadequately responsive to human need.

Twenty-third-century scholars agreed on these facts but they disagreed as to the implications. One school of thought said the big mistake had been to let aspirations loose in the first place. Human aspirations, they said, should be kept under tight control. The opposing school of thought argued that human aspirations were a dynamic force that held enormous potential for good. They insisted that the main requirement was to make human institutions less sluggish. The only error of the mid-twentieth century, they said, was to release aspirations without designing institutions responsive enough to satisfy those aspirations.

After years of debate, the two schools of thought began to come together, and a common doctrine began to emerge. The first thing they agreed upon was that human aspirations *were* capable of contributing enormously to the dynamism of the society and therefore should not be tightly bottled up. But they also agreed that there must be procedural bounds within which the aspirations could express themselves.

Some were quick to point out that in the mid-twentieth century such procedural bounds did exist and functioned quite well, permitting extraordinary scope and variety of dissent until the last third of the century, when the bounds were increasingly rejected and the dissolution of the society began. Back of the rejection was the impatient hostility that late-twentieth-century man felt toward his institutions. Those who consciously sought the destruction of their society were never more than a small minority, but they found it easy to trigger the latent hostility of larger numbers of people. Many, of course, were ignorant of the long, painful evolution of procedures for the expression of dissent, for the protection of individual rights, for the maintenance of that framework of order without which freedom is impossible. Others were not ignorant but very angry. The result was the same.

The second thing twenty-third–century scholars came to agree upon was that if society is going to release aspirations for institutional change—which is precisely what many twentieth-century societies deliberately did—then it had better be sure its institutions are capable of such change. In this respect they found the twentieth century sadly deficient.

Most institutions were designed to obstruct change rather than facilitate it. And that is not really surprising. The institutions were, after all, designed by human beings, and most men most of the time do not want the institutions in which they themselves have a vested interest to change. Professors were often cited as an interesting example of this tendency, because they clearly favored innovation in other parts of the society but steadfastly refused to make universities into flexible, adaptive, self-renewing institutions.

There were, of course, a good many people in the twentieth century who did want change, but they were curiously indifferent to the task of redesigning their institutions so that change could be readily accomplished. Many of them were moral zealots who expended their total energy in headlong combat between themselves (whom they believed to be very, very good) and specified others (whom they believed to be very, very bad); and the object of the combat was to do in the bad ones, even if it meant doing in oneself. This led to endless hostilities, especially when those marked for assault had equally strong convictions about their *own* moral superiority. It was particularly difficult when the two groups spoke a different language or were separated by an ocean or thirty years in age.

There were other reformers who were considerably more discriminating and saw that to achieve their ends they *must* change human institutions. But even these often misconceived the fundamental task.

Each such reformer came to his task with a little bundle of desired changes. The society is intolerable, he would assert, because it has these specifiable defects: *a, b, c,* and so on. The implication was that if appropriate reforms *a', b',* and *c'* were carried through and the defects corrected, the society would be wholly satisfactory and the work of the reformer done.

That, as twenty-third–century scholars plainly saw, was a primitive way of viewing social change. The true task, they saw, was to design a society (and institutions) capable of continuous change, continuous renewal, continuous responsiveness. They understood that this was entirely feasible; indeed, they noted that the twentieth century had hit upon a number of partial solutions to the problem of designing self-renewing institutions but had never pursued the task with adequate vigor. (I might add that I, myself, wrote a book on this subject, back in the twentieth century. It was entitled *Self-Renewal.* I won't review its findings here, because I wouldn't want to spoil your enjoyment of the book.)

Because of their failure to design institutions capable of continuous renewal, twentieth-century societies showed astonishing sclerotic streaks. Even in the United States, which was then the most adaptable of all societies, the departments of the federal government were in grave need of renewal; state government was in most places an old attic full of outworn relics; in most cities municipal government was a waxwork of stiffly preserved anachronisms; the system of taxation was a tangle of dysfunctional measures; the courts were crippled by archaic organizational arrangements; the unions, the professions, the universities, the corporations—each had spun its own impenetrable web of vested interests.

Such a society could not respond to challenge. And it did not. But as one twenty-third–century scholar put it, "The reformers couldn't have been less interested in the basic adaptability of the society. That posed tough and complex tasks of institutional redesign that bored them to death. They preferred the joys of combat, of villain hunting. As for the rest of society, it was dozing off in front of the television set."

The twenty-third–century scholars made another exceptionally interesting observation. They pointed out that twentieth-century institutions were caught in a savage crossfire between uncritical lovers and unloving critics. On the one side, those who loved their institutions tended to smother them in an embrace of death, loving their rigidities more than their promise, shielding them from life-giving criticism. On the other side, there arose a breed of critics without love, skilled in demolition but untutored in the arts by which human institutions are nurtured and strengthened and made to flourish. Between the two, the institutions perished.

The twenty-third–century scholars understood that where human institutions were concerned, love without criticism brings stagnation, and criticism without love brings destruction. And they emphasized that the swifter the pace of change, the more lovingly men had to care for and criticize their institutions to keep them intact through the turbulent passages.

In short, men must be discriminating appraisers of their society, knowing coolly and precisely what it is about the society that thwarts or limits them and therefore needs modification. And so must they be discriminating protectors of their institutions, preserving those features that nourish and strengthen them and make them more free. To fit themselves for such tasks, they must be sufficiently serious to study their institutions, sufficiently dedicated to become expert in the art of modifying them.

Having arrived at these judgments, twenty-third–century leaders proceeded to redesign their own society for continuous renewal. Commenting on the debt they owed to the twentieth-century experience, one of them said: "It is not just that we have learned from twentieth-century mistakes. We have learned from twentieth-century insights. For in that troubled time there were men who were saying just what we are saying now. Had they been heeded, the solutions we have reached would have come 300 years earlier. But no one was listening."

"If you want to be loved, you'll be coopted. People often ask me how I choose people to work with me. Well, you start off by saying they have to be bright, hard-working, the usual traits. But the one key probably is how willing they are not to be loved. We've had raiders who will start off on an investigation, say, of the Food and Drug Administration; and after a while one or two come back and say the people over there were so nice to them that they just can't write reports that are critical. . . .

"The most important quality for this kind of work is to have no anxiety to be loved."

Ralph Nader
quoted in Time, *May 10, 1971*

PEGGY SEEGER
EWAN MacCOLL

the
space girl's
song

My mama told me I should never venture into space
But I did, I did, I did;
She said no Teran girl could trust the Martian race,
But I did, I did, I did.
A rocket pilot asked me on a voyage to go
And I was so romantic I just couldn't say no,
That he was just a servo robot, how was I to know,
So I did, I did, I did.

My papa warned me never to trust a space engineer
But I did, I did, I did.
He said free-fall and super drive would surely cost me dear
And they did, they did, they did.
I've been as far in hyper-space as anybody can,
I've traveled through the time-warp on the psycho-plan,
They say a gal must travel for to find her spaceman
So I did, I did, I did.

They said to find a man out there and try to settle down
So I did, I did, I did.
They said my kids might grow up one-eyed,
green or bald or round,

And they did, they did, they did.
My cosmic husband died of mumps a hundred years ago,
My daughter's in the Milky Way a-tracking down a beau,
And I'm so old and doddering, I've nothing for to show
What I did, I did, I did.

JOHN BOARDMAN

the
asteroid
light

My father was the keeper of the Asteroid Light,
He slept with a Martian one fine night,
Out of this match came children three,
Two were mutants and the other was me.

Chorus: Yo ho ho, the jets run free,
Oh for a life at the speed of *c*!

When I was but a space cadet,
They put me in charge of a proton jet,
I cleaned the tubes and filled them with fuel,
And picked my teeth with an old slide rule.

   Chorus

One night as I was heading for the Moon,
And singing a well-known spaceman's tune,
I heard a voice cry out of the void,
And there sat my mother on her asteroid.

Chorus

Oh, what has become of my children three,
My mother she then asked of me,
One is on exhibit in a zoo on Venus,
And the other keeps a telepathic link between us.

Chorus

The deuterons flashed in her hydrogen hair,
I looked again, and my mother wasn't there,
But she telepathed angrily out of the night,
Then to hell with the keeper of the Asteroid Light.

Chorus

"I'm not worried. By the time the population crunch really hits, we'll be sending the excess off to Earth or somewhere."

Drawing by Lorenz from *The New Yorker,* August 23, 1969. Copyright © 1969 by The New Yorker Magazine, Inc. Used with permission.

MALVINA REYNOLDS

what have they done to the rain?

Just a little rain falling all around,
The grass lifts its head to the heavenly sound,
Just a little rain, Just a little rain,
What have they done to the rain?

Just a little boy standing in the rain,
The gentle rain that falls for years.
And the grass is gone, the boy disappears,
And rain keeps falling like helpless tears,
And what have they done to the rain?

Just a little breeze out of the sky,
The leaves pat their hands as the breeze blows by,
Just a little breeze with some smoke in its eye,
What have they done to the rain?

In this piece, Edwin L. Dale states some "iron laws" which relate the economy to the environment. You will have to decide whether you agree that no changes are possible in these laws or whether Dale has missed some possibilities of change.

EDWIN L. DALE, JR.

the economics
of
pollution

Now that environment has become a national concern, it might be well to clean up some of the economic rubbish associated with the subject. There are, alas, a few "iron laws" that cannot be escaped in the effort to reduce the pollution of our air and water, in disposing of solid waste and the like. The laws do not necessarily prevent a clean environment but there is no hope of obtaining one unless they are understood.

We have all become vaguely aware that there will be a cost—perhaps higher monthly electric bills, perhaps higher taxes, perhaps a few cents or a few dollars more on anything made from steel—if there is a successful and massive effort to have a better environment. But that is only a beginning. There are other problems.

This article will describe the three iron laws that matter. There is no point in hiding that all three are very depressing. The only purpose in adding more depressing information to a world already surfeited with it is a small one: to avoid useless effort based on false premises. A classic example has already arisen in wistful congressional inquiries into whether we might think of a future with somewhat less electric power, or at least less growth in electric power.

From *The New York Times Magazine,* April 19, 1970. Reprinted with the permission of the New York Times Company © 1970 and Edwin L. Dale.

In shorthand, the three laws are

1. the law of economic growth
2. the law of compound interest
3. the law of the mix between public and private spending

We can count on the output of the average worker to continue to rise in the years ahead, as it has in the past. Nearly all current forecasts put this rise in productivity much closer to 3 per cent than to 2, and 3 per cent has been our average in the years since World War II. So without any change in the labor force at all, our national output will go on rising by some 3 per cent a year.

What does output mean?

It means electric power produced—and smoke produced.

It means cans and bottles produced.

It means steel produced—and, unless something is done about it, water and air polluted.

It means paper produced—with the same result as for steel.

And so on and on.

But that is not the end, for there will not be a static labor force. As noted, the force for the next 20 years is already born and it is going to grow year by year (with a caveat, to be described below).

Obviously, we want to offer these people employment opportunity. So, in addition to a 3 per cent productivity growth, there will be an added growth of at least 1 per cent a year in the number of workers. The result is that we are almost "condemned" to a rise in our total output of 4 per cent a year. The only escape, it seems, would be a national decision either to have high unemployment or to try to be less efficient. Both are absurd on their face.

The law of economic growth says, then, that we already know that the national output in 1980 will be, and almost must be, some 50 per cent higher than it is now. President Nixon has said so publicly, and he is right. That is the result of an annual rate of real growth of about 4 per cent, compounded. It is terrifying. If an economy of $900 billion in 1969 produces the pollution and clutter we are all familiar with, what will an economy half again as large produce?

Is there no escape from this law? The answer, essentially, is no. But there is one possible way to mitigate the awesome results. We might reduce the labor input (but, we hope, not the productivity input), without creating mass unemployment.

Each working person has a workday, workweek, workyear and worklife. Any one of them could be reduced by law or otherwise. We could reduce the legal workweek from the present 40 hours. We could add more holidays or lengthen vacations to reduce the workyear. We are already shortening the worklife, without planning it that way: increased participation in higher education has meant later entry into the labor force for many, and retirement plans, including Social Security, have brought about earlier retirement than in the past for others.

If, by chance or by law, the annual man-hours of employment are reduced in the years ahead, our output will grow a little less rapidly. This is the only way to cut our economic growth, short of deliberate unemployment or deliberate inefficiency.

There is a cost. It is most easily seen in a union-bargained settlement providing for longer vacations without any cut in annual wages, or a legal reduction in the workweek from 40 to 35 hours, with compulsory overtime payments after that. In each case, more workers must be hired to produce the same output, and if the employer—because of market demand—goes on producing at the same level, wage costs for each unit of output are higher than they otherwise would have been. Prices will therefore be higher. This is widely recognized. Maybe we would be willing to pay them.

But we cannot guarantee less output. Only if employers produce less—because of the extra cost—would that happen. And in the larger sense, the cost of a reduction of our annual labor input is simply less production per capita because the labor force is idle more of the time.

But less production was the objective of the exercise—the antipollution exercise. If we start with the proposition that the growth of production is the underlying cause of pollution, which has merit as a starting point, the only way we can get less growth in production, if we want it, is to have more of our labor

force idle more of the time. In that case, we will have more leisure without mass unemployment, as we usually think of the
term. Our national output, and our standard of living, will rise
less rapidly.

That last idea we may learn to take, if we can cope with the
leisure. But under any foreseeable circumstances, our output
will still go on rising. With the most optimistic assumptions about
a gradual reduction of the workday, workweek, workyear and
worklife, we shall undoubtedly have a much higher output in
1980 than we have in 1970. To a man concerned about the environment, it might seem a blessing if our economic growth in
the next 10 years could be 2 per cent a year instead of 4 per
cent; he cannot hope for zero growth.

The law of economic growth, then, tells us a simple truth:
"we" cannot choose to reduce production simply because we
have found it to be the cause of a fouled environment. And if
we want to reduce the rate of growth of production, the place to
look is in our man-hours of work.

the law of compound interest

It is a fair question to ask: Why weren't we bothered about
pollution 12 or 15 years ago? In October, 1957, to pick a date,
the Soviet Union sent the first earth satellite into orbit. The
American economy had just begun a recession that was to send
unemployment to 7 per cent of the labor force. The late George
Magoffin Humphrey, who had just resigned as Secretary of the
Treasury, was warning of what he saw as vast Government
spending, at that time $77 billion, and saying it would bring "a
depression that would curl your hair." There were plenty of
things to think about.

But nobody was worried about pollution. Conservation
groups were properly bothered about parts of the wilderness
(the Hell's Canyon Dam in Idaho, for example), but that was an
entirely different thing. That was an issue of esthetics, not health.
Nobody seemed to mention air pollution or waste that might
overwhelm the space in which to put it. In a peculiarly sad

irony, the late Adlai E. Stevenson had fought and lost an election against Dwight D. Eisenhower in 1956 partially on a "pollution" issue—radiation in the atmosphere from the explosion of atomic weapons.

The question, to repeat: why didn't we worry about pollution then? The answer is that, relatively speaking, there was no pollution. Yes, there were electric power plants then, too. Yes, there were paper mills polluting streams. Yes, there were tin cans and paper and bottles. Some snowflakes, though we didn't know it, were already a bit black, and Pittsburgh got national attention because it tried to do some cleaning up.

But here we come to the law of compound interest. In 1957 —*only 13 years ago*—our gross national product was $453 billion. In 1969, in constant dollars, it was $728 billion. That is an increase of nearly $300 billion in tin cans, electric power, automobiles, paper, chemicals and all the rest. It is an increase of 60 per cent.

So what? That was not the result of an unnaturally rapid growth rate, though a bit more rapid than in some periods of our past. The *so what* is this: in the preceding 13 years the growth had been *only $100 billion.* We were the same nation, with the same energy, in those preceding 13 years. We invested and we had a rise both in productivity and in our labor force. But in the first 13 years of this example our output rose $100-billion, and in the second 13 it rose $300 billion.

In the next 13 it will rise more than $500 billion.

That is the law of compound interest. These are not numbers; they are tin cans and smoke and auto exhaust. There is no visible escape from it. Applying the same percentage growth to a larger base every year, we have reached the point where our growth in one year is half the total output of Canada, fully adjusting for inflation. Another dizzying and rather horrifying way of putting it is that the real output of goods and services in the United States has grown as much since 1950 as it grew in the entire period from the landing of the Pilgrims in 1620 up to 1950.

Most investors know the law of compound interest. There is a magic rule, for example, known as the Rule of 72. It says, with mathematical certainty, that money invested at a 7.2 per cent rate of interest, compounded each year, doubles in 10 years. Our GNP, happily, does not compound at 7.2 per cent. But it compounds at between 4 and 5 percent, and it has been compounding. The result is that the same routine, full employment, desirable, nationally wanted, almost unavoidable percentage increase in our national output in 1970 means precisely twice as many extra tin cans, twice as much additional electric power, and so on, as the same rate of growth in 1950. And that is only 20 years ago! We are not doing anything different, or anything awful. We are the same people. Granting approximately the same amount of human carelessness and selfishness, we are the victims solely of the law of compound interest.

the law of the mix between public and private spending

Robert S. McNamara, the eternally energetic and constructive former Secretary of Defense and now president of the World Bank, gave a speech in February about the plight of the poor countries. In the speech he understandably criticized the United States for reducing its foreign aid effort. But in supporting his point he adopted, almost inadvertently, a piece of partly fallacious conventional wisdom:

"Which is ultimately more in the nation's interest: to funnel national resources into an endlessly spiraling consumer economy—in effect, a pursuit of consumer gadgetry with all its senseless by-products of waste and pollution—or to dedicate a more reasonable share of those same resources to improving the fundamental quality of life both at home and abroad?"

Fair enough. It means tax increases, of course, though Mr. Namara did not say so. That is what the "mix" between public and private spending is all about. But for our purposes the point is different. Let us look more closely at the phrase: ". . . a pursuit of consumer gadgetry with all its senseless by-products of waste and pollution . . ."

As it stands, it is true. Private consumption does create side effects like waste and pollution. But now, assume a Brave

New World in which we are all happy to pay higher taxes and reduce our private consumption so that the Government may have more money with which to solve our problems—ranging from poor education to poverty, from crime to inadequate health services. We shall not examine here the issue of whether more Government money solves problems. It is obviously more effective in some areas than in others. But anyway, in our assumption, we are all willing to give the Government more money to solve problems, including pollution.

Now let us see what happens.

• The Government spends the money to reduce pollution. Sewage plants are built. They need steel. They need electric power. They need paperwork. They need workers. The workers get paid, and they consume.

• The Government spends the money on education. New schools are built, which need steel, lumber and electric power. Teachers are hired. They get paid, and they consume. They throw away tin cans.

• The Government spends the money on a better welfare system that treats all poor people alike, whether they work or not. Incomes among the poor rise by some amount between $4 billion and $20 billion, and these people consume. Electric power production rises and appliance and steel production rises, and so on and on.

The point is obvious by now. A shifting in our national income or production between "public goods" and "private goods" hardly changes the environment problem at all because it does not reduce total spending, or output, in the economy.

Lest a careful economist raise a valid objection, a slightly technical point must be conceded here. Government spending is done in three categories:

1. Purchase of goods (tanks, typewriters, sanitation trucks, and school buildings).
2. Transfer payments to people outside government (Social Security, veterans' benefits, welfare).
3. Purchase of services, meaning the services of the people it employs (teachers, policemen, park rangers, tax collectors).

To the extent that a shift to more public spending, through

higher taxes and a resulting reduction of private consumption, involves the first two of these categories, the point stands as made: there will be just as much production of steel, tin cans, electric power, and toasters as before. To the extent that the higher public spending goes to the third category, employment of more teachers, policemen and the like, there will be slightly less production of goods, even though these people spend their paychecks like everyone else. Essentially what happens in this case is that the society has chosen, through higher taxes, to have more services and fewer goods. If we assume that goods production brings pollution, a society with fewer auto- or steel-workers and more cops will crank out less pollution.

But this remains a relatively minor matter. Hardly anyone who proposes a solution to our problems thinks in terms of vast armies of Government workers. Reforming welfare through the President's new family-assistance plan is the perfect example; this will be a simple expansion of transfer payments. And, for that matter, building more sewage plants will be a purchase of goods. The overriding fact is that we can spend 30 per cent of our GNP for public purposes, as we do now, or 50 per cent, and the GNP will still be there. The law of compound interest will apply, forcing the GNP upward. To the extent that the environment problem is caused by ever-expanding output, the third law says that it will not be essentially changed by altering the mix between private and public spending.

conclusion

Three nice, depressing laws. They give us a starting point for any rational discussion of the environment problem. Our output is going to go on growing and growing under any conceivable set of choices we make.

But the starting point does not mean despair. It simply means that trying to solve the problem by reducing output, or the growth of the output is waste of time and energy. It won't and can't work.

How is the problem solved then? The purpose here is not,

and has not been, to solve any problems. It has been to try to head off useless solutions. But a few things can be said:

There is, first, technology itself. The very energy and inventiveness that gave us this rising output—and got us to the moon—can do things about pollution. A fascinating case is the sulphur dioxide put into the air by coal-burning electric power plants. A very strong argument can be made that under any foreseeable circumstances we will have to burn more and more coal to produce the needed growth of electric power. And the ground does not yield much low-sulphur coal. Thus, somebody is going to have to have the incentive to develop a way to get the sulphur out before it leaves the smokestack; and if this costs the utilities money, the regulatory commissions are going to have to allow that cost to be passed along in electric bills.

Next, there is the related idea—being increasingly explored by economists, regulators and some legislators—of making antipollution part of the price-profit-incentive system. In simplest terms, this would involve charging a fee for every unit of pollutant discharged, with meters used to determine the amount. There would be an economic incentive to stop or reduce pollution, possibly backed up with the threat to close down the plant if the meter readings go above a specified level. The company—say a paper company—would be faced with both a carrot and a stick.

There is also the simple use of the police power, as with poisonous drugs, or, lately, DDT. It is the "thou shalt not" power: automobiles can emit no more than such-and-such an amount of this or that chemical through the exhaust pipe. Once again, if the engineers cannot find a way out, the car simply cannot legally be sold. There will be, and should be, all sorts of debate "at the margin"—whether the higher cost of the different or improved engine is worth the extra reduction of pollution. The argument exists now over DDT; there are clearly costs, as well as benefits, in stopping its use. But the "thou shalt not" power exists.

Finally, there are many possibilities for using a part of our public spending for environmental purposes. Sewage plants are the obvious case. President Nixon has proposed a big expansion of the current level of spending for these plants, though not as much as many interested in clean water—including Senator Edmund Muskie— would like to see.

In this case, and only in this case a greater effort at curing pollution must be at the expense of some other Government program unless we pay higher taxes. It is proper to point out here the subtle dimensions of the issue. There are all sorts of possible gimmicks, like tax rebates for antipollution devices for industry and federally guaranteed state and local bonds. One way or another, spending more for pollution abatement will mean spending that much less for something else, and the something else could mean housing or medical services. Every local sewage plant bond sold means that much less investment money available for mortgages, for example.

A final reflection is perhaps in order, though it is almost banal. Our rising GNP gives us the "resources" to do the antipollution job. These resources include rising Government receipts. Our technology, which has given us the rising GNP, might find the way out of one pollution problem after another— and they are all different.

But, in the end, we cannot be sure that the job will be done. Growth of total output and output per capita will continue. The long-term relief is perfectly obvious: *fewer "capita."* That sort of "solution" might help, in our country, by about 1990. If we survive until then, the law of compound interest will be much less horrifying if the population is 220 million instead of 250 million.

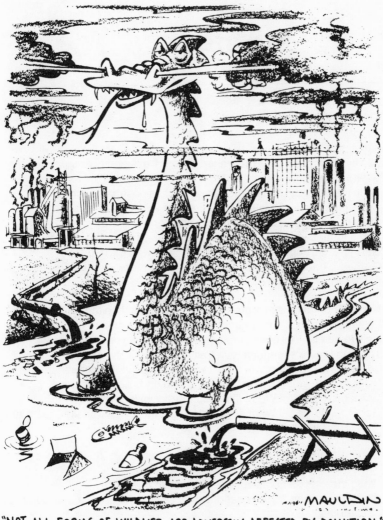

"NOT ALL FORMS OF WILDLIFE ARE ADVERSELY AFFECTED BY POLLUTION."

BILL STEELE

garbage

Mister Thompson calls the waiter, orders steak and baked potato
But he leaves the bone and gristle and he never eats the skins;
Then the bus boy comes and takes it, with a cough contaminates it
As he puts it in a can with coffee grounds and sardine tins;
Then the truck comes by on Friday and carts it all away;
And a thousand trucks just like it are converging on the bay.
Garbage, garbage! We're filling up the sea with garbage.
Garbage, garbage! What will we do when there's no place left to put
    all the garbage?

Mister Thompson starts his Cadillac and winds it up the freeway track,
Leaving friends and neighbors in a hydrocarbon haze;
He's joined by lots of smaller cars all sending gasses to the stars
There to form a seething cloud that hangs for thirty days
While the sun licks down upon it with its ultraviolet tongues
'Til it turns to smog and settles down and ends up in our lungs.
Garbage, garbage! We're filling up the sky with garbage.
Garbage, garbage! What will we do when there's nothing left to breathe
    but garbage?

Getting home and taking off his shoes he settles down with evening
    news
While the kids do homework with the TV in one ear;
While Superman for thousandth time sells talking dolls and conquers
    crime,
They dutifully learn the date of birth of Paul Revere.
In the paper there's a piece about the mayor's middle name
And he gets it done in time to watch the All-Star Bingo Game.
Garbage, garbage! We're filling up our minds with garbage!

Garbage, garbage! What will we do when there's nothing left to read,
    and there's nothing left to hear
    and there's nothing left to need
    and there's nothing left to wear
    and there's nothing left to talk about
    and nothing left to walk upon
    and nothing left to care about
    and nothing left to ponder on
    and nothing left to touch
    and there's nothing left to see
    and there's nothing left to do
    and there's nothing left to be—but garbage?

J. M. SCOTT

clean-up program

My water's distilled in the basement,
I use no other liquid to drink,
The food is all germ-proofed by boiling,
The robot gets rid of the stink,
I've already got a trash-masher,
I'm getting a sani-flush sink,
My kitchen will be,
Bacteria-free,
When I just throw out messy old me.

A prototype four bedroom, 1,500 square-foot home with walls of three-inch polyurethane core, faced on the outside with rough sawn aluminum siding, and inside with tempered hardboard. Being introduced in California, it is said the components for a complete shell can be factory produced in 42 minutes and erection of complete house takes two to three weeks. No wood or nails are used.

Photograph reproduced courtesy of Kaiser *News* © 1970.

W

ill anyone living, live to see our little light burn out?

After 100 years of constant use, it may lose only half its brightness.

That's because we don't use a bulb, a filament or a vacuum.

We use a tiny crystal chip called a light-emitting diode. It works something like a transistor, but let's not get into all that.

Our diodes are already in use on computer panels, freeing the man who used to look for burned-out bulbs among all those hundreds of winking lights.

That's a good market. But let's look at markets to come.

How about a flat head-light as wide as your car, to evenly light the road?

Or an inch-deep color TV set?

Or a wrist watch without a dial, that shows the time in numbers at the instant you push a button?

That's part of the future we see in our crystal chips. And just a small part of the future we see in **Monsanto: the science company.**

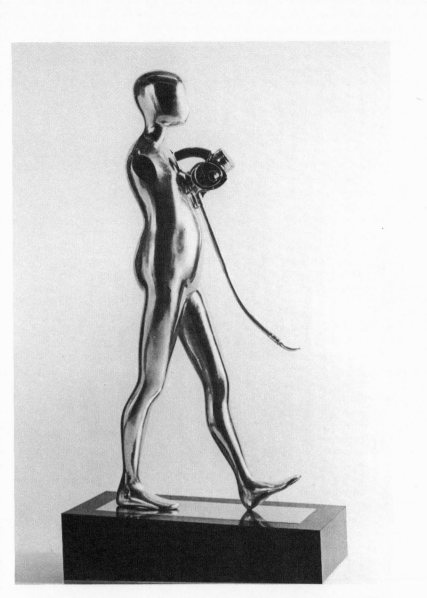

Photograph of *Study from Falling Man series: Walking Man* by Ernest Trova, 1964. Reproduced with the permission of The Museum of Modern Art, New York. Chromium plated bronze (cast 1965), 59⅝ x 11⅜ x 26½". Gift of Miss Viki Laura List.

J. M. SCOTT

chic in
black

How shall we dress in the Year 2000?
What shall we wear?
We could go bare,
Or take pills and grow hair,
Beige, perhaps, or black,
Or white with a stripe down the back.

Still from the motion picture *THX–1138*. Copyright © 1970 by Warner Bros., Inc.

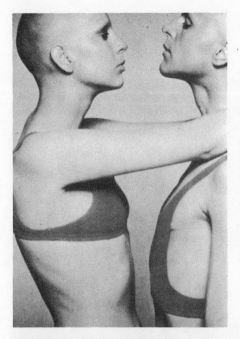

Rudi Gernreich is America's designer of fashions for the future. Instead of clothes being decorative, he says they will become functional . . . fashion will go "out of fashion" among the young—male and female alike. Clothing will accentuate the form of the body. He predicts we may lose our hair, eyebrows, and eyelashes. We will wear helmet-shaped dynel wigs—white in summer, black in winter. To protect us from pollution, we'll wear contact lenses, body stockings that extend over the mouth and nose, and waterproof hip boots. Clothing will be made of cheap and disposable synthetic materials.

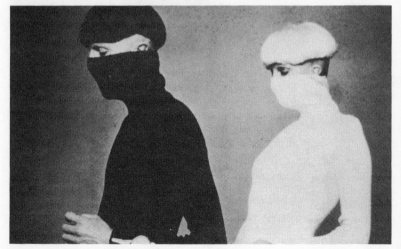

Photographs by Hideki Fujii reproduced courtesy of the designer, Rudi Gernreich, and the owner, Max Factor & Co.

A new "cult of the elderly" will also emerge in an era when the embarrassment of old age will fade away. The elderly will wear big bold prints, abstracting a body which can no longer be accentuated.

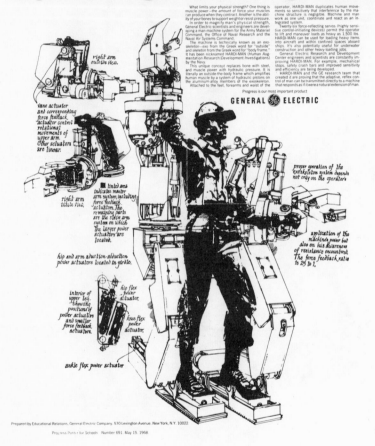

Poster reproduced courtesy of General Electric.

Science is full of broken laws. In the Middle Ages, it was impossible to sail around the earth for the world was flat. The earth was the center of the universe and man was the master of everything he surveyed.

Laws change when the structure of perceived reality changes. There is no set of conclusions which is not based on some unprovable first assumption—whether in mathematics or the social sciences.

In the next piece, Willis Harman argues that there is a fundamental shift taking place in the world view of Western man. Does he convince you? Would the "iron laws" of Edwin Dale apply in the world which Harman sees coming into existence?

WILLIS HARMAN

the new copernican revolution

As future historians look back on our times what will they conclude to have been the most significant event of the present
decade in terms of its impact on the future? The riots in the
cities? The Vietnam War? The Great Society programs? The
hippie movement? Student protest? Technological and scientific advances? Man to the moon?

None of these, I would make bold to guess. Nor any of the
events or trend discontinuities which the in-vogue forecasters
are picking out with their current methodologies. I will suggest
below that it will be something quite different from any of these,
an event perhaps well symbolized by an obscure scientific conference to be held in Council Grove, Kansas, in April 1969.

What follows is a report on research in process. It does not
pretend to present demonstrated conclusions. Rather, it raises
questions and advances possible interpretations which are so
momentous in their possible implications for the future that the
fullest possible amount of responsible dialogue is called for.

Let us suppose for a moment that we are back in the year 1600,
concerned with forecasting probable future trends. In retro-

Reprinted from *Stanford Today,* series 2, no. 1 (Winter 1969), courtesy of
Stanford University and Willis W. Harman. Copyright © by the Board of
Trustees of the Leland Stanford Junior University.

spect it is clear that one of the most significant events in progress was what came later to be called the Copernican revolution. Would our futurist researches have picked this up? They might have, if we were looking at the right things. What was the essence of this remarkable transformation that started with the brash suggestions of Nicholas Copernicus and Giordano Bruno and led to consequences as diverse as a tremendous acceleration in physical science and a decline in the political power of the Church? One useful interpretation is that a group of questions relating to the position of the Earth in the universe, and the nature and significance of the heavenly bodies passed out of the realm of the theological and philosophical and into the realm of empirical inquiry. No longer were these questions to be settled by referring to this or that ecclesiastical or scholarly authority: rather they were to be subjected to illumination by systematic observation and experiments. The consequences of such a shift are manifold. New research activities are started: familiar phenomena are given new interpretations; educational approaches are altered; power structures in society undergo change: new bases for consensus are applied to conflicts between belief systems.

A later similar event occurred with the work of the geologists, paleontologists, and biologists of the nineteenth century culminating in the controversial evolutionary hypotheses. Questions relating to the origin of the earth and of man were relabeled "empirical" instead of "theological." Again the consequences reverberated throughout the worlds of research, education, and politics.

I believe there is good reason to suspect that we are in the midst of another such saltation today. Much evidence suggests that *a group of questions relating to the commonality of and interpretation of man's subjective experience, especially of the "transcendental," and hence to the bases of human values, are shifting from the realm of the "philosophical" to the "empirical." If so, the consequences may be even more far-reaching than those which emerged from the Copernican, Darwinian, and Freudian revolutions.*

The evidence is of various sorts. The most obvious kind, of

course, is simply the indications that scientists—that is, persons with recognized scientific training, on the staffs of research organizations and universities with high standards, and holding membership in good standing in recognized scientific associations—are manifesting more and more interest in developing an adequate science of ordinary and extraordinary subjective experience. This is not completely new, of course. The phenomena of hypnosis have been studied in a scientific way, off and on, for at least a century and a half. Phenomenology has been a sometime influence in psychology. Freud's psychoanalysis and its offshoots have attempted to probe the unconscious processes. Pioneering books in the exploration of supraconscious processes include F. W. H. Myers' *Human Personality and Its Survival of Bodily Death,* Richard Bucke's *Cosmic Consciousness,* William James' *Varieties of Religious Experience,* and Pitirim Sorokin's *The Ways and Power of Love,* the first three being approximately two-thirds of a century old. Early in 1969 the first issue will appear of the *Journal of Transpersonal Psychology,* dedicated to the systematic exploration of "transpersonal experience." The April 1969 Council Grove (Kansas) conference on "voluntary control of inner states," cosponsored by the Menninger Foundation and the American Association for Humanistic Psychology, represents an unprecedented assemblage of scientists working with altered states of consciousness through such techniques as autohypnosis and group hypnosis, aural feedback of alphawave signals, and psychedelic drugs.

In the field of clinical psychology several scientists are proposing to formulate through their researches "a natural value system, a court of ultimate appeal for the determination of good and bad, of right and wrong" (A. H. Maslow), "universal human value directions emerging from the experiencing of the human organism" (Carl Rogers).

An ever-increasing number of students, now in the millions at least, are involved with "awareness-expanding" activities in free university courses and elsewhere. This concern is intimately related to student demands for a person-centered, rather than scholarship-centered, education.

The science of man's subjective experience is in its infancy.

Even so, some of its foreshadowings are evident. With the classification of these questions into the realm of empirical inquiry, we can anticipate an acceleration of research in this area. As a consequence there is new hope of consensus on issues which have been at the root of conflict for centuries (just as earlier there came about consensus on the place of the Earth in the universe, and on the origin of man). The new science will incorporate the most penetrating insights of psychology, the humanities, and religion. These developments will have profound impacts on goal priorities in society, on our concepts of education, on the further development and use of technology, and perhaps (as in the case of the Copernican revolution) on the distribution of power among social institutions and interest groups.

Young and incomplete as the science of subjective experience is, it nevertheless already contains what may very well be extremely significant precursors of tomorrow's image of man's potentialities. Space does not permit documenting them here: however, the following three propositions have accumulated an impressive amount of substantiating evidence:

The potentialities of the individual human being are far greater, in extent and diversity, than we ordinarily imagine them to be, and far greater than currently in-vogue models of man would lead us to think possible.

A far greater portion of significant human experience than we ordinarily feel or assume to be so is comprised of unconscious processes. This includes not only the sort of repressed memories and messages familiar to us through psychotherapy. It includes also "the wisdom of the body" and those mysterious realms of experience we refer to with such words as "intuition" and "creativity." Access to these unconscious processes is apparently facilitated by a wide variety of factors, including attention to feelings and emotions, inner attention, "free association," hypnosis, sensory deprivation, hallucinogenic and psychedelic drugs, and others.

Included in these partly or largely unconscious processes

are self-expectations, internalized expectations of others, images of the self and limitations of the self, and images of the future, which play a predominant role in limiting or enhancing actualization of one's capacities. These tend to be self-fulfilling. Much recent research has focused on the role of self-expectations and expectations of others in affecting performance, and on the improvement of performance level through enhancing self-image. On the social level research findings are buttressing the intuitive wisdom that one of the most important characteristics of any society is its vision of itself and its future, what Boulding calls "organizing images." The validity of the self-fulfilling prophecy and the self-realizing image appears to grow steadily in confirmation.

Assuming that the evidence substantiating these propositions continues to mount, they have the most profound implications for the future. For they say most powerfully that we have undersold man, underestimated his possibilities, and misunderstood what is needed for what Boulding terms "the great transition." They imply that the most profound revolution of the educational system would not be the cybernation of knowledge transmission, but the infusion of an exalted image of what man can be and the cultivation of an enhanced self-image in each individual child. They imply that the solution to the alienation and widespread disaffection in our society is not alone in vast social programs, but will come about through widespread adoption of a new image of our fellow man and our relationship to him. They suggest that the most pervasive illness of our nation is loss of the guiding vision, and the cure is to be found in a nobler image of man and of a society in which his growth may be better nurtured. They reassure that an image of fully-human man and of a new social order need not be built of the gossamer of wishful thinking, but can have a sound foundation in the research findings of the most daring explorers of the nature of man and his universe.

It is perhaps not too early to predict some of the characteristics of the new science. Preliminary indications suggest at least the following:

Although we have been speaking of it as a science of subjective experience, one of its dominant characteristics will be a relaxing of the subjective-objective dichotomy. The range between perceptions shared by all or practically all, and those which are unique to one individual, will be assumed to be much more of a continuum than a sharp division between "the world out there" and what goes on "in my head."

Related to this will be the incorporation, in some form, of the age-old yet radical doctrine that we perceive the world and ourselves in it as we have been culturally "hypnotized" to perceive it. The typical commonsense scientific view of reality will be considered to be a valid but partial view—a particular metaphor, so to speak. Others, such as certain religious or metaphysical views, will be considered also, and even equally valid but more appropriate for certain areas of human experience.

The new science will incorporate some way of referring to the subjective experiencing of a unity in all things (the "More" of William James, the "All" of Bugental, the "divine Ground" of Aldous Huxley's *The Perennial Philosophy).*

It will include some sort of mapping or ordering of states of consciousness transcending the usual conscious awareness (Bucke's "Cosmic Consciousness," the "enlightenment" of Zen, and similar concepts).

It will take account of the subjective experiencing of a "higher self" and will view favorably the development of a self-image congruent with this experience (Bugental's "I-process," Emerson's "Oversoul," Assagioli's "True Self," Brunton's "Overself," the Atman of Vedanta, and so on).

It will allow for a much more unified view of human experiences now categorized under such diverse headings as creativity, hypnosis, mystical experience, psychedelic drugs, extra-sensory perception, psychokinesis, and related phenomena.

It will include a much more unified view of the processes of personal change and emergence which take place within the contexts of psychotherapy, education (in the sense of "know thyself"), and religion (as spiritual growth). This view will possibly center around the concept that personality and behavior patterns change consequent upon a change in self-image, a modification of the person's emotionally felt perception of himself and his relationship to his environment.

John Rader Platt has argued in *The Step to Man*—as have Kenneth Boulding and Teilhard de Chardin before him—that the present point in the history of man may well, when viewed in retrospect by some future generation, appear as a relatively sudden cultural step. The portentous impact of the new technology is the heady yet sobering realization that we have the future in our hands, that man recognizes his role as, to use Julian Huxley's phrase, "a trustee of evolution on this earth." The new man, "homo progressivus" in Teilhard de Chardin's words, is described by Lancelot Law Whyte as "unitary man," by Lewis Mumford as the "new person," and by Henry A. Murray as an "ally of the future." The challenge of our time is whether we make "the step to man" or our Faustian powers prove our undoing and the whole vast machine goes off the track through the strains of internecine conflict and degradation of the environment.

To become the new man and to construct the new moral order require a guiding image which is worthy of the task. Man's highest learning has seemed to comprise, in C. P. Snow's terms, not one culture but two. And the noblest of the images of man to be found in the culture of the humanities appeared somehow alien to the culture of the sciences. The preceding arguments suggest that this state of affairs is probably a temporary one. For example, Ernest Becker proposes that the two cultures can be joined in a true science of man through admission of the universal value statement that that which estranges man from himself is unwholesome. Whether this or something else becomes the unifying principle, the reconciliation may soon take place. On the one hand, we will come to use comfortably many pluralistic images of aspects of man—one for his biochemical functioning, another perhaps for dealing with his pathologies, still another for encompassing his most fully human actions and proclivities. But on the other hand we will find nothing incompatible between any of these and an overarching image of what man can be, or perhaps more accurately, can come to realize that he is already.

The social significance of our dominant basic assumptions regarding the interpretation of subjective experience can be made more specific. At the surface level, so to speak, the nation is beset by numerous social problems which we point to with the terms poverty, crime, racial discrimination, civil disorder, unemployment, pollution, and the like. Experience with attempts to deal straightforwardly with these problems—to tackle discrimination with civil-rights legislation, to alleviate the ills of poverty with minimum-wage laws and welfare payments, to eliminate ghettos with urban-renewal programs, to deal with civil disorders by increasing police power—indicates that such direct measures typically have unexpected and unintended outcomes. It is as though an "ecology of situations" were upset by a piecemeal approach.

    The reason appears to be intrinsic. It seems that these manifest problems are in a sense symptoms of underlying conditions that are more pervasive and less easy to objectify. At another level these problems reside in the institutions of the society, in built-in power distributions, in the traditional roles to which persons are trained, in the time-hallowed structures and processes. At a still deeper level they involve the most basic assumptions, attitudes, and felt values held by the individual and promoted by the culture. The most carefully designed social measures will not achieve their desired goals unless they involve not only rationally designed programs and structures, but also changes in deeply-rooted beliefs, values, attitudes, and behavior patterns, both of the individuals who constitute "the problem populations" and of the self-righteous others who assume that they are not implicated.

    An analogy with the process of psychotherapy may reassure that in attending to these underlying conditions we are dealing with that which is more, not less, real and relevant. In the end the neurotic discovers that he was divided against himself, and in a sense lying to himself to conceal that condition. So it may be with our social problems that the significant constructive change is first of all an inner one rather than outer, and in the direction of recognizing the hidden lies and resolving the hidden divisions. To put it in somewhat different terms, just as it is possible for a person to have a pathological set of beliefs about himself, so it may be possible for our society to possess a dysfunctional belief and value system.

In fact, much of today's student unrest centers around the accusation that the society's operative assumptions about man's deepest desires are indeed not consistent with individual inner experience nor in the long-term interest of man or society. A dominant theme among disaffected students is that the American corporate capitalist system manipulates and oppresses the individual.

Thus it is not solely in an idealistic vein that the new science of subjective experience is hailed as having profound significance. It has survival value as well.

Several recent scholars of the future such as Robert Heilbroner, Kenneth Boulding, and Fred Polak have made much of the concept that it is the *image* of the future which is the key to that future coming into realization. "Every society has an image of the future which is its real dynamic." As previously noted, much evidence has been accumulated to indicate that the power of the image may be far greater than we have heretofore suspected.

To whatever extent the science of the past may have contributed to a mechanistic and economic image of man and a technocratic image of the good society, the new science of subjective experience may provide a counteracting force toward the ennobling of the image of the individual's possibilities, of the educational and socializing processes, and of the future. And since we have come to understand that science is not a description of "reality" but a metaphorical ordering of experience, the new science does not impugn the old. It is not a question of which view is "true" in some ultimate sense. Rather, it is a matter of which picture is more useful in guiding human affairs. Among the possible images that are reasonably in accord with accumulated human experience, since the image held is that most likely to come into being, it is prudent to choose the noblest.

It is strange to observe that at this point in history when we literally have the knowledge and material resources to do almost anything we can imagine—from putting a man on the moon, to exploring the depths of the oceans, to providing an adequate measure of life's goods to every person on earth—we also seem the most confused about what is worth doing. The great problems facing us are a sort where we need belief in ourselves and will to act even more than we need new technologies, creative social program concepts, and program budgeting. At a time when the nation may well be in its gravest peril in over a century, and Western civilization may hang in the balance, it could even come to pass that a new "Copernican revolution" might provide a missing balance in some four-century-old trends started by the first one.

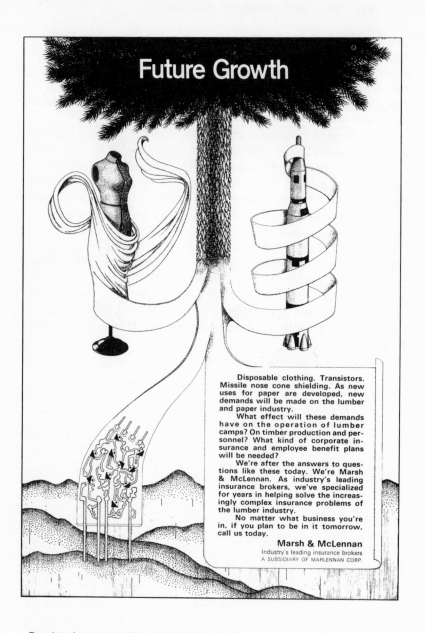

Future Growth

Disposable clothing. Transistors. Missile nose cone shielding. As new uses for paper are developed, new demands will be made on the lumber and paper industry.

What effect will these demands have on the operation of lumber camps? On timber production and personnel? What kind of corporate insurance and employee benefit plans will be needed?

We're after the answers to questions like these today. We're Marsh & McLennan. As industry's leading insurance brokers, we've specialized for years in helping solve the increasingly complex insurance problems of the lumber industry.

No matter what business you're in, if you plan to be in it tomorrow, call us today.

Marsh & McLennan
Industry's leading insurance brokers
A SUBSIDIARY OF MARLENNAN CORP.

Reprinted courtesy of Marsh & McLennan Co.

BERTOLT BRECHT

to
posterity

1

Indeed I live in the dark ages:
A guileless word is an absurdity. A smooth forehead betokens
A hard heart. He who laughs
Has not yet heard
The terrible tidings.

Ah, what an age it is
When to speak of trees is almost a crime
For it is a kind of silence about injustice!
And he who walks calmly across the street,
Is he not out of reach of his friends
In trouble?

It is true: I earn my living
But, believe me, it is only an accident.
Nothing that I do entitles me to eat my fill.
By chance I was spared. (If my luck leaves me
I am lost.)

They tell me: eat and drink. Be glad you have it!
But how can I eat and drink
When my food is snatched from the hungry

From *Selected Poems of Bertolt Brecht,* trans. H. R. Hays. Reprinted with the permission of Harcourt/Brace Jovanovich, Inc. Copyright 1947 by Bertolt Brecht and H. R. Hays.

And my glass of water belongs to the thirsty?
And yet I eat and drink.

I would gladly be wise.
The old books tell us what wisdom is:
Avoid the strife of the world, live out your little time
Fearing no one,
Using no violence,
Returning good for evil—
Not fulfillment of desire but forgetfulness
Passes for wisdom.
I can do none of this:
Indeed I live in the dark ages!

2

I came to the cities in a time of disorder
When hunger ruled.
I came among men in a time of uprising
And I revolted with them.
So the time passed away
Which on earth was given me.

I ate my food between massacres.
The shadow of murder lay upon my sleep.
And when I loved, I loved with indifference.
I looked upon nature with impatience.
So the time passed away
Which on earth was given me.

In my time streets led to the quicksand.
Speech betrayed me to the slaughter.
There was little I could do. But without me
The rulers would have been more secure. This was my hope.
So the time passed away
Which on earth was given me.

Men's strength was little. The goal
Lay far in the distance,

Easy to see if for me
Scarcely attainable.
So the time passed away
Which on earth was given me.

3

You, who shall emerge from the flood
In which we are sinking,
Think—
When you speak of our weaknesses,
Also of the dark time
That brought them forth.

For we went, changing our country more often than our selves,
In the class war, despairing
When there was only injustice and no resistance.

For we knew only too well:
Even the hatred of squalor
Makes the brow grow stern.
Even anger against injustice
Makes the voice grow harsh. Alas, we
Who wished to lay the foundations of kindness
Could not ourselves be kind.

But you, when at last it comes to pass
That man can help his fellow man,
Do not judge us
Too harshly.

JAMES THURBER

the unicorn
in
the garden

Once upon a sunny morning a man who sat in a breakfast nook looked up from his scrambled eggs to see a white unicorn with a gold horn quietly cropping the roses in the garden. The man went up to the bedroom where his wife was still asleep and woke her. "There's a unicorn in the garden," he said. "Eating roses." She opened one unfriendly eye and looked at him. "The unicorn is a mythical beast," she said and turned her back on him. The man walked slowly downstairs and out into the garden. The unicorn was still there; he was now browsing among the tulips. "Here, unicorn," said the man, and he pulled up a lily, and gave it to him. The unicorn ate it gravely. With a high heart, because there was a unicorn in his garden, the man went upstairs and roused his wife again. "The unicorn," he said, "ate a lily." His wife sat up in bed and looked at him, coldly. "You are a booby," she said, "and I am going to have you put in the booby hatch." The man, who had never liked the words "booby" and "booby-hatch," and who liked them even less on a shining morning when there was a unicorn in the garden, thought for a moment. "We'll see about that," he said. He walked over to the

From James Thurber, *Fables For Our Time,* published by Harper & Row, New York. Copyright © 1940 by James Thurber; Copyright © 1968 by Helen Thurber. Reprinted with the permission of Helen Thurber. Originally printed in the *New Yorker.*

door. "He has a golden horn in the middle of his forehead," he told her. Then he went back to the garden to watch the unicorn; but the unicorn had gone away. The man sat down among the roses and went to sleep.

As soon as the husband had gone out of the house, the wife got up and dressed as fast as she could. She was very excited and there was a gloat in her eye. She telephoned the police and she telephoned a psychiatrist; she told them to hurry to her house and bring a strait-jacket. When the police and the psychiatrist arrived they sat down in chairs and looked at her, with great interest. "My husband," she said, "saw a unicorn this morning." The police looked at the psychiatrist and the psychiatrist looked at the police. "He told me it ate a lily," she said. The psychiatrist looked at the police and the police looked at the psychiatrist. "He told me it had a golden horn in the middle of its forehead," she said. At a solemn signal from the psychiatrist, the police leaped from their chairs and seized the wife. They had a hard time subduing her, for she put up a terrific struggle, but they finally subdued her. Just as they got her into the strait-jacket, the husband came back into the house.

"Did you tell your wife you saw a unicorn?" asked the police. "Of course not," said the husband. "The unicorn is a mythical beast." "That's all I wanted to know," said the psychiatrist. "Take her away. I'm sorry, sir, but your wife is as crazy as a jay bird." So they took her away, cursing and screaming, and shut her up in an institution. The husband lived happily ever after.

Moral: Don't count your boobies until they are hatched.

a riddle

A man and his child are in an auto accident. The man is killed. The child is taken to a hospital, seriously injured. A surgeon is called and looks at the child and says, "I can't operate. That's my child." How can that be?

The surgeon is the child's mother. Did you get it? Experience shows that many people do not. Why not? Would you have got it more easily if the person who had been with the child in the car had been a woman and the husband had been the surgeon? Try it on your friends and find out who does see through the riddle and who does not.

NEIL POSTMAN

once upon
a time

A FABLE OF STUDENT POWER

Once upon a time in the City of New York civilized life very
nearly came to an end. The streets were covered with dirt, and
there was no one to tidy them. The air and rivers were polluted,
and no one could cleanse them. The schools were rundown, and
no one believed in them. Each day brought a new strike, and
each strike brought new hardships. Crime and strife and disorder and rudeness were to be found everywhere. The young
fought the old. The workers fought the students. The whites
fought the blacks. The city was bankrupt.

When things came to their most desperate moment, the
City Fathers met to consider the problem. But they could suggest no cures, for their morale was very low and their imagination dulled by hatred and confusion. There was nothing for the
Mayor to do but to declare a state of emergency. He had done
this before during snowstorms and power failures, but now he
felt even more justified. "Our city," he said, "is under siege, like
the ancient cities of Jericho and Troy. But our enemies are sloth
and poverty and indifference and hatred." As you can see, he
was a very wise Mayor, but not so wise as to say exactly how
these enemies could be dispersed. Thus, though a state of emergency officially existed, neither the Mayor nor anyone else

could think of anything to do that would make their situation better rather than worse. And then an extraordinary thing happened.

One of the Mayor's aides, knowing full well what the future held for the city, had decided to flee with his family to the country. In order to prepare himself for his exodus to a strange environment, he began to read Henry David Thoreau's "Walden," which he had been told was a useful handbook on how to survive in the country. While reading the book, he came upon the following passage:

"Students should not play life, or study it merely, while the community supports them at this expensive game, but earnestly live it from the beginning to end. How could youths better learn to live than by at once trying the experiment of living?"

The aide sensed immediately that he was in the presence of an exceedingly good idea. And he sought an audience with the Mayor. He showed the passage to the Mayor, who was extremely depressed and in no mood to read from books, since he had already scoured books of lore and wisdom in search of help but had found nothing. "What does it mean?" said the Mayor angrily. The aide replied: "Nothing less than a way to our salvation."

He then explained to the Mayor that the students in the public schools had heretofore been part of the general problem whereas, with some slight imagination and a change of perspective, they might easily become part of the general solution. He pointed out that from junior high school on up to senior high school, there were approximately 400,000 able-bodied, energetic young men and women who could be used as a resource to make the city livable again. "But how can we use them?" asked the Mayor. "And what would happen to their education if we did?"

To this the aide replied, "They will find their education in the process of saving their city. And as for their lessons in school, we have ample evidence that the young do not exactly appreciate them and are even now turning against their teachers and their schools." The aide, who had come armed with statistics (as aides are wont to do), pointed out that the city was spending $5-million a year merely replacing broken school windows and that almost one-third of all the students enrolled in the schools did not even show up on any given day. "Yes, I know," said the Mayor sadly. "Woe unto us." "Wrong," said the aide brashly. "The boredom and destructiveness and pent-up energy that are now an affliction to us can be turned to our advantage."

The Mayor was not quite convinced, but having no better idea of his own he appointed his aide Chairman of the Emergency Education Committee, and the aide at once made plans to remove almost 400,000 students from their dreary classrooms and their even drearier lessons, so that their energy and talents might be used to repair the desecrated environment.

When these plans became known, there was a great hue and cry against them, for people in distress will sometimes prefer a problem that is familiar to a solution that is not. For instance, the teachers complained that their contract contained no provision for such unusual procedures. To this the aide replied that the *spirit* of their contract compelled them to help educate our youth, and that education can take many forms and be conducted in many places. "It is not written in any holy book," he observed, "that an education must occur in a small room with chairs in it."

Some parents complained that the plan was un-American and that its compulsory nature was hateful to them. To this the aide replied that the plan was based on the practices of earlier Americans who required their young to assist in controlling the environment in order to insure the survival of the group. "Our schools," he added, "have never hesitated to compel. The question is not, nor has it ever been, to compel or not to compel, but rather, which things ought to be compelled."

And even some children complained, although not many. They said that their God-given right to spend 12 years of their lives, at public expense, sitting in a classroom was being trampled. To this complaint the aide replied that they were confusing a luxury with a right, and that, in any case, the community could no longer afford either. "Besides," he added, "of all the God-given rights man has identified, none takes precedence over his right to survive."

And so, the curriculum of the public schools of New York City became known as Operation Survival, and all the children from 7th grade through 12th grade became part of it. Here are some of the things that they were obliged to do:

On Monday morning of every week, 400,000 children had to help clean up their own neighborhoods. They swept the streets, canned the garbage, removed the litter from empty lots, and hosed the dust and graffiti from the pavements and walls. Wednesday mornings were reserved for beautifying the city. Students planted trees and flowers, tended the grass and shrubs, painted subway stations and other eyesores, and even repaired broken-down public buildings, starting with their own schools.

Each day, 5,000 students (mostly juniors and seniors in high school) were given responsibility to direct traffic on the city streets, so that all the policemen who previously had done this were freed to keep a sharp eye out for criminals. Each day, 5,000 students were asked to help deliver the mail, so that it soon became possible to have mail delivered twice a day—as it had been done in days of yore.

Several thousand students were also used to establish and maintain day care centers, so that young mothers, many on welfare, were free to find gainful employment. Each student was also assigned to meet with two elementary-school students on Tuesday and Thursday afternoons to teach them to read, to write, and to do arithmetic. Twenty thousand students were asked to substitute, on one afternoon a week, for certain adults whose jobs the students could perform without injury or loss of efficiency. These adults were then free to attend school or, if they preferred, to assist the students in their efforts to save their city.

The students were also assigned to publish a newspaper in every neighborhood of the city, in which they were able to include much information that good citizens need to have. Students organized science fairs, block parties and rock festivals, and they formed, in every neighborhood, both an orchestra and a theater company. Some students assisted in hospitals, helped to register voters, and produced radio and television programs which were aired on city stations. There was still time to hold a year-round City Olympics in which every child competed in some sport or other.

It came to pass, as you might expect, that the college students in the city yearned to participate in the general plan, and thus another 100,000 young people became available to serve the community. The college students ran a "jitney" service from the residential boroughs to Manhattan and back. Using their own cars and partly subsidized by the city, the students quickly established a kind of auxiliary, semipublic transportation system, which reduced the number of cars coming into Manhattan, took some of the load off the subways, and diminished air pollution—in one stroke.

College students were empowered to give parking and litter tickets, thus freeing policemen more than ever for real detective work. They were permitted to organize seminars, film festivals, and arrange lectures for junior and senior high school students; and on a UHF television channel, set aside for the purpose, they gave advanced courses in a variety of subjects every day from 3 P.M. to 10 P.M. They also helped to organize and run drug-addiction rehabilitation centers, and they launched campaigns to inform people of their legal rights, their nutritional needs, and of available medical facilities.

Because this is a fable and not a fairy tale, it cannot be said that all the problems of the city were solved. But several extraordinary things did happen. The city began to come alive and its citizens found new reason to hope that they could save themselves. Young people who had been alienated from their environment assumed a proprietary interest in it. Older people who had regarded the young as unruly and parasitic came to respect them. There followed from this a revival of courtesy and a diminution of crime, for there was less reason than before to be angry at one's neighbors and to wish to assault them.

Amazingly, most of the students found that while they did

not "receive" an education, they were able to create a quite adequate one. They lived, each day, their social studies and geography and communication and biology and many other things that decent and proper people know about, including the belief that everyone must share equally in creating a livable city, no matter what he or she becomes later on. It even came to pass that the older people, being guided by the example of the young, took a renewed interest in restoring their environment and, at the very least, refused to participate in its destruction.

Now, it would be foolish to deny that there were not certain problems attending this whole adventure. For instance, there were thousands of children who would otherwise have known the principal rivers of Uruguay who had to live out their lives in ignorance of these facts. There were hundreds of teachers who felt their training had been wasted because they could not educate children unless it were done in a classroom. As you can imagine, it was also exceedingly difficult to grade students on their activities, and after a while, almost all tests ceased. This made many people unhappy, for many reasons, but most of all because no one could tell the dumb children from the smart children anymore.

But the Mayor, who was, after all, a very shrewd politician, promised that as soon as the emergency was over everything would be restored to normal. Meanwhile, everybody lived happily ever after—in a state of emergency, but quite able to cope with it.

What would happen if you took this fable seriously? Would it be possible for you to convince your teachers and the city fathers that you can learn more in the streets of your community than in the classroom?

What sort of arguments would you muster if you had the opportunity to explain this proposal to your TV station, your newspaper, your church, your synagogue? Would you use the same arguments in each case?

Would you make your proposal as shocking as possible or would you, on the contrary, try to show that it was only a development of practices which were already going on? What people do you think would be in favor of this plan in your city and who would be against it?

Would you, yourself, be in favor of the proposal or against it? What would you do to improve your education, or that of the children you know who are in school at the present time? What does education mean in today's world?

This is the range of issues that another task force in Hawaii tried to deal with. Their conclusions are reported in the next piece.

JANE EVINGER

education
in
hawaii 2000

The Hawaii of the 21st Century may be an "educational resort" to which people come "not simply for recreation, but for the re-creation of their selves through serious learning activities."

This is one of the possibilities envisioned by the Education Task Force in a preliminary report it has prepared for the Governor's Conference on the Year 2000.

Noting that during the Chautauqua movement "many people went to camp grounds to spend their leisure 'improving themselves,'" the report says that in the future, "some communities will very likely become major educational resorts."

Hawaii could be such a center "for people with leisure who would like to spend a couple of weeks or several years in learning or re-learning," it suggests.

"Hawaii has few raw materials for heavy industry, agriculture is rapidly growing unprofitable, simple tourism will soon pall as other locations become the prestige place to vacation.

"Perhaps education could be one of our major 'crops,' particularly bringing together people from both the East and the West. Not only would they profit, but they would bring a rich resource of talent and interest to our community.

"Another task force has suggested that combining hotels

Review article from the Honolulu *Advertiser*, July 31, 1970. Reprinted courtesy of the Honolulu *Advertiser*.

with the University and the East-West Center might be a new direction for tourism in Hawaii. We second the motion."

guaranteed income

Within the coming 30 years, the report assumes, technology will provide far more leisure and everyone, whether he works or not, will receive a guaranteed annual income.

As a result, says the task force, "since there will be plenty of time to learn, there will be no need for compulsion."

Rather, the year 2000 will see schools "crowded with people, young and old, who want to learn."

The schools themselves "will not be at all like the present complexes of classrooms and offices and playgrounds. They will not be segregated by ages into elementary, middle, intermediate, secondary, or higher education," according to the report.

"The school of the future will be an educational center where people of all ages gather to learn together or individually.

"The buildings will not be crowded for six hours a day, five days a week, thirty-six weeks a year and empty the rest of the time. They will be open virtually all the time.

"Some people will want to study at night, on week-ends, during holidays or vacations. Others will want to be absent between nine in the morning and three in the afternoon Monday through Friday. That may be their time to work—or the surf may be up!

"Schools must be open for the convenience of those who want to learn, not restricted to an arbitrary set of hours when the brain cells are required to get into gear and do in six hours all the thinking that should be spread over twenty-four."

In the schools of the future, "the purpose of learning will be identical with the purposes of living, for learning and living will be inseparable," said the task force.

"The searching for answers to life's problems will define the subjects, the structure of education."

The task force stresses that "learning in the schools of

the year 2000 must not be limited to the acquisition of literacy."

Work skills must be a part of the program, since "with the rapid changes in technology, many people will be completely retrained several times in the course of their short work career.

"More importantly, we must include in all vocational training concern for maintaining an environment which will make possible the survival of mankind," says the report.

The schools also "must give more attention to helping people learn to understand self"—which will be an important step in cutting down on mental illness.

Related to this, "schools must give attention to the critical problems of learning to live with others."

dependence to go on

"One aspect of the future which is not likely to change is man's dependence—socially as well as economically—upon others. We cannot tolerate a world where man preys upon man, individually or by ethnic groups, economic classes or nations," says the task force.

It warns that "this will probably be one of the most controversial aspects of education, for there is much about learning to live with others that we have refused to bring out in the open.

"We have been too afraid or too ashamed to examine our religious beliefs honestly and admit that religious irrationalities can be just as destructive of humanity as any other form of irrationality.

"We must be prepared to admit that churches have often promoted religious persecution and wars in the name of gods who supposedly offered all mankind love. But candor in examining man's religious relationships will demand that the evil be weighed with the good.

"Another taboo which must be broken if we are to be fully educated about human relationships is the reluctance to discuss sexual relationships," says the task force.

To learn about their political responsibilities as citizens in a democracy, "people must be able to practice democratic citizenship in the school setting, where they might be helped to analyze the successes and failures of their practice and thus improve themselves in effective citizenship."

With the increasing hours of leisure, schools must "provide opportunity for people to learn many forms of creative expression—music, games, individual sports, painting, drama, dance, conversation—as a performer as well as a passive appreciator."

In the schools of the future, "arbitrary divisions between bodies of subject matter must be broken down," says the task force.

"Problems in life do not come in neat textbook isolation. If schools are to be related to living, the problems that the learner encounters in his actual life must be the starting point for his education."

Required courses should be abolished.

"With all the knowledge and skills to be learned today, no one can possibly learn all that somebody may assume to be important," says the report. "The effort to preserve some courses in the curriculum and require everyone to take them is pointless.

"If a subject is important enough for someone to be interested in it, he will learn it. If he isn't interested then let him learn what he is interested in."

Much of the learning in the year 2000 will take place as a student works individually with programmed materials—books, slides, tapes, films.

Depending on what he wants to learn, "he may be in a classroom, a library, a sound-proof listening booth, a laboratory, a concert hall, a gymnasium, a swimming pool, a conference room, a lecture hall, a private study carrel, his bedroom, or under a tree with a good book," says the task force.

variety in schools

Just as hospitals have many kinds of workers so that "when a patient needs his back rubbed, he doesn't expect to have it done by a surgeon," the schools of the future also will have a variety.

There will be technicians to keep the learning machines in operating condition, instruct students in their use, and help other members of the staff develop new units of learning materials.

Specialists in various subject fields will be on call whenever their expertise is needed.

"Central to the whole system will be specialists who know how to help students understand what problems they really want to learn about and to give them guidance in accomplishing their goals," says the task force. "They will be the counterparts to present day teachers."

Students themselves will help others learn, an arrangement "of value to both the learner and the 'teacher.' As anyone who has ever taught knows, you learn most effectively when you try to help someone else learn."

Part-time volunteer teachers on the staff also will play a part.

The task force says perhaps the most glamorous aspect of the schools of the future will be the fantastic advances in technology. The computers, projectors, recorders, language laboratories, multi-media auditoriums and carrels, science laboratories and gymnasiums will be matched by an almost infinite number of combinations of learning materials.

"It will take a computerized information retrieval system to be able to select the proper set of materials for a particular student at the particular state of his development.

"Undoubtedly the biggest problem will be to produce the generation of teachers and other staff members who know how to utilize the full arsenal of weapons against ignorance."

The report acknowledges that "suggesting radical changes" for the schools of 2000 "will rock some boats and make some people very uncomfortable, particularly teachers who have their lesson plans all worked out from 20 years of experience."

can we afford it?

Can society afford the kind of education suggested by the task force?

"We answer that the concern for the intangibles such as learning will soon become more socially desirable than for the tangibles such as more cars, boats, bigger houses, etc.," says the report.

"For example, no one wants to live in huge mansions today —those of 50 years ago are being demolished for convenient condominiums. The housewife freed from the drudgery of keeping a huge house will place greater value on learning new aesthetic skills, developing new ideas, integrating a life view.

"Society will pay for what it values. Today we pay billions to kill Southeast Asians, to put men on the moon for a few brief minutes. A supersonic transport plane will cost billions just in development costs.

"If we turned those sums into providing education, we could afford the kind of schooling we are to describe, and begin to build it now."

Education, says the task force, "is the most productive form of leisure, not only in intangible satisfaction for the individual, but in improving the ways in which man may continue to progress materially with the least amount of destruction of our all too finite resources of raw materials and energy sources.

"Intelligence for conserving our planet must be developed to replace the attitude of unrestricted exploitation of irreplaceable resources."

The education it describes, says the task force, "is not only possible, but it is necessary for the prolongation of life on this small planet."

DENISE LEVERTOV

the
artist

(From the Spanish translation of Toltec Códice de la Real Academia, fol. With the help of Elvira Abascal who understood the original Toltec.)

The artist: disciple, abundant, multiple, restless.
The true artist: capable, practicing, skillful;
maintains dialogue with his heart, meets things with his mind.

The true artist: draws out all from his heart,
works with delight, makes things with calm, with sagacity,
works like a true Toltec, composes his objects, works dexterously, invents,
arranges materials, adorns them, makes them adjust.

The carrion artist: works at random, sneers at the people,
makes things opaque, brushes across the surface of the face of things,
works without care, defrauds people, is a thief.

el artista

El artista: discipulo, abundante, múltiple, inquieto.
El verdadero artista: capaz, se adiestra, es hábil;
dialoga con su corazón, encuentra las cosas con su mente.

El verdadero artista todo lo saca de su corazón
obra con deleite, hace las cosas con calma, con tiento,
obra como un tolteca, compone cosas, obra hábilmente, crea;
arregla las cosas, las hace atildadas, hace que se ajusten.

El torpe artista: obra al azar, se burla de la gente,
opaca las cosas, pasa por encima del rostro de la cosas,
obra sin cuidado, defrauda a las personas, es un ladrón.

toltecatl

In toltecatl; tlamachtilli, tolih, centozon, aman.
In qualli toltecatl: mozcaliani, mozcaliz, mihmati;
moyolnonotzani, tlalnamiquini.

In qualli toltecatl tlayollocopaviani,
tlapaccachivani, tlaiviyanchivani, tlamavhcachiva,
toltecati, tlatalia, tlahimati, tlayocoya;—
tlavipana, tlapopotia, tlananamictia.

In xolopihtli toltecatl; tlailivizviani, teca mocayavani,
tlaixpachoani, iixco quihquiza,
tlailivizvia, teca mocayava, ichtequi.

J. M. SCOTT

dead
season

The falling leaves
Screen me from my mistakes
And cover yesterday's errors.

But these woodsy piles
Block my path to tomorrow.

ROBERT THEOBALD

why discuss?
how to
dialogue

why discuss?

Man lives today caught between the possibility of a truly human future and the possibility of unlimited catastrophe. Each one of us is trying to create his own personal understanding of the freedom gained by man's development of power over his own environment. In general terms it seems that mankind is no longer caught in a system in which he is a mere cog. Today we have the ability to free ourselves to direct the future course of "Spaceship Earth," within the realities we have inherited as one human race from our biological past.

We are moving from one period in history to another. The confusion and crisis of the present time are the inevitable result of our early efforts to come to grips with this change. Mankind is moving out of the industrial phase of the agricultural era into the cybernetic era, just as he moved from hunting animals and gathering plants into the use of agricultural techniques.

The earlier great change was slow and immensely painful. Mankind had centuries—indeed thousands of years—to change from living off the free production of the land and sea to controlling it for his own benefit: his social practices, economic thinking and his religions evolved slowly. Today the pace of change is so great that we must bring about a similar overall change in

213

the society and the economy in one generation and we must involve all the world in it.

In effect, we must move away from trying to increase further our technological power to take actions. We must now learn to determine what we should do with the power we have today and will have increasingly tomorrow. That we shall increase our power is certain: a decision to cease to concentrate on technological change does not mean that our technological power will no longer grow, but rather that we can treat technological change as a given, built into our society. Nor does it mean that we shall no longer have a problem of choice: we will never be able to do *everything* we wish, but we have already reached the point where we can do what is most important to us. Do we need to go to the moon or to develop better methods of transportation on earth? Do we need new consumer gadgets or do we need to feed the hungry? Today, time and space are our scarcest products: this will force radical changes in our priorities.

It is such changes which can emerge from successful discussion or dialogue.

Today invitations to join discussion groups are common: whites want to meet blacks, Protestants to meet Catholics, the middle class to meet the poor. To many it seems as though talk is replacing actions and that we are drowning in a sea of words.

"We know the problems," many say. "All we have to do is to carry through certain programs and we can eliminate present social ills." Unfortunately, however, there are many factions—right and left, young and old, black and white among others—who are all equally convinced that their answers are correct. It is obvious that these groups usually do not agree!

Discussion is needed, then, if we are to create agreement about the steps we should be taking at the present time. If we should fail to discuss the issues in intelligent ways, the polarization which is already developing between groups must inevitably become more serious.

There are some who argue that change does not automatically follow from agreement. "The power structure," they argue, "make all the decisions about the area where we live, as well as national directions and international attitudes. They determine what needs to be done in terms of their own interests. We cannot change the power structures through discussion. Why then discuss?"

If this is indeed true, one must certainly abandon any idea that discussion can be relevant. But one must also, if one is to be logical, abandon any hope of significant change, for direct actions designed to achieve change will certainly fail unless there is growing understanding of the need for change. This must obviously develop from discussion, whether formal or informal. If there are no common interests which can be discovered, our society is indeed certain to fly apart.

There are two reasons, however, for challenging the preceding argument. First, one may examine the thought of Pogo, "We have met the enemy and we are they," as well as the words of Shakespeare, "The fault, dear Brutus, lies not in the stars but in ourselves." Each of us has far more potential power than we exercise: we fail to exercise it because we do not know what we really desire and we do not therefore develop the energy required to create real change.

Second, while it is true that power structures follow their own interests, such a statement is not really significant for it is also true of each one of us. Each person will always do the thing which seems best to him given all the circumstances of which he is aware at the time he acts. But is it obvious that this statement applies to the person who saves a child from being run over in the street as well as to the individual who mugs a woman to get money for his dope habit? The relevant question is, "*what will seem best to each person?*"

If we really desire change, we must alter our own and other people's perception of their own self-interest. This can be done in two ways. First, we may discover new patterns of thinking and behavior which make old ways of thinking and behavior obsolete and challenge us to alter our present action patterns. This change in patterns of action can be voluntary or it can be forced by the reactions of our neighbors and the laws of the society.

Those in power structures are subject to the same pressures as each one of us: they can perceive better ways of be-having or they can be forced to change. Indeed, in many ways those in power structures are more constrained by public opin-ion than anyone else. Politicians must be reelected if they are to survive: changes in public opinion therefore force them to alter their position, as the recent debate over the antiballistic missile shows. Businessmen can only sell a product which ap-pears pleasant and safe: Ralph Nader forced a new stance on the automobile industry by making Congress take note of the lack of safety features on automobiles. The churches have al-tered their sense of priorities as the need for reconciliation has been brought home to them. The universities are seeking new structures to provide the student with additional potentials for learning, as logical pressure is brought to bear.

Is it possible, then, that we continue to blame the ob-stinacy of power structures because the alternative view is too destructive of our own self-image? Perhaps the barrier to more rapid change in many areas has not been an unwillingness to change in response to pressure, but rather the failure of those who are discontented with the present system to develop the ideas which would result in significant improvements if applied. This does not mean, of course, that those wanting to bring about change will ever be greeted with open arms: every human being—including oneself—resists alterations in his patterns of life, for change disturbs long-developed habits. But there is now sufficient recognition of the reality of the crisis we face that peo-ple in many parts of our society are looking for new ideas and concepts.

Discussion can lead to new and significant ideas which can be communicated. Will this truly cause change? The answer to this question depends on our view of human nature. In effect, an agreement to discuss involves a view that human beings are motivated to discover their changing needs. One must be-lieve that others—and above all oneself—are open to a changed view of human needs and requirements: that the future can be better than the past.

Abraham Maslow, the psychologist, has developed the reasons why this vision of man is justified far more today than ever before. When each one of us had to strive for food, clothing, and shelter and to overcome others to attain them, this had to be our immediate priority. Today, however, most of us in Western countries are assured of the minimal requirements for life and we are now looking for ways in which we can develop ourselves.

It is important that we not lose sight of this optimistic starting point as we discuss and dialogue. It is always easy to conclude that change of the necessary scope is impossible and to ensure failure through our inaction.

how to dialogue

Let us now assume that the person who continues to read this document is convinced of the validity of the process of discussion, of the possibility of change and of his own necessity to participate in the change—or is at least willing to suspend his disbelief. What do we know about the process by which change in people's views of their own self-interest takes place, with consequent change in the society? (It is essential to use the word self-interest here, although it can be misunderstood. We have seen that self-interest can be expressed at various levels of human growth, but it is always self-interest: each person will always do the thing which seems best to him given all the circumstances of which he is aware at the time he acts.)

The first reality we must recognize is how ill-prepared we are for the forms of discussion we need: these forms are often called dialogue and this word will therefore be used in the remainder of this document. We have been exposed in the past to authoritarian learning situations in which it was assumed that one member of the group knew and that the others should learn. Dialogue, however, assumes that we are looking for new patterns, many of which may not be consciously known to any member of the group.

We must therefore get beyond the basic learning patterns we have so far experienced in most cases, particularly in our formal education, where the teacher usually expects his students to ingurgitate knowledge and then regurgitate it without change. Rather we must look for a creative meshing of ideas between unique people who are all interested in the same topic and are willing to spend time together to develop their ideas and to create new patterns of action.

Most people and groups do not recognize the fundamental difference between a situation in which one person can state what needs to be done and the profoundly new reality of today where we need the joint efforts of all if we are successfully to invent the future. Because we use an old-fashioned understanding of "education," we set up our groups in such a way that they cannot be truly effective: indeed many of the basic rules of thumb we apply in creating groups are actually counterproductive. In the remainder of this pamphlet, therefore, I will first set out the reasons for which people can be expected to come together for dialogue; second, the very few rules we know which help to create—but do not guarantee—dialogue; and, third, the criteria for evaluation of a successful dialogue group.

It seems as though people can be brought together for three types of purposes or for combinations of them: first, to perceive how they can personally act more effectively within the conditions in which they are living; second, to increase their understanding of the functioning of the world; and third, to decide what changes need to be made in the socioeconomic structures. These three starting points seem to cover all the possibilities, although the degree of specialization will be very different for groups of types two or three. It is also clear that any fully successful groups would involve the introduction of each of these elements.

It is always tempting to place absolute priorities on certain types of action or at least to suggest that certain steps must necessarily precede others. This fails to recognize that human beings have different needs at different times and that their growth does not follow neat, tidy intellectual lines. We need to provide as many alternate routes for personal growth as we can.

The first type of group, devoted to facilitating individual growth, will be most likely to appeal to those who feel that their personal lives are presently unsuccessful. A number of techniques have now been created to help people to be more effective: one of the most developed is the Human Potential Seminar, created by the Stone-Brandel Center which circulates this document. The Seminar operates on the assumption that people grow by developing their strengths rather than directly overcoming their weaknesses. The sessions start off by helping people to perceive what they have "going for them" and they try to create "success experiences" in planning one's personal life. This is group psychotherapy but with positive rather than negative assumptions about the nature of man: it challenges fundamentally the patterns of sensitivity training being developed by the National Training Laboratories.

The second type of group is likely to appeal to those who presently perceive their opportunities for self-development in terms of greater understanding of the universe in which they live and who perceive, however incompletely, that fuller understanding of the universe will inevitably increase their capacity to act on the use of dialogue techniques to discover the new truths in the new world in which we live. These classes challenge directly the disciplinary structure of present school and university thinking.

The third style of group will involve those who are dissatisfied with various parts of the socioeconomic system within which they live, who want to understand it better with a view to changing it and who feel that they have the action skills to help bring about change. Groups of this type, which take the total neighborhood or city as their concern, are of relatively late development and are only now learning how to mesh the specialized interest of the various agencies: they challenge fundamentally all the fragmented organizations whether private or public.

Each of these three approaches is useful for the individual whose present felt needs accord with them; we must not try to choose between them. Each type of group and every experience of true individual learning must, however, recognize the constraints of the past, must hold a hope/belief for the future, and must act in the present, for it is only in this way that we can mesh the necessities of the past with the potential of the future.

The future is not determined: it is created out of our actions and in light of our hopes and fears.

GROUP FORMATION AND MEETING.

There are many forms of groups created for many purposes. The central distinction between them for the purpose of this document is whether we assume that goals are fixed and the only relevant question is how to achieve them or whether we are concerned with setting goals as well as finding means to achieve these goals.

This document—and, in particular, the rules which follow —apply to groups which must find out what they wish to do before they go about creating means to do it and *not* to those who are given a set task.

Make sure that people get to know each other before dialogue starts.

This rule has often been reduced to: "Be sure to make introductions," but such a limitation destroys its purpose.

Discussion of real issues requires a degree of trust for otherwise there will be surface and superficial chatter rather than meaningful dialogue. One needs to know who one is talking to in order to perceive the range of skills and the range of concerns present in the room as well as the possible power relationships which may complicate or facilitate discussion. Each person present should spend at least one minute—and preferably five—in setting out the reasons why they are present, what they would like to achieve and what they think they can contribute. Each person present should beware—both for himself and others—of self-deprecating comments such as, "I'm Joe's wife," or, "I'm just a housewife."

People will undoubtedly object that many discussions are set up in such a way that they don't have time for lengthy self-introductions. The only possible response to this comment is that nothing significant will take place until people feel comfortable with each other and that this process cannot be rushed. (The efficient examination of structured situations which can be carried out without real insight into others' views—for personal values are not involved—has been excluded from our concern.)

Real discussions require the commitment of significant amounts of time. The fact that this reality is difficult to deal with in our hectic world does not make it less real. If you want to teach others about the future—or learn from them—you must take the time to get to know them.

Limit the size of your group.

Experience has taught us that there is an optimum size for dialogue groups with eight normally the lowest size and twelve the largest. These limits result from the fact that with less than eight people there is not a sufficiently wide range of experience. With more than twelve people, the range of relevant experience is so great that it cannot be easily handled. (Experienced people can, of course, interact successfully even though the numbers are far greater.)

Even with this small a group the period you spend together can be broken up. Some people talk best in two's and three's; others like a larger group.

Role of the discussion leader.

Don't.

This is a terribly difficult piece of advice which is not always relevant. But it is still the best single rule of thumb.

A self-aware group does not need a discussion leader, for the members of the group know how to lead their own discussion. If the group is not yet self-aware, the task of the discussion leader is to ensure that the group develops self-awareness rather than substituting his own partial self-awareness for that of the total group. This can only be done by permitting the group to chart its own course with the leader participating as an equal.

There are, of course, ways that the discussion leader can "steer" the group toward more rapid self-awareness, but the more he uses his "authority," the slower the process will be.

Thus, the "group" should draw out the silent person: one or more people should have become aware of the skills of the silent individual and ask him to comment when he will be relevant and when he will not feel it an imposition. The talkative individual, if he is really dominating the group and not acting as the most knowledgeable person in the group for a brief or lengthy period of time, should be informed of his behavior by another member of the group who knows him—or eventually by a collective explosion of frustration. The group itself will learn to determine what the relevant point is at a particular moment in time and will control itself for its own purposes—which will seldom coincide perfectly with the limited purposes of the discussion leader.

The group should be particularly alert to inherent assumptions about the skills of particular classes of people. There is a tendency today to assume that males between forty-five and sixty-five have most to contribute and thus allow them to speak for as long as they wish while cutting off women and young people. The group as a whole should act to prevent this common pattern from developing.

Each group is different: each situation requires a different style. Those who have grown up with authoritarian styles will be lost if they are given too much freedom too rapidly. The practicable methods of creating group integration, as every other effort, must be based on the past and the future—in this case, the history of the individuals concerned and the hopes which are held for the future. The effort must be to find the immediate, feasible step which will move people the maximum distance from where they now are to where they want to be.

In every case, too little is irrelevant and too much is dangerous: one rule of thumb is to find ways to permit people to do what they already can plus ten percent for risk: such structuring is only possible if people know "where others are." This rule of thumb has relevance in determining who should meet with whom. If one presently holds a relatively narrow white "middle-class" point of view, it will probably be destructive for both sides if one tries immediately to understand the view of a black-power advocate, for the interaction will be both "irrelevant" and threatening. One should dialogue with people whose world one can enter fully and by entering it enlarge one's own world and at the same time one's capacity to understand worlds which are more radically different. (Young people who act from their personal beliefs and not on the basis of an ideology can get to know each other far more rapidly.)

A group starts to function effectively when it has created its own collective experience to which it can refer. The way the group states this understanding may be serious but it is far more likely to be seen as a joke, a misunderstanding, a disaster turned into a success. This collective experience is often called a myth for it ceases to be the recitation of a set of facts and becomes a method of bringing the group together when it threatens to fall apart. (This is the only way a group can have cohesion if one excludes the possibility of an external threat: i.e., if the group does not exist to fight against another group.)

HOW TO MEASURE THE SUCCESS OF YOUR GROUP, OR DON'T BE AFRAID OF "FAILURE"

In our statistical society, we like to measure the number of groups created, the number who continued throughout the program, the actions taken. Unfortunately, these formulas do not accord with the reality of individual growth.

People get involved in projects for many reasons: some positive and some negative. Up to now, because of our fascination with numbers we have tried to hold everybody whether they were truly interested or not. The lack of enthusiasm of those who were not truly interested then always acted to limit and even destroy the potential development of those who wished to think, study or work intensively.

A good analogy for a successful group is an atomic pile. Energy is produced when the pile goes "critical": that is to say when sufficient uranium rods are pulled sufficiently far out of a surrounding material which prevents their interaction. Similarly, a human group gives off energy when people are sufficiently freed from the negative forces which presently surround them.

But, one may object, if people leave our group we will have failed to provide them with the opportunity for learning. Such a statement, although it appears to be responsible, is in fact profoundly arrogant for it assumes that only one style of learning exists. Let us remember our elementary mathematics: two negative signs multiplied together are positive. People who interact badly with one person or a group may react well with another which we may help them find or which they may find for themselves.

This is an enormously freeing vision if we take it seriously. The liberty it provides was expressed best by a young girl of seventeen who thought she was doing her "duty" by attending meetings of those with whom she totally disagreed. "You mean," she said, "it's all right to just go to those meetings where one can groove, where one likes the other people?"

The psychic energy needed to create change can be created by working with others with whom we agree or it can be wasted in battles which we cannot presently hope to settle but which will probably become irrelevant as the future emerges. Dialogue assumes that the future can only be invented when we join together to celebrate our human potential and we accord to others the same right. We are all searching for a truth which will permit all of us to live creatively—our different pasts ensure that we will reach it along many different routes.

J. M. SCOTT

lass-
étude

I'm trying to think of the future
But tomorrow's too far away,
And if I don't get going there's right
                    now no knowing
If I'll ever get up today.

STANFORD ERICKSON

i too
sing

I too shall sing!
I too shall challenge the stars at night,
Call them down to me,
Capture that brilliant light
In a single twinkling thought of pure delight.

I too shall sing!
Bang the bell that's me,
Let the resonance of my individual being ring
Throughout a land of individual beings.

I too shall be one of those
Who make the world take note of them.
I too shall paint the sky in orange and red,
Eclipse the sun with a knowing wink,
Sip in the wind like a dry white wine.

I too shall be one of those
Who seek the Grail of Holy Light
In the darkness of themselves . . .
And finding it
Drink the goblet dry.

I too shall sing!
I too shall scratch my nails in the face of time,
Leave foot prints in the sandy wastes of self,
And discover desire for life on the shores of others' seas.
I too, I too will sing!

Printed with the permission of Stanford Erickson.

DEUTERONOMY 30

the
choice

See, I have set before thee this day life and good, and death and evil;

In that I command thee this day to love the Lord thy God, to walk in his ways and to keep his commandments and his statutes and his judgments, that thou mayest live and multiply; and the Lord thy God shall bless thee in the land whither thou goest to possess it.

But if thine heart turn away, so that thou wilt not hear, but shalt be drawn away, and worship other gods, and serve them;

I denounce unto you this day, that ye shall surely perish, and that ye shall not prolong your days upon the land, whither thou passest over Jordan to go to possess it.

I call heaven and earth to record this day against you, that I have set before you life and death, blessing and cursing: therefore choose life, that both thou and thy seed may live.

PART THREE

refining your view of the future

There is no way to come to understand the real options involved in the future unless you start to become involved in creating them. This part of the book provides a number of ways in which you can work at imagining the future you think is probable as well as the future you would desire.

Some of the ways you can think about the future require no more than a pencil and paper, a tape recorder, or a camera —anything which will record your ideas. Some of them require research. What you do will depend on the time you have, the energy you want to put into imagining your own future, and your own priorities.

There is, however, no way to teach the future without your participation. You must be involved if you want to get any real sense of your possibilities, those of the society, and those of the world. The time when you could be objective and noninvolved and still learn has passed.

At least, this is the view that I hold. Probably you will not have come so far in this book unless you too believe that man has to create his future for himself. This last section is certainly based on this belief and will appear, therefore, nonsensical or irrelevant to the positive extrapolators, negative extrapolators, and romantics.

i
the life-style
of various
occupations

We have seen that people hold different world views. Try to decide what world views are held by various occupations at the present time and, also, whether it is possible for people to hold a different world view and still operate within this occupation.

For example, most educators at the present time are positive extrapolators. What would happen to them if they became negative extrapolators, romantics, or system thinkers. Are there examples of each of these types of teachers at the present time?

Cartoonists normally seem to be negative extrapolators. Can you imagine a society in which the cartoonist would be a systems thinker—or would the cartoonist not exist at all?

What about the newspaperman, the lawyer, the policeman, the crook, the economist, the sociologist, the nurse, the doctor, the clergyman? What would happen to the engineer, the computer scientist, the gardener?

What were the priest, the oracle, the medicine man, the farmer, the fisherman, the shaman in other cultures? What occupations would you like to invent or reinvent? Would you like to recreate the court jester, what are the uses of the ombudsman?

ii
positive and
negative
scenarios

"I do not wish to seem overdramatic, but I can only conclude from the information that is available to me as Secretary-General that the Members of the United Nations have perhaps ten years left in which to subordinate their ancient quarrels and launch a global partnership to curb the arms race, to improve the human environment, to defuse the population explosion and to supply the required momentum to development efforts. If such a global partnership is not forged within the next decade, then I very much fear that the problems I have mentioned will have reached such staggering proportions that they will be beyond our capacity to control."

These were the words of U Thant in May 1969. In October 1970, the United Nations Center for Economic and Social Information published a pamphlet entitled The Challenge of a Decade: Global Development or Global Breakdown *in which it explored the nature of the probable breakdown if trends should continue. A series of news stories dated in 1980 showed the consequences of failure to act imaginatively.*

Stories which showed the potential for the future were also published. Both are included here. You may want to write your own news stories which set out your vision of the probable and possible course for the world over the next decade.

RICH-POOR SPLIT ENDS PLANNING FOR DEVELOPMENT DECADE
Collapse of UN System Now Widely Predicted

October 12, 1980—Political negotiations to save the Third United Nations Development Decade broke down today. Secret talks could not bridge the gap between the minimal demands of the developing countries and the maximum willingness of the developed countries to provide resources.

As the news broke, glum United Nations diplomats discussed whether the UN system could survive the latest blow. Even the most optimistic feared that the economic and social activities of the UN would be destroyed by this failure.

Spokesmen for the developing countries argued that the developed nations had failed to honour their moral obligations and to perceive their immediate self-interest. They pointed out that the gap between the rich and the poor countries had widened even faster during the seventies than in the sixties.

The developing countries blamed the failure of negotiations on the consistently negative attitude of the developed countries. In particular, they argued that "the abundant countries had repeatedly placed their concerns about the environment ahead of the needs of starving, un-housed human beings and that they had tried to dominate the decision-making process in the developing countries by forcing them to adopt nineteenth-century patterns of growth."

Spokesmen for the developed countries rejected the charges. They argued that they had to be concerned about the expressed needs of their citizens for a better quality of life. In addition they stated that while they were willing to accept a responsibility to provide resources to developing countries they were only justified in doing so if the resources were effectively used. In their view, the "requests of the developing countries for aid had been increasingly based on a fundamental misunderstanding of the nature and process of development."

The few development experts still trusted by both developed and developing countries claim that the present crisis results from a tragic misunderstanding. They believe that in many cases the proposals of the developing countries would indeed lead to effective development in modern technological conditions but that the representatives of the developed countries have failed to perceive the validity of any development process which follows lines different from their own.

EMPLOYMENT RIOTS IN LARGE AREAS OF WORLD
Firms, Embassies Bombed

October 31, 1980—During the past month, employment riots spread to many countries which have not previously suffered from them. Authori-

Reprinted from *The Challenge of a Decade: Global Development or Global Breakdown.* United Nations Center for Economic and Social Development (October 1970).

ties fear that further worsening is inevitable.

It is not only the amount of violence which is increasing, but attitudes appear to be hardening daily. During the initial attacks, there were significant attempts to prevent human casualties and to ensure that only property was damaged. Increasingly, patterns of violence ignore dangers to human life—indeed some attacks seem to be designed to maximize casualties.

The most serious unemployment problem is, of course, in the poor countries of the world where 50 per cent or more of the people in the large cities have no jobs and no other means of obtaining income. Despite the attention given to the employment issue during the past decade, the situation has continued to worsen rapidly. The increase in the efficiency of machines has been so rapid that it has been impossible to absorb more than a very limited part of the increase in the available labour force in the developing countries.

The pattern in the developed countries was not considered critical until recently although unemployment rates in many developed countries far exceed the levels considered desirable. Transfer mechanisms based on unemployment compensation and other welfare measures had continued to provide minimal incomes to all those affected.

However, there is now clear-cut evidence that employment riots are spreading to the developed countries. Those workers who have already lost their jobs are demanding higher incomes. Those who are still employed are demanding job security. While the amount of violence in the developed areas has so far been limited, its consequences are often more extensive because of the vulnerability of highly developed industrial systems to sabotage.

EPIDEMICS SUSPEND MANY INTERNATIONAL FLIGHTS
Measures Demanded by America, Australasia and Europe

October 5, 1980—Flights to large areas in Asia, the Middle East and Africa were indefinitely suspended today. An enraged public in America, Australasia and Europe demanded protection against the risk of cholera, yellow fever, plague and other contagious diseases. These have reached pandemic proportions in many of the poorer areas of the world.

International organizations which co-ordinate activities in the fields of aviation and health argue that the measure will be ineffective and exceptionally damaging to the interests of all countries in the world. They have been trying for many years to prevent this situation from becoming critical by securing greatly enlarged budgets to control the spread of disease: they have never been able to obtain the enormous sums of money required.

The decision to suspend flights was taken reluctantly, officials of the various rich countries emphasized. "We were forced to act by the attitude of our citizens who have come to fear that the growing number of cases of tropical diseases imported into the abundant countries might set off a general epidemic."

While national authorities continue to officially deny this possibility, some public health officials state, off the record, that there are real dangers. There is fear in certain circles that the rising number of strikes in essential services and the growing shortage of medical personnel could make the rich countries vulnerable to diseases which have been eradicated in the past or effectively controlled. Already venereal diseases are causing severe problems and there is a constant threat of the emergence of a strain of these diseases which will be resistant to available antibiotics and other drugs.

Nobody knows how, or when, the suspension of flights will be lifted. The proportion of the population with access to clean water supplies has been falling rather than rising in many developing countries. The threat of epidemics is therefore a permanent danger for a lengthy period into the future.

PERCENTAGE OF LITERATES IN WORLD DECLINES
Funds for Education Totally Inadequate to Needs

October 7, 1980—Recent surveys show that the rapid increase in population in the developing countries has overwhelmed the efforts of governments to provide even primary education to all of their citizens. The cost of ensuring literacy for everyone has far exceeded the financial capacity of governments in the poor countries.

The possibility of this development was already visible in surveys taken by UNESCO at the end of the sixties and the beginning of the seventies. Although the number of people "in school" was still rising, it was clear that the quality of education and teaching was declining steadily despite the willingness of many governments to spend an ever-greater proportion of the national income on education.

During the seventies, funds available for education only grew at the same rate as national income. The consequence of this development would have been less serious if there had been effective global cooperation to develop the potential of such techniques as programmed learning, television-assisted instruction, educational radio, etc.

The educational crisis has been increased by the fact that many of the available teachers are urban-oriented. The most visible result of "education" in many rural areas is to make children dissatisfied with their surroundings and to cause them to emigrate to the already-overcrowded cities.

An additional reason for the failure to revise educational strategy in the developing countries has been the growing disagreements about the meaning of education in the abundant world. There has been an increasing challenge to the effectiveness of schools and universities as the proper way to provide children and adults with the skills required to live in the communications era.

"We have lost a whole generation of children from the educational process in many areas," a high UNESCO official stated. "Modern communications technology provided us with the means to inform all the people of the world and we have failed to take advantage of the available possibilities. The consequences for the future are incalculable."

IS DEATH OF SEAS NOW INEVITABLE?
Question Posed by International Scientists

October 24, 1980—The destruction of all life in the seas could occur in the immediate future. Such a development would cause the death of mankind. This was the conclusion of an international group of scientists meeting under the auspices of the United Nations.

Questioned at a press conference following the release of the conclusions, a spokesman for the group stated that only immediate international agreement on radical measures would confront the danger. "Effective techniques for dealing with some of the most severe threats are still not known," he said.

"The progressive deterioration is now so severe that it is no longer a question of whether we will survive in the absence of corrective measures but whether the most extreme policies which we presently know how to take will be sufficient."

The extent of the threat to man's reserves of water began to be recognized in the late sixties. By this date, large bodies of water, such as Lake Erie in North America, were losing many species of plant and animal life. At this point in time most of the damage was believed to be due to the consequences of excessive dumping of industrial and human wastes and the destruction caused by long-lived pesticides such as DDT.

Some limited efforts were made to get these problems under control in developed countries during the seventies but, on a global basis, these efforts were offset in large part by the rise in population. In addition, the agricultural green revolution which did succeed in preventing widespread famine in the seventies depended on new varieties of grain which required heavy applications of pesticides such as DDT, thus worsening the problem.

The seventies have proved that the problem of pollution is far more complex than was originally believed. It was discovered that highly dangerous consequences could result if

trace-elements of various products were present. Mercury was one of the first of these elements to be discovered: many others were later found to be lethal.

THIRD DEVELOPMENT DECADE PROCLAIMED
Sufficient Food and Protein for All by 1990

October 24, 1980—The Third Development Decade was proclaimed today by the United Nations General Assembly. The targets include the final abolition of hunger and protein deficiencies throughout the world before 1990 to improve further on the progress already made. New varieties of pulses and grains are critical to the successful achievement of this goal as are the contributions of new food preservation techniques based on irradiation.

The Second Development Decade's goal of a 6 per cent growth rate was surpassed due to the rapid increase in transfer of resources from the developed to the developing countries and the imaginative use of the potential of science and technology. The actual rate of growth was over 7 per cent and this ensured a doubling of Gross National Product during the seventies.

The successes of the Second Development Decade are blurring the sharp distinctions between the rich and the poor countries. Rapid structural changes in many parts of the world have dramatically altered the patterns of trade and the need for aid. Countries which were receiving aid at the beginning of the Decade are now substantial donors.

It would, however, be misleading

to concentrate on economic indicators. During the Decade, social concerns have come to be seen as equally important as economic growth. Progress in such fields as health, housing, education has been dramatic. Agricultural and industrial production have grown together. In addition, rapid progress has been made in building up telecommunication, weather, postal and transportation networks whose availability has been recognized as crucial.

The Secretary-General of the United Nations stated: "It is impossible to overestimate the extent of the achievement during the Second Development Decade. The pace of economic growth is, in itself, dramatic evidence of the change in climate during the past ten years. However, I should like to draw attention to the underlying reasons for the changes in trends.

"The Second Development Decade served, I believe, to clarify the issues involved in worldwide development and to create global consciousness of the needs of the human race. Without the present good-will it would have been impossible to deal with the major structural changes which have been required to support the process of growth in both the developing and the developed countries.

"At the beginning of the seventies, the tensions between market-economies and centrally-planned economies were still preventing effective cooperation. In addition, there was growing tension between the abundance and scarcity countries. The abundance countries felt that their aid was being wasted: the scarcity countries felt that the rich countries of the world were unwilling to make even minimal sacrifices.

"There is still no real agreement about the process by which the world came to commit itself to the goal of global solidarity. The fact remains that no country today would wish, or indeed be able, to opt out of the effort toward global development. The 1 per cent target for transfer of resources was met early in the seventies and is now, of course, largely exceeded."

The rate of growth in Gross National Product in the developing countries has led to greatly increased exports of both agricultural and industrial goods. Policies have had to be invented in the abundance countries to permit a steady rise in imports from the scarcity countries while minimizing the hardship felt by those who lost their jobs.

In the scarcity countries there have been significant changes in patterns of land settlement but changes in agricultural technology and methods of distributing resources have made this problem less unmanageable than was originally expected. On the other hand, the problem of excessively rapid growth of cities and rural depopulation has required highly imaginative decision making. Even this has not been effective in all cases: some cities on all continents are now so large that they cannot be effectively managed. Securing control of the urbanization process remains one of the critical priorities of the Third Development Decade.

The world still faces enormous challenges: the goals of the Third Development Decade are monumental. It is only because we have the successful experience of the Second Development Decade behind us that it seems reasonable to accept them. Interviews with people throughout the UN system show, however, that there is a general belief that the goals will be achieved. Every individual will therefore have access to the resources and services required to live in dignity by the beginning of the next century—now only twenty years away.

UN DAY CELEBRATED
AS TRANSNATIONAL HOLIDAY
World Population Salutes
Progress during Decade

October 24, 1980—The thirty-fifth anniversary of the United Nations is being celebrated today by the peoples of the world. Every country now considers this a legal holiday.

For the first time, worldwide TV programming will cover a 24-hour period. Noon has been set as the time for celebrations of UN Day and the cameras will move around the world with the sun.

The more than 4,250,000,000 people who are members of the United Nations will be able to see parades and listen to speeches—simultaneous translation into local languages will, of course, be provided. This will, however, be a small part of the total programme.

Countries throughout the world have commissioned their artists to add new depth to the vision of man as a cooperative, creative individual. Music, painting, dance, sculpture, cinema, theatre and other old and new media will be used to express hopes for development, peace and harmony.

Planners of this programme voice three concerns about their activities: their fears are nevertheless minor compared to their hopes for a greater sense of transnational unity.

First, and most serious, they recognize the extraordinary technological difficulty of the task they are proposing. While stand-by arrangements have been created, the producers will be extremely surprised if they can get through the day without some serious breakdown.

Second, they are worrying about the transferability of some of the forms of cultural expression. Will many Westerners still find the dance and music of Asia too slow and elliptical—as well as discordant?

Third, there are concerns about the possibility of violence. Despite the positive alterations in conditions over the last decade and the profound change in attitudes, there are still areas where riots and demonstrations occur constantly. Will groups in these areas try to break up the programming?

RATE OF POPULATION RISE
HALVED DURING DECADE
Further Rapid Reductions
Predicted

October 24, 1980—The fall in the worldwide birth rate is becoming even more rapid, the most recent available statistics show. An increasing number of countries have decided that a rapid rate of increase in population is against their interests and they are making greater efforts to provide their populations with methods of limiting births to the level desired by parents.

The surprising shifts on this issue can be traced to a number of causes. Perhaps the most important is the increased life-span in the developing countries and the growing probability that infants will survive. This has altered the wishes of parents throughout large parts of the world: in many areas the desire was more for the certainty of some children surviving than for the largest possible family.

It is now generally agreed that any attempt to limit births without the full consent of husband and wife has highly undesirable consequences. Despite the fact that birth rates, even at the present level, pose acute problems, there is no longer any discussion of forced contraception by adding birth-control products to water supplies, etc. Those most directly involved agree that the problem is not any lack of desire to control births but rather to develop culturally acceptable birth-control methods. They are convinced that the potential for further rapid decline in births exists.

The shift in individual values has been reinforced by a change in the view of governments. Even those governments which have no problems of density of population are now concerned by the fact that a rise of 1 per cent in population is equivalent in very rough terms to cutting the rate of increase in income per head by 1 per cent. In addition, population increases often prevent concentration on the strategy required for further development.

Finally, our greater understanding of other organisms in the environment has contributed to a shift in perspective. We have discovered that the number of young born to a given species is often limited not by reproductive capacity but by the number which can be effectively raised in given conditions. The recognition that "instinctive" birth-control mechanisms exist in some species has certainly played its part in altering our view of the issue.

EDUCATION CAPABILITIES ENLARGED
Wide Use of Modern Technologies

October 24, 1980—The concept of education has changed dramatically during the seventies. "Permanent education" advanced as a goal by UNESCO in the sixties has affected the thinking of national governments throughout the world. Education is no longer perceived as a process lasting for a certain number of years at the beginning of an individual's life: rather it is believed that education is a continuous process.

Schools and universities are no longer seen as the only places where education can occur. Education is believed to be possible when people read magazines, listen to television or the radio, or receive information from the government. It is now generally defined as any process which helps the individual to live more effectively within his present environment and permits him to participate in the process of improving his conditions.

Change in policies was to some extent forced upon the developing countries. It was clear at the beginning of the seventies that it was impossible to increase the number of places in schools and universities sufficiently rapidly to provide every citizen with the right to an education. Once the shift had been made, it was discovered that many forms of learning could take place more effectively by using non-conventional means.

The shift was made easier by the fact that there was growing agreement in the abundant countries that gross overexpansion of the formal education system had taken place in these countries. It came to be understood that schools actually often prevented students from learning what was necessary if they were to live effectively. Trends in both developed and developing countries have been similar during the decade: a far greater appreciation has been created of the educational potential inherent in the process of life itself.

It is now generally accepted that the educational process must be designed to provide the individual with knowledge about the ways in which he can develop his own potential to the maximum. "Education" in this sense is seen as the inalienable right of all: it will be possible to provide it to every human being before the end of the next decade.

TWENTY-FIFTH MEETING OF WORLD'S WISE MEN
Third Development Decade Discussed

October 24, 1980—The twenty-fifth meeting of the Terran Communication Council (TCC) closed today. Since 1971, a worldwide group of individuals chosen for their breadth of vision has met on a regular basis to examine—and report on—the issues crucial to global development. While many of these individuals were originally educated in a specific discipline, they now recognize that we must find a new overall framework of analysis if we are to continue to solve world problems.

The ideas and reports of the TCC have formed the basis for many of the discussions in the United Nations family during the preparation of the Third Development Decade. The individual stature of each member of the TCC and their joint prestige—as well as the representation of all areas of the world—ensures that their reports receive wide attention.

It is clear that their conclusions have changed the agreed definition of many problems and created many new possibilities. For example, it was the first report of the TCC which effectively clarified the fact that the developed and developing countries would necessarily see the environmental issue in different ways. Similarly the TCC defined—and thus eventually helped to compromise—the differences in the way that the developed and developing countries saw the process of development and the evaluation procedures they therefore believed to be appropriate.

One of the reasons for the success of the TCC was almost accidental. The stature of the members of the group forced a procedure for bringing them together which has since been recognized as one of the chief reasons for the success of the group. None of its members gave up their normal activities to participate in it. Their broad range of national and international activities ensures that the results of their thinking are widely and rapidly diffused.

Members of the TCC who were interviewed today gave much of the credit for their success to those young people who have worked with them over the last decade. The secretariat for the group has been composed predominantly of individuals aged from 25–30. "They have been extremely successful in researching the information needed for our work and, where it was not available, they have helped us to create it," TCC members said.

iii
the revision
of
the constitution

America's political system is based on a written constitution. Since it was created almost 200 years ago, it has often been bent to fit new conditions but it is still used as the basis for the American system of law. What changes need to be made in the constitution if it is to be appropriate to the new conditions in which we shall live?

Some, of course, claim that there is no need for change. Such a belief would not be acceptable to the founding fathers who were fully aware that they wrote for a specific period of history—even though they hoped the principles on which they based their thinking would remain valid.

In a forthcoming book, Arthur Waskow sets out a revised constitution; he places the date of its creation at 1990. Waskow assumes that the following conditions will exist: "By 1990 there are autonomous Black, Chicano, Jewish, Indian, Quebecois, Puertoriqueno, and Italian commonwealths in North America; there are Autonomous Regions in the Bay Area, the Northwest, New England, and about six other areas; there are Workers Control Alliances in all major industries on the continent; there is democratic and *socialist planning, initiated by a Congressional Congress of recallable delegates, the White House is a museum and the Pentagon a vast Department of the History of the American Empire, wherein all the people are busy publishing and evaluating all the documents they formerly kept secret. The USA in any recognizable sense is, in short, gone. The American peoples and workers are free. Political struggle continues but in new forms—particularly between technocrats and nonprofessionals over control of the newly 'workers controlled' economic and industrial institutions."*

Waskow's constitution appears very different on the surface from the present one. But, in the comments which follow Waskow's piece, is Steve Nickeson right when he argues that there has been little real change in the style of thinking? What criticisms are Todd Gitlin, Jim Stenzel, Merrill Jackson, and the Eleanor Burns Women's Collective making? Which of them are positive extrapolists, which negative extrapolists, which romantics, which system thinkers?

There is no lack of different views here. Some people are saying that the proposals in Waskow's constitution are unwise. Some people are saying that the future cannot be controlled by a static constitution. What do you think? Could you write your own constitution?

Do you believe that the constitution created in the eighteenth century should serve as the underpinnings for the future? If you believe this, have you really studied the constitution or have you simply assumed its value?

Some people have suggested that we should call a consti-

tutional convention to revise the constitution in 1976—the bicentennial of America's founding. What do you think of the idea? Would you like to create a constitution? Or do you think that the idea of a written constitution will fail to solve the problems of the future?

ARTHUR WASKOW

draft
constitution

Preamble. The Federal Commonwealths of America are not a Nation or a Sovereign State. They shall not claim sovereign power to conquer or oppress other countries, or sovereign authority to maltreat the citizens of other countries whether resident among the Commonwealths or elsewhere, or sovereign immunity as against their own citizens. The Federal Commonwealths of America are rather a free association of free human beings grouped according to their own will. We the workers and peoples of America who propose to live by this Constitution, reserve to ourselves the right of revolution against it or reconstruction of it.

I. Every person who is at least 13 years old, lives among the Federal Commonwealths of America, spends 30 hours a week in productive work and chooses to belong to a Work Collective shall be a citizen of the Federal Commonwealths. Any person under 13 who lives among the Federal Commonwealths and is a member of a Living Collective shall be a citizen. A person born in the Federal Commonwealths but living elsewhere may reenter and reclaim citizenship at any time.

II. The basic politico-social units of the Federal Commonwealths shall be three kinds of Collectives: Work Collectives,

From Arthur Waskow, *The 1990 Draft Constitution,* forthcoming, January 1972, by arrangement with The New American Library, New York.

Ethno-Collectives, and Living Collectives. Persons living in the United Commonwealths may choose to create, join, or belong to one collective in each category, but no more. Work Collectives shall be made up of people working together in the same area of production for at least 30 hours a week. Ethno-Collectives shall include collectives built around an identity in a racial, national, religious, philosophical, or sexual group. Living Collectives shall be made up of persons living close together, and if possible shall operate as a family. A Collective shall be made up of at least 10 and no more than 50 persons. Membership in all Collectives shall be wholly voluntary in both directions. All Collectives shall by three-fourths vote adopt a Statement of Internal Self-Government which shall define their decision-making process.

III. Any group of at least 200 Collectives with at least 5,000 total membership, but no more than 600 Collectives with no more than 25,000 total membership, may join together in a Comradery in the following ways: such a group of Work Collectives in the same area of production may form a Work-union; such a group of Ethno-Collectives may form a Tribe; such a group of Living Collectives sharing the same geographic area may form a Neighborhood. Each Collective in a Comradery shall elect one recallable delegate to a Comrades' Congress, which shall decide according to majority vote of the delegates on matters delegated to the Comradery by the member Collectives. Work-unions shall govern the working pace and conditions at a given workplace, choose managers, etc. Tribes shall shape and celebrate ethnic or other identities, may provide schools, etc. Neighborhoods shall govern local planning, zoning, parks, recreation, housing, transportation, etc.

IV. Any group of at least 100 Comraderies with at least 500,000 total membership may form itself into a Commonwealth in the following ways: A group of 100 Work-unions may form a Workers' Alliance; a group of 100 Tribes may form a People; and a group of 100 Neighborhoods may form a Territory. Representation of the Comraderies in Commonwealth Congress, and other rules for internal government shall be decided within each Commonwealth. Workers' Alliances shall govern industries, make decisions within the norms set by the Continental Congress as to production and prices, develop new technologies, etc. Peoples shall form ethnic, sexual, or other identities and safeguard the rights of national, sexual, or other minorities. Territories shall plan the physical future of a geographic area and govern such other institutions within it as are delegated to it by the Neighborhoods.

V. The Commonwealths shall be represented in a Continental Congress according to their membership, with one Member of Congress up to 1,000,000 members and one additional Member of Congress for each additional 1,000,000 members of the Commonwealth. Each Member of Congress shall be elected by and subject to immediate recall by his or her Commonwealth and no Member shall serve for more than three years of his or her life. The Congress shall legislate on matters within its jurisdiction by majority vote. But whenever any People with at least 10 million members interposes a veto, the measure shall fail, and whenever any Territory or Workers Alliance with at least 10 million members interposes a veto, the vote required for passage shall be two-thirds.

VI. The Continental Congress shall each January choose by majority vote a Cabinet of 10 persons who shall jointly execute and administer the laws, and may remove them at any time. No person shall serve in the Cabinet more than three years of his or her life.

VII. Wherever this Constitution prescribes election of a delegate, Congressman, or Cabinet member, the delegate may instead be chosen by lot from all those who would be eligible to elect, but shall in any case be recallable by majority vote.

VIII. All persons living in the Federal Commonwealths shall be guaranteed the following rights:
1. All citizens over 13 shall have equal personal yearly in-

comes, and all citizens under 13 shall receive two-thirds of that income.

2. Every person who is not a citizen shall receive a personal income that is half what he would receive if he were a citizen.

3. All labor shall be voluntary. No person shall be conscripted to labor or service, military or civilian, or held to a contract for personal labor or service to or by any institution whatsoever, except through the processes of justice. But no person over 13 years of age who refuses to work shall be a citizen.

4. All property shall be owned by a Collective, Comradery, or Commonwealth, or by the Continental Congress. No person shall own any property. No public body shall own any property outside the Federal Commonwealths, except vehicles of transportation and non-capital goods that are sold within 90 days of leaving the United Commonwealths. The Federal Commonwealths shall hold no colonies or any other territory in which this Constitution does not apply.

5. All persons shall be wholly free to speak, associate, publish, assemble, celebrate, worship, and carry on sexual and familial relations in any fashion they please so long as it involves no coercion of another to do likewise. An Ethno-Collective, a Tribe, or a People may set limits upon these activities in regard to its members, enforceable only by expulsion. But no Work Collective, Work-union, or Workers Alliance, and no Living Collective, Neighborhood, or Territory may set such limits.

6. The distinction between "criminal" and "civil" law is hereby abolished. All cases in which harm by one person or institution to another is alleged shall be treated as public issues in which the complainants shall be a presiding jury. Any redress may include the payment of money or of services from a public body or person to a public body or a person. No act except a physically violent attack upon another person which seems likely to be repeated shall be punished by the confinement of the

wrongdoer, and then for no more than one year unless a jury shall unanimously, at the end of that year, conclude that the person is likely to repeat the violence, and extend the confinement for no more than two more years. All confinement shall be under conditions intended solely to make a violent attack unlikely, and all persons confined shall remain possessed of all their Constitutional rights. There shall be no punishment by death or physical violence, other than confinement. No person shall be required to testify against himself or herself, and every person shall have an attorney of his or her choice in all stages of the process of justice.

7. No person may be subjected to the processes of justice except by an initial presentment by two-thirds vote of a jury of 12 persons chosen at random from among the members of any Comradery of which he or she is a member, or if not a member of any Comradery by a jury chosen at random in the neighborhood where he or she lives. If it is charged that a person who claims citizenship is not performing 30 hours of productive work a week, the case may be presented only by the person's Work Collective or by a jury chosen at random from his Work-union.

8. Trial in all cases shall be by a jury of 12 persons chosen at random, of whom at least 4 shall be of the Neighborhood where the presented person lives, 4 of his Tribe if he belongs to one, and 4 of his Work-union, if he belongs to one. If the alleged wrong act was related to a person who was not of his own Neighborhood, Tribe, or Work-union, half the jury shall come from his own Comraderies and half from those of the other party. The jury shall decide by unanimous vote, and shall hear advice from the judge but shall itself be the ultimate judge of both the law and the facts.

9. All police forces shall be under control of a Comradery, shall be chosen at random from its members, and shall not have more police than one-thousandth of the Comradery's whole membership. All police shall be publicly

known and their names, addresses, photographs and biographies published every year. No person shall serve in the police more than three years of his or her life. No person shall be arrested (except during the actual commission of a felony); no house shall be entered bodily or by any visual, aural, electronic, or similar device; no conversation shall be recorded; no effects sequestered; and no similar police action undertaken in regard to a person without the actual service of a warrant, drawn upon probable cause and issued by a judge of proper jurisdiction, upon the persons affected. No police may question any person unless the person has an attorney actually present. No police may carry any firearm or other lethal weapon, except upon issuance and public announcement of a special warrant particularly naming the person and case requiring the issuance. If any police shall violate these provisions, he or she shall be dismissed from the police and prohibited permanently from serving therein, and the person accused shall go free and receive an indemnity of one year's income from the Continental treasury and another from the Comradery treasury. If any Comradery shall abolish its police force entirely and rely upon its ordinary membership for self-policing, it shall receive a bonus payment from the United Commonwealths of one-tenth of its regular yearly public grant, for each of the next ten years. There shall be no Continental or Commonwealth police forces.

IX. The Continental Congress shall have jurisdiction over the following subjects:
1. The level of the personal income of citizens, to be set in January each year.
2. The proportion of the gross national product and resources to be allocated each year to public purposes; provided that this proportion shall not be less than half and that once this amount is established, it shall be divided as follows: one-tenth to foreign nations whose populations live on one-fifth or less the average income

(personal plus public) of Americans, this amount to be subdivided solely according to the populations of said countries; one-tenth at the disposal of Congress; five-tenths to be divided among the Commonwealths according to their membership; and three-tenths to be divided among the Comraderies according to their membership.

3. The management of the civilian administrative service of the Federal Commonwealths, provided that no person shall serve in it more than three years of his or her life and that at no time shall it exceed 100,000 persons.

4. The setting of prices and production quotas for major basic industries.

5. The preservation of a Continental environment in which human, animal and vegetable life is safeguarded.

6. The preservation of peace with other nations and the pursuit of world arrangements to make war impossible, provided that any Commonwealth may directly negotiate on behalf of peace with any foreign government or group.

7. The proportion of gross national product to be allocated each year to armaments for defense against domestic tyranny or actual foreign invasion of or attack on the territory of the Federal Commonwealth, *provided* that the proportion shall never be more than three percent; that there shall be no nuclear weapons or other weapons of mass destruction; and that once the total amount is decided, half the arms themselves be divided among the Comraderies according to their membership, and the other half among Collectives according to their membership. There shall be no Continental or Commonwealth armed forces. No arms or armed persons shall go outside the territory of the Federal Commonwealths, except a maximum of 2,000 persons lightly armed from any single Commonwealth, if requested by the United Nations and approved by a two-thirds vote of all members of the Commonwealth, no more than five Commonwealths to be providing such forces at any one time.

X. There shall be a Supreme Court of 36 persons chosen by lot from the Continental Congress, 4 chosen each January to serve for 9 years, to interpret the laws and this Constitution, in particular cases on appeal from other courts. It may issue advisory interpretations of this Constitution at the request of the Continental Congress or any Commonwealth. It shall have power to nullify laws, acts of Collectives, Comraderies, and Commonwealths, executive acts, or court decisions that contravene this Constitution. Any decision it makes under Article VIII that upholds the Constitutional rights of persons against the Continental Congress or a Commonwealth or Comradery shall be final. But any other decision may be reversed by a four-fifths vote of the Continental Congress, unless vetoed by a People with more than 10,000,000 members.

XI. The Congress may by two-thirds vote (except if vetoed by a People with more than 10,000,000 members) submit amendments to this Constitution to the whole citizenry, who may adopt them by two majority votes cast at least 12 months apart.

JIM STENZEL

tokyo:
an asian critique
of "1990"

Art Waskow's article including the "1990 Draft Constitution" landed here two weeks ago, and my personal reactions to it have changed continually. First I thought the piece was quite radical, probably because of the newness of such concepts as collectives, comraderies and commonwealths applied to the U.S. My next reaction was that I needed to hear much more about the revolution itself: how it would happen, to what extent people would decimate each other in civil war, whether people would risk their lives to fight for equal incomes, how in fact the super-structure would be brought down, etc. Finally I decided that, despite the missing information, the article was valuable: it showed that the Movement was beginning to do some important thinking and would no longer leave long-term planning to the inner circles of the super-structure.

However, most of these reactions proved to be as American as spiked cider outside the Yale Bowl. My education, or gentle upbraiding, took place during a two-hour discussion of the article with Moonkyu Kang, Asia Secretary for the World Student Christian Federation. Moonkyu, in addition to his intimate knowledge of revolutionary struggles in Asia, has two strong traits: an ability to cut through irrelevancies and get to the essence of a problem, and an ability to present radical ideas without diluting them with emotional fervor or loud rhetoric.

During our talk, Moonkyu repeatedly touched on three basic criticisms of Waskow's article. I have combined his references into one statement in each of the three areas.

All the critiques of Arthur Waskow's proposal were published in *motive* (March and April, 1971). Reprinted with the permission of *motive* magazine.

the article is arrogant

"I understand that Mr. Waskow is speaking to the American Movement about primarily domestic matters. Even so, if I may be very frank, this is an arrogant proposal, because it assumes continued affluence and privilege of Americans—affluence and privilege that is based on international exploitation. If the U.S. would pull back all its capital and all its military from abroad, and if it would stop all exploitive trade, then the U.S. wouldn't have the 10 percent of GNP to give away as foreign aid. But U.S. radicals don't talk much about giving up the whole world market.

"The only international reference in the paper concerns foreign aid. But I'm not really interested in a figure like 10 percent. First, I do not think any nation-state will ever give so much aid. Second, if they did, it wouldn't solve the economic problems of the world. One economist has said that developed countries would have to give 20 percent of GNP just to keep the gap from widening. Since Mr. Waskow is dreaming in his proposals, why not say 25 percent or 50 percent of GNP for foreign aid? But this might cut into the affluence and privilege of Americans, and their unwillingness to do this is my basic anger.

"Privileged Americans always see foreign aid as a crusade. Even U.S. radicals insult me with their sense of messianic responsibility to liberate the world after they assure their own affluent comfort. Their concept of domestic justice is more developed than their concept of international justice, even though they use this phrase a lot these days. The Vietnam War is one example. Much of the U.S. Movement's war opposition is personal ('the draft is unjust') or economic ('it's bad for business') or political ('it's dividing the country'). Americans may say they oppose the war because of international justice, but they are more committed to personal and domestic interests.

"How about proposing international control of U.S. capital and of such things as the Ford Foundation? What are Waskow's international economic assumptions? Perhaps it's possible that, after 20 years of continuous American revolution, and presumably much bloodshed, the commonwealths will need foreign aid from each other and from foreign countries! And what if Mao or Castro refuses?

"This paper represents the dilemma of liberal-minded people: they dream of socialism in which they do not sacrifice liberal and capitalist privilege. Besides assuming the ongoingness of affluence, the paper suggests the continuation of power in the American super-state. Why should three per cent of GNP —$30 billion today—go to the military? This is more than the GNP of most of Asia, and it would maintain the U.S. as a super-military power. If the U.S. stops exploitation abroad and at home, it will not need such expenditures. Also, Waskow suggests to me that a powerful super-welfare state will be needed to guarantee all those nice new sewers, hospitals and houses. This again is a liberal response to a purely domestic concern, and it assumes affluence.

"Waskow discusses the reorganization of political power more than the assumptions behind economic power. I believe economic power is much more important as a force to free or oppress people internationally. To concentrate on talk about new communities is, I think, one of the luxuries of affluent Americans."

the article is naive

"I think it is terribly naive for any American to assume that revolution will happen of its own accord. Revolution is the struggle for power, and power is gained only through carefully-mapped-out strategies and goals. Revolutions don't just happen automatically, and they don't succeed without superior organizing and superior power. Romantic ideas of revolution never succeed.

"My feeling about this paper is that it enjoys, even unconsciously, the capitalistic freedom to dream socialism. His intentions are fine and his dreams interesting, but I would prefer a clear ideology, a clear frame of reference—it's too easy just to assume that there will be a general strike of the workers and the people. The workers are the most conservative element in society! Does Waskow really believe the opposite of Marx when he says the sub-structure collapses before the super-structure? Does Waskow recognize that the greatest power in the West isn't political but technological, and does he want to give this up or accept its decline?

"I criticize those liberal or post-liberal or even radical thinkers in the U.S. who think revolution will happen without a blueprint based on clear ideological and historical understanding. Americans prefer a neo-laissez-faire attitude based on spontaneity and optimism that something new will come about. They do not question the liberal tradition about the goodness of man and the good uses of power; they simply remain optimistic that history will move in that direction.

"This proposal reminds me of a sort of pre-Marxist, idealistic idea of socialism in the fantasy. You can't just dream of a Robinson Crusoe-type of idealistic island where you live peacefully making no distinction between civil and criminal. Such thinking is too naive to me because it doesn't understand man and history or power and structures. One who dreams such dreams might better migrate to Sweden than to die disillusioned in America."

the article is one-dimensional

"Waskow says that he wants to relieve 'white, male, middle-class Americans' of their spiritual and psychological oppression. But I don't sense any great amount of such liberation in his Constitution, because it's so preoccupied with functional mechanisms and structures. Now, a functional understanding of society is important, but I don't think the understanding here will provide enough identity for the nation-state.

"The sense of community here is restricted to functional groupings. The problem is the lack of integration—that's always the problem. A community or nation-state historically is where an individual—through a synthesis of history, culture, values and so forth—can transcend himself and find meaning. I don't think the functional units, the ethnic and work groups, can provide such integration or identity. In reality, this identity comes first and then structures are built which express it; but here we have the structures first with the assumption that integration will somehow emerge from the structures. This is illogical and tends to absolutize the structures.

"What the U.S. needs is a healthier nationalism: not in the destructive sense of economic or militaristic nationalism, but in the constructive sense of an integrated and inclusive concept of person, of community, of the uniqueness of its culture and history and so forth. Inclusive nationalism is behind all struggles for liberation. Asians are keen to emphasize their own culture and history and to build revolutions as well as societies upon these.

"Americans have failed to find a new integrity, a new unity incorporating their technology and their pluralism. I'm afraid Waskow doesn't really begin this process of integration. For example, pluralism has to do with a lot more than just ethnic and racial groupings with equal income—just as international justice has to do with much more than just 10 per cent in foreign aid."

Throughout the interview with Moonkyu, I felt the recurring implication that he felt revolution was not very likely in the U.S. In both the middle and the end of the interview, I asked him about this. The first time he said, "Because of the super-power of the super-state, even Marcuse thinks that the U.S. will still be pre-revolutionary in the year 2000." To close the interview he said, "Maybe we should think of it as an impossible possibility —we can't give up on it, can we?"

STEVE NICKESON

toward a
civil
future

It is self-contradictory to keep the 1990 Constitution in the futuristic framework where Art Waskow placed it. The already entrenched phenomenon of continuous change forced me to view the constitution *not* as where the Movement dreams to be in 20 years, but where it stands today. It is a pleasing and optimistic summation of where the Movement is in 1971. That is the strength of the document. It is today's prescription and prophecy, and Waskow is underestimating the Constitution's current value by postdating its functions to 1990.

But that is not my criticism, nor do I have any quarrel with the basic structures of the Constitution. It is the document's revolutionary windowdressing that is wrong; it is misleading and potentially self-destructive. The advertising in the coverletter sets us out in the wrong direction because the document itself is simply not *that* revolutionary. The important beauty of the 1990 Constitution is the fact that it is as All-American as the Wednesday night bowling league. To deny that is to deny its greatest selling point and its present-day integrity and usefulness.

Look at the Constitution again and mentally pencil out words like "revolution," "radical," "commune," "Comradery," "Collective," "Worker's Alliance," "Tribe," etc. In other words, take off its contextual style and let its functions stand there naked. What does it do?

It memorializes (as does the 1789 Constitution) the long-standing American suspicion of professional governments and politicians.

It continues the founding fathers' sentiment that ideology and abstracted high principles play a greater cohesive role in a society than the economic and governmental functions.

It institutionalizes the present American religiosity for cultural or group acceptance.

It furthers the American distrust of police and indignation at their existence, and recalls the romantic frontier days by placing the peace keeping functions in the hands of temporary amateurs.

Its grouping of the people suggests that it was influenced by the typically urban American belief in the agrarian myth.

It perpetuates the belief that each new American generation represents a redeeming and messianic force.

It reminds us that America has a longer standing history and stronger tradition of isolationism than internationalism.

It reaffirms America's concerned, but not overwhelming, benevolence toward underdeveloped nations.

And throughout runs the traditional optimistic faith that Americans can apologize to history and reclaim their innocence and destiny if only they can find some way of purifying themselves.

The Constitution's ties with Americana should not be areas of shame, but points on which to capitalize. The biblical cliche that has the actions of the fathers (I hope not just their sins) being visited on the children is not a moral judgment. It is a fact that puts to the sons and daughters (our sisters and brothers) the liberating responsibility of reconciling themselves to their breeding and making the most of their parentage.

This is where the Waskow document is the strongest. It prescribes to the present day sons and daughters a realistic and liberating future that contains benefits for the rest of the world as well.

After seeing what the document is, we should look at how it will function, or how the last two generations of American daughters and sons can best continue in their nation's traditions.

The 1990 Constitution is a wise and compassionate document. To the wisest and most compassionate child of most modern American families falls the unpleasant job of arranging for the old folks' journey to the rest home or the grave. We can be sure it is now time for that. The old patriarch America is ready to retire and is preparing for death in full history book tradition. It has rationalized away its unfulfilled and now hopeless dreams. It has built a technology that will come in and do the daily chores and it has made all the proper arrangements so the sons and daughters will inherit the richest estate on the face of the globe. The old patriarch is the last of that breed of immoral commoners who managed to pull themselves up to the vulgar level of the *nouveau riche* in order to bequeath the children and grandchildren lifetimes full of genuine refinement, education, sophistication, culture, security, and good health. We will inherit the material wealth to buy it all and an adject poverty of spirit that will isolate us for ever.

In the 1990 Constitution I see the children are fully prepared to accept that inheritance in true tradition. We will soon be free to phase out the old man's business before it becomes our liability. We should do so soon and with a clear conscience because it is doomed to failure now and has long been a public nuisance. It is just that much better that we will be able to live (with careful planning) on the liquidated assets for many a generation before anyone has to start looking for a job.

In the meantime we will be able to do what tradition usually requires of the children of such an illustrious parent. We will seclude ourselves in our retreats and bring into them culture and education. We will be free to make new acquaintances among people of the same general means. We will have the opportunity to build new and livable communities that truly reflect all the noble aspirations of people with our status and liberated circumstance. We can be free to worry over and experiment with the structure of our new environment while at the same time be dilettante about our own individual duties in the operation and maintenance of those communities.

Our liberated time will allow us to do occasional charity work when called upon, but mostly we will be free to do what we like the best, and which we are best at . . . studying ourselves. Our liberation will give us the final excuse and the justifiable right to be self-centered (we will, no doubt, change the traditional American accent on that custom from the individual to the commune). We will be able to all live free, honorable, and happy lives complacently secure in the center of a series of all-protective concentric rings of Community.

And above all that, it will give the rest of the world what it has long desired and deserved; the permanent retirement of that big rich family on the North American Continent.

TODD GITLIN

comments on the 1990 constitution

My first feeling about Art Waskow's 1990 Constitution was that it is a smorgasbord; some is tasty, some is ingenious (the veto provisions), some would go nicely on crackers (where *are* those damn crackers?), some is better as decoration than as food, and a bit is not even good as decoration. (You'll forgive the *bar mitzvah* memories, but Art brought them up with his 13-year-old citizenship clause.) My second feeling was a qualified celebration: it is past time for a revival of utopian thinking, even if first starts are partial, overly schematic, or insufficiently utopian. To change the metaphor, the instruments of utopian speculation haven't been used for a long time; they have to be tuned; and the notes sounded in tune-up are necessarily off-key. The point, however, is to get to the concert.

But something troubles me about Art's Constitution, more than my questions about this or that item. In fact, altogether I agree with most of his particulars, but that is not the point. Utopian novels have traditionally floundered in trying to explain how the utopia was achieved. More's original *Utopia,* as I recall, offered no explanation whatsoever. Huxley's *Island* offered the collusion of a farsighted Rajah and a canny Scots doctor—a happy unopposed alliance of Eastern and Western wisdom. William Morris' *News from Nowhere* is unique, to my knowledge, in presenting a hundred years of class warfare as the necessary condition of the decentral utopia, but even Morris was unable to explain, with feeling and precision, how the particular features of his utopia stemmed from the real configuration of social and ideological forces. He, like Huxley, finally had to presuppose some remarkable and confounding Enlightenment, though in Morris' case it was an enlightenment that accompanied political struggle. . . .

Let me try to clarify the point by illustrating it. Take the classical prescription, now updated: "All property shall be owned by a Collective, Comradery, or Commonwealth, or by the Continental Congress. No person shall own any property." Now what shall become of my writing desk if I don't choose to belong to a Living Collective (at least ten members, remember)? Will it fall to my Work Collective? But what if—being a post-Calvinist freak—I choose not to work 30 hours a week (will that be time-clocked, by the way?), and therefore disdain membership in a Work Collective? Suppose I don't belong to an Ethno-Collective either. Maybe I'm just cantankerous, maybe shy, maybe I differed with my last Ethno-Collective; there could be any number of reasons. But here I am alone with my desk, at which I write angry manifestos calling for revolution (or, for that matter, counter-revolution). Can I own my desk? Or does someone else have the right to take it to use as firewood?

I bring this up not to be clever, not to punch holes in the Constitution for the sake of punching holes. Beneath the logical problem is a problem of *social definition.* Is it to be supposed, in Art's historical projection, that by 1990 someone like me will have revamped his life-style to the point where certainly he would join a Living Collective? Is it to be supposed, in other words, that monogamous living as we know it will have become obsolete? If so, it can't be assumed, it must be argued that social and ideological forces are in the works to abolish privatist monogamy. For surely the Constitution would not propose to do so by fiat. That is to say, the Constitution would only make sense as a revolutionary—as opposed to bureaucratic— document if it recorded and institutionalized the common social sense of the people as of 1990—recorded, in other words, the direction in which social forces were already clearly moving.

The same point applies to the question of joining a Work Collective. Is it to be supposed that people like me would have overcome their bone-deep alienation to the point of wanting to work 30 hours a week, when we could live (presumably the half-wage for non-citizens would be sustaining) without it? The answer to that question requires a social analysis. In the next twenty years, what will have become of a youth culture in which many people choose not to labor? Will the movement have helped me overcome my alienation, or will it have heightened it, or left it untouched?

Or suppose it was a car, that vile private form of transportation, instead of a desk? What will have to have happened to the mental structure of most Americans *in twenty years* to lead them to prefer bicycles for short hauls and public transportation (presumably available) for longer? For a revolution takes place in the mental structure as it works in the political and institutional; the two take place together, or a revolution is merely a Grand Inquisitor's *coup d'etat.* To make the Constitution's property cause plausible, then, the book will require social and psychological and ideological analysis of the richest and most penetrating order.

With this in mind, I have to add that I find the twenty-year timetable almost grotesquely optimistic. Art's four-point agenda for political organizing, with which I agree utterly, makes it plain how far we have to go. My own analysis of the movement's first ten years, which I've already belabored in *motive,* indicates that the movement must overcome its own self-estrangement as it overcomes its own terribly limited class position. This interlocking project is almost unspeakably difficult. The level of organization, even among students and in the ethnic communities, is still primitive. The level of consciousness in the movement is still primitive, for consciousness is something much deeper than verbal gymnastics and breast-beating, of which there is plenty. (Think of how little progress has been made, among white males at least, in uprooting racism and sexism, despite all the talk.) And we are not even speaking yet of the epochal transformation which lies before the American people

—those people whom we love to invoke and of whom we know so precious little—if they are to *mobilize themselves* and thereby obviate the movement's wretched isolation. It is fine for the phrase "general strike" to be "heard on American lips" in the '70s, but that is not the same as the implications of revolutionary transformation being felt in American hearts.

It also strikes me as giddy to think that by 1990 there will be "autonomous Black, Chicano, Jewish . . . (etc.) Commonwealths in North America." The decay of the old order seems to be proceeding much more vividly than the construction of the new. But if Art's proposition is to be made plausible, histories have to be offered, taking account of repression and self-repression and all the shit we've been subjected to and inherited. I cannot imagine that history. (If Arthur can, more power to him.) The same point applies to the "Workers Control Alliances in all major industries"—right now there are none, with the possible exception of the League of Revolutionary Black Workers in Detroit, and there is not much talk about workers' control in America, least of all by the movement's authoritarians.

China's revolution took thirty years, from the founding of the party to the seizure of power, with the enormous "advantage" of an anti-colonial war to cement the nation. I don't know how to measure the duration of the Russian Revolution, but it's worth pointing out that before the army became riddled with Soviets (which were crucial in the taking of power), five million casualties had to be suffered in the war, including 1½ million deaths. Both were revolutions in a pretechnological pattern. Now we propose an unprecedented revolution for this country, sweeping beyond socialism: a revolution against centralism, against racism and sexism and ecocide, against industrial progress itself, *and against the totality of our heritage of ideas.* Maybe it does make sense to talk about twenty years, to act as if it were possible, but in my head it feels like a millenium, with only the first century completed.

MERRILL JACKSON

weaknesses and
problems
of the
1990 constitution

1. Is there sufficient guarantee that weaker units will not be exploited by stronger units?

2. Who handles the inter-commonwealth concerns?

3. How are responsibilities to the rest of the world met?

4. Cultural marginability is hardly dealt with at all.

5. The anti-death machine is certainly inadequate as a focus for political coalition.

6. Who controls the mode of production?

7. Why are 30 hours a week of productive work necessary from all citizens or from *any* citizens? With the galloping pace of automation even now in the 1960s and 1970s and the rapidly narrowing gap between automation and cybernation (not to mention the state of affairs following the end of the Vietnam War) it would seem that the burden of 30 hours of work in the 1990's would unnecessarily press down the autonomy, esteem and freedom of the population.

But there may be a confusion in language here. Does Waskow distinguish between "work" and "worthwhile activity" as James Boggs does in his writings in the early 1960s, where work means the process of production and worthwhile activity refers to such things as music, dancing, art, science, performing ritual, partaking in various religious activities, etc.? The question is: how does Waskow define work?

8. How are larger identity blocks created, encouraged, and strengthened given the tremendously dangerous uneven distribution of power, wealth, resources, skill, and influence in the world today? I take it the revolutionary period from 1959 to 1989 has rectified the grossest inbalances; but how does the 1990 Constitution deal with the fact that the problem is perennial?

9. Domestic imperialism, Waskow assumes, has been to a significant degree eliminated on the North American continent by 1989; and he provides appropriate and powerful obstacles to its reoccuring. But how is North American foreign imperialism dealt with? The internal American collapse Waskow refers to which occurs sometime between 1970 and 1989 of course greatly limits American potential to keep up its foreign imperialism. Still I would like to see the whole series of economic, political, military, and cultural problems dealt with more effectively in the 1990 Constitution. The most revelant section is the stipulation that the federal commonwealths have no army or police force, etc. But we have long ago learned to dominate by subtler means than policing or war. For example by fiscal policy, by making international agreements which bring all currencies in the world to be based on the American dollar, by trade agreements, by a series of seemingly innocent and agreeable alliances with foreign powers—a criss-cross of alliances—which can add up to an enormous ability to "put on the squeeze" when circumstances call for it.

10. Can the federation expand to include other areas and peoples?

11. Does it in its present form include Mexico and Central America? (I doubt it.)

12. It seems to me, power has to be redefined. I wonder how a number of Waskow's hopes will be achieved otherwise. And of course I mean a true change in the nature of our understanding of power, a shift in its base and dynamics.

13. How is "aid" to be supplied by the more affluent commonwealths to those in distress? And in what form is it to be supplied? Will it increase dependency as it so prevalently does

today? Will it deprive the "receivers" of experience (with their environment) as it so prevalently does today? Will it break up and destroy kin units as it so commonly does today?

14. How is the Constitution to be adopted and put into effect?

15. Who cleans up the ghetto wastelands that are now being created in the center of metropolises?

16. How is mass migration to be handled?

17. What happened to the enormous cities of the continent, by the way? I see how they can technically be taken into account by the Constitution, but one would expect them to be more of a concern than they apparently are to Waskow in the 1990 Constitution. The question has some additional importance since many other "future society designers" put cities at the center of their plans. Some even go so far as to say that the building blocks of the future in the USA will be the metropolitan area.

18. Will liberated zones be called for at some point in the 1959 to 1989 Revolution as some writers, Tom Hayden for example, argue?

ELEANOR BURNS
WOMEN'S COLLECTIVE

in a new society why do we have to have a boring constitution?

Trying to write this has been really good for us as a collective. We've found ourselves supporting each other's ideas and encouraging each other rather than criticizing what each of us says. We got really excited as our own ideas bounced off each other's ideas and the whole thing grew.

The "real part" for us was discovering what we thought about Waskow's constitution—or ANY constitution. Writing it out has just been an attempt to pass on to you some of what happened between us. It should not be seen as an attempt to present a critique within an analytical framework. A tape recording would give a truer representation of our reactions, but we've tried to reduce our several levels of feeling to linear form —mainly questions. We invite our sisters in other cities to join us in thinking about what kind of society we want, and to let us know their responses to our questions, their criticisms, and their own ideas.

The first thing that struck us was the whole tone of Waskow's constitution. We didn't like it. We found it technical, boring, inhuman and totally lacking in spirit, joy and celebration. In other words, it's no different from the one we've got. We felt threatened by it. It operates on fear and on a negative view of us. We felt it assumed that we would never be better people than we are now, and that we would never relate to each other any differently than we do now. And this made us angry—because we're trying to learn to care about each other and to work out our differences cooperatively rather than in the competitive way we've learned in this society.

The way the constitution would organize the society would be more divisive than unifying. It's based on a contemporary vision of what people seem to want. It assumes that the divisions our capitalist society has emphasized (black-white, male-female, gay-straight) are good and should be preserved rather than seeing such groups as female caucuses, as ways for oppressed people to survive within and to begin to fight the present system. In a new society, we would hope there would be men to whom we could relate in ways that we can't now as women. And that white people would no longer be oppressing everyone else, so we wouldn't need "ethno-collectives" based on blackness, femaleness, etc. (We don't want a completely homogeneous society to the point that no differences are permitted. We want a society where people are free to choose.)

Waskow doesn't make clear what kind of people his constitution governs. We need to know whether they're just like most of us are now—aggressive, competitive, sexist, racist—in short, products of present society—or whether people's ideas and personalities will have changed by the time of this constitution.

It's hard to believe any of this (revolution, new constitution, new consciousness) could happen when sitting in front of a fire in a Nashville living room, smack in the middle of the present. We can see that things are beginning to change (waitresses are wearing pantsuits at Elliston Place Soda Shop), but it's really hard to dream of a future when the present demands so much of our attention. Maybe it's harder for us because as women we've learned that it's up to us to provide for immediate needs—like what to have for supper. We have a hard time imagining a time when such things will be the concern of the whole society.

In a new society, we hope that everyone will be encouraged and helped to develop to her fullest potential—whatever that means. To us it means that everyone accepts responsibility for everyone else's growth as well as for her own. Even though Waskow says he's working toward a state of continuous revolutionary change, we see no way provided in his constitution for this to happen. The structure of the constitution itself, with its provision for traditional forms of amendment, would be as hard to change as the one we've got. There is no sense of the society moving and changing and needing new guidelines. It's hard to express fluidity and growth in a static document. Perhaps that means that so definitive a thing as a constitution should not exist at all. (Cuba began her revolution demanding enforcement of the constitution she already had, and as yet, hasn't written a new one. We, too, have better things to do with our time than sit around and dream up documents for an as-yet imaginary new society. But when people like Waskow—white, male, middle-class intellectuals—start drawing up such documents and asking for our comments and criticisms, they are going to HEAR our comments and criticisms.)

What the society really needs is not so much a constitution as goals and directions. As women, we have some specific interests in this area. There are basic principles that we would like to see a new society based on. First, let's put some warmth and some concern in this society. We would like to live in a society where everyone's basic needs are met, in order that we can move toward the elimination of sexism, racism, individualism and class privilege. We would like to live in a society where people really care about each other and are gentle, kind, supportive, patient, tolerant—in short, loving.

Whether Waskow intends the constitution to govern people like us or new people with changed consciousness, we have lots of questions about the constitution, either way. Questions not directed at Waskow, but as guides for thinking. We divided our questions into general categories in order to make them easier for us to deal with. Beyond our general problems with the constitution, we saw the rest of our questions in the categories of membership in collectives, work, enforcement, imperialism, and a bill of human rights.

membership in collectives

Why are we limited to only one of each kind of collective? What if we're women and black?

How do we get to know people unlike ourselves?

Why is ten the minimum number in order for a collective to be represented? Some of us live in very happy collectives of five. How does a person initially join a collective? Is she born into one? Do her parents decide for her?

Why is the age of decision set at an arbitrary thirteen? People develop at different rates and should be able to decide for themselves when they're ready. Where do we live before we join a living collective? With our parents? In groups by age? In community childcare centers? Who decides?

The constitution says living collectives don't have to live together, but should operate as a "family." Could "family" mean the nuclear model? What if everyone is getting along fine (in mixed collectives as opposed to ethno-collectives) and white men still somehow dominate the congress? Why is there no provision to insure the representation of those groups which have been historically left out?

How are members added to or subtracted from a collective? Do we place an ad in the paper? ("We need one Puerto Rican 5′3″ Marxist-Leninist grandmother immediately! We're about to lose our representation!")

How do we change collectives?

How do we change jobs? Do collectives trade members like baseball teams?

Are people free to form White Citizen's Councils?

work

What is the economic structure?

How has the society reached full employment? There aren't enough jobs for women, blacks, Indians, children and other "marginal people" now.

Who decides what counts as work?

Who decides what work needs to be done?

Does housework count? Does singing? Does studying?

Under the Constitution, work unions control work conditions and the congress controls prices and quotas. Shouldn't the workers decide how much they can do?

Why are there prices to be set?

What is money needed for? Aren't basic needs guaranteed?

Why is an arbitrary number of 30 hours set for a work week?

Why is citizenship tied to work? Do we believe people need an economic incentive to work?

What constitutes refusal to work? And who decides?

What's wrong with refusing to work now and then? Or ever?

Do we do the same work for all 30 hours?

Do some people have "creative" jobs and others boring jobs? Shouldn't poets cork bottles sometimes and corkers sing?

Will there be collectives of secretaries and collectives of executives? Will those jobs still exist? Who wants control of the same old job? Is work not done in new ways? We would make a revolution about fulfillment and creativity and becoming a new person—not to get control over the same old shit.

If we're children or old or sick in bed or don't want to work, why do we get only half what workers get and why are we denied citizenship? Can we assume that half is enough? Then why do workers get twice "enough"?

Who protects the environment?

Who decides where factories go, if we have factories? Workers or neighborhoods?

Do we get any vacation from our 30 hours of work?

How are our basic needs cared for when we're away from home?

Do we need penpal collectives wherever we plan to visit?

enforcement

Will crime not become a thing of the past? If it doesn't, isn't there something wrong with the society?

How soon after an accusation would a trial be held? Where would the accused person wait for trial? Is she held somewhere and by whom? With no provision for the length of a trial, can a person be held indefinitely while the jury deliberates?

If a decision has to be unanimous and the juries are chosen by, in effect, choosing up teams, what is to prevent one side from stalling and delaying a person indefinitely?

Are jurors free to ask questions and to participate in finding out what happened?

Why is redress of grievances on an economic basis?

Is there no provision for resocialization?

Why is economic incentive used to encourage abolition of police?

imperialism

What does the rest of the world look like?

Have we given up all our exploitative relationships with other countries?

If so, what has that done to our economy? If not, why not?

If we've really redistributed resources, do we have 10% of our GNP to give to other countries?

If anyone anywhere is living on $\frac{1}{5}$ what we live on, is this a socialist revolution?

Shouldn't the GNP be redefined to take into consideration damage to the environment in the process of production and also our technological knowledge?

Is our national goal still production and economic growth? This sounds like a superindustrial work-work-work society.

How industrialized are we? How technological?

If no public property can be owned outside the country, can private or collective property be owned elsewhere?

Why do we need any weapons at all?

Why are we still thinking nationalistically?
Does the UN function the same as now? Why?

bill of human rights

In addition to the rights mentioned in the constitution, we want
to insure:
Free nutritional, interesting, natural food—to be distributed
according to need and availability.
Free adequate, comfortable, attractive housing.
Free health care including preventive medicine. Free safe birth
control for men and women. Free abortions on demand. Free
sterilization on demand. No forced sterilization or abortions
ever.
Right to clean air, clean water and ecologically balanced environment for us and other animals and vegetation. No people
have the right to destroy or alter the environment.
Right of children to loving care and education which permits
them to develop to their fullest—whatever they think that means,
including the right to make their own decisions as soon as possible.
Right to free lifetime continuing education (whenever you can
fit it into your thirty hours and all the meetings all those collectives will require).
Right to free ecologically sound transportation—if there is such
a thing.

We don't expect all our questions to be answered in a constitution, but there must be some way provided for them to be answered.

In closing, we have one more question: Have you ever tried
to write one sentence with five other people? When we under-
took this project, we weren't sure it could be done, but now
we know it is possible and productive. Now, sisters, we'd like
to hear from you. If this is our revolution, and we're determined it will be, then we have to be heard.

iv
ideas to
play with

At this point you should be ready to create your own ideas. Write a poem, a science-fiction story, make an audio-tape, write an advertisement, draw a cartoon or a picture around the single sentences which follow.

PUBLICITY
IS THE ENEMY
OF CHANGE

WAR
is the continuation of
DIPLOMACY
by other means
(1905)

DIPLOMACY
is the continuation of
WAR
by other means
(1969)

abundance
is a free
gift.

We are always getting ready to live.

We have met the enemy and we are they.

insistence on
birth   at
      the wrong
            time
is the source
of all
evil

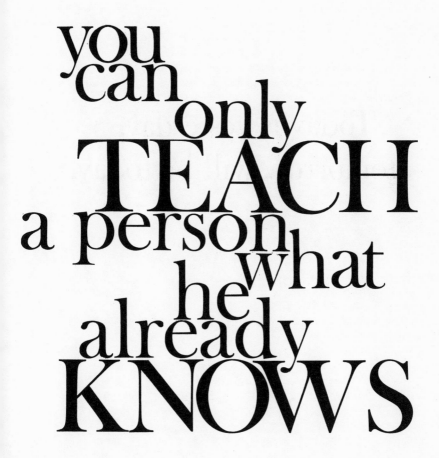

Today is yesterday,
tomorrow will be today.

(whose
today
will it be?)

*Communication
is a life-style.*

Decision-making is
a time-consuming and
often painful
process.

POWER *inevitably distorts information.*

"I have set before you life and death, blessing and curse; therefore choose life, so you and your children may live."

"The characteristics that lead a person to criminal behavior may be the same as those that bring success in business," a Rutgers University team of sociologists said in a report.

Telephones are faster than airplanes.

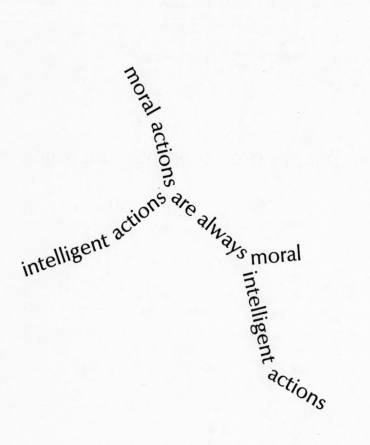

HIGHER
education
is
everybody's
rite

STYLE

is content.

v
looking
backward

The material which follows was written by a girl in 1994. She reacts negatively to the school and university systems as they existed in the sixties and seventies. Do you feel her criticisms are justified?

Can you imagine yourself into the 1990s? How would you expect to write about the church, or politics, or law, or any other social practice seen from a perspective of twenty years on?

ROBERT THEOBALD
J. M. SCOTT

letter from teg to friends of teg's age in quebec

Queries and
Comments

Dearpeers,

After breakfast, April 14, 1994. (Betty's birth-
day, Best Wishes.)

Conditions. Calcutta is very depressing! There
was population pressure in the part of China
where I was but there was no social breakdown. I didn't see Shanghai, of course, but it's
apparently in exactly the same situation as
Calcutta.

Effective, culturally-acceptable contra-
ceptives for Asia were developed so late that
the size of population cohorts only stabilized
around 1984. Cultures collapsed in many areas
and people were increasingly driven to the
urban areas as the least bad of the available
possibilities. Calcutta today is a conglomerate

of twenty-five million people: efforts to reconstruct functioning communities within Calcutta fail through sheer weight of numbers.

Emigration to Australia, Africa and North America is beginning to make a difference but only slowly. Even the most optimistic see the year 2000 as the date for the beginning of real progress; those who have been attempting community facilitation for decades seem to have given up all hope.

Since arriving in Calcutta I've begun to understand fully the extent of the tensions caused by restrictions on travel and emigration to abundance-regions. This wasn't obvious in B's community in China because the residents find their environment supportive. Ecofact availability is rising rapidly there and any remaining shortages are more than compensated by a highly synergetic community myth and the consequent wide availability of desired sociofacts.

Few, however, would want to stay here in Calcutta if they had *any* alternative, however unsatisfactory. Provision of ecofacts from the abundance-regions is satisfying minimal needs but the absence of any opportunity to improve personal or family conditions deepens the pervasive despair: sociofact production is, of course, rare in these conditions. Under these circumstances, the possibility of emigration is the sole remaining hope for those who have initiative.

Personal attitude. It's a long way from home. I'm learning but I'm tired. Now I *know* why people told me the year would be difficult.

Text. I must share what I've just learned with

Queries and Comments

Queries and Comments

somebody and it had better be somebody of my own age. During yesterday's facilitation session with C I learned about the "education system" of the sixties. If I tell anyone who was "at school" then how entropic it was, they may feel attacked.

After the session with C, one of the apprentices here and I were having a relaxed evening. We'd set the computer on random search among sixties films on the first three life-periods. We discovered a behavior-pattern which amazed us: during the sixties protest about educational conditions was expressed in a way which could not possibly have been expected to bring about change.

I'm sure I've been told about this reality in a dozen different ways but somehow I never really got inside the system before listening to C. During the sixties it appears that *only one form of "education"* was valued—"authoritarian teaching" and "rote assimilation of materials": inside schools for those up to eighteen and inside colleges for those up to 22 and in many cases beyond.

Schools and colleges contained large numbers of "students" who were taught in classes of up to 40 and even of 1,000 and beyond in colleges. This size of class was considered practical because people were expected to rote-memorize what previous scholars had taught and then reinform the teacher about existing theories. Apparently no one expected that students would retain the knowledge beyond the "exam" period designed to test people for recent-information-recall.

I can't make sense of this pattern. If the object had been to train people in a specific skill, classes of this size would have been a possible technique, given the fact that auto-training with computers and robots did not exist at that time. But then those involved would have continued practicing the same skill until it became automatic and their constant need for the skill would have ensured that it was retained. Tests to discover information-recall would have been unnecessary. On the other hand, if the object was education, repeatedly forcing existing concepts on the student would prevent him from internally rearranging the information into new patterns and perceiving new insights which is the function of any effective educational process.

In the sixties the confusion about appropriate techniques of learning was not apparently due to any lack of concern. In addition, the films we saw made it clear that many of those involved in education as teachers and learners saw how dysfunctional the entire educational system was. But those who protested didn't seem to have any idea of the way in which change is achieved. They held "rallies" and "sit-ins" protesting the actual detailed functioning of the educational system without recognizing that changes in part of a system are not possible without changing the total system and that it is not possible to change total systems unless those involved comprehend a changed perception of the nature of the universe.

The increasing disruption and violence which accompanied student "rallies" and "sit-ins" during the late sixties set in motion two forces which led to the collapse of many government and private universities. First, private donors and government agencies cut back on

Queries and Comments

Queries and Comments

the funds they applied. Second, an increasing number of young people no longer saw college as essential to their life-development and sought alternative patterns of learning.

By the mid-seventies, colleges and universities were attempting to develop programs which would attract both new donors and students. It was unfortunate that many of the colleges which had the clearest comprehension of the new approach to learning, and which were therefore able to attract students, did not have the merchandising skills to attract funds. By the end of the seventies, a large proportion of colleges and universities had disbanded.

In a few cases the buildings of a college or university were purchased by groups of individuals who created new forms of communities in which learning was an integral part of the community style: the sharp age-breaks between those learning and those working began to disappear. These new institutions, often organized consentives, and those colleges which did survive moved in one of two directions: they became either local or transnational nodes in the de-Chardinian noosphere. As such they acted as transmission points for information.

The local nodes began to develop ways in which they could serve their immediate community. These local organizations used, among other innovations, patterns of learning interaction developed by the Street Universities and also brought in by individuals from India and other nations with traditions of personal facilitation. They were able to demonstrate how real education could take place within the community rather than cut off from it in schools and colleges.

In the second case, when institutions and colleges moved toward being transnational nodes in the noosphere, they concentrated increasingly in a single problem/possibility (p/p) area. It was made clear to those who wished to join these emerging institutions that their purpose was to elucidate a specific p/p area and that nobody should seek admission if they were not interested in this area of knowledge. As this process of moving toward being a transnational node continued, it was understood that information structured around p/p areas required new forms of presentation. It became necessary to replace those methods which had been used for deduction and transfer of data within "disciplines," such as rote learning texts and personal interpretation of facts written by an "authority" for his followers. . . .

I see that I've got, as usual, way beyond what I intended to write. But I'd never understood till I talked to C that the learning pattern we take for granted was so recent in origin. Nor had I realized the irony of the present degenerated state of Indian education in view of the fact that the traditional Indian attitude toward education contributed so much to the beginnings of present learning patterns in the abundance-regions.

C is working on the reorganization of the Indian learning process along traditional lines. Given the evolution of education in the abundance-regions she is able to use, for this purpose, the present abundance-region techniques. The communicators and other equipment are plentifully available but there are very few here who understand how to facilitate. C has established a program for educa-

Queries and Comments

**Queries and
Comments**

tional facilitators and she suggested that I look at the outline of the introductory film to see the elementary level at which she has had to begin.

I wish I were going to see you before November,

Forward,
Teg

vi
a timetable
for
your future

You may now feel able to summarize the events you expect to take place between now and the year 2000, or 1990, or 1980. To help you do this we include a couple of timetables —one specially written for this volume and another representing the key events in Teg's 1994. As you will see by looking at them, they represent not only different events but the type of events which are included are different in kind.

What events do you think will happen in the future? What type of events do you think we shall see as important?

BILLY ROJAS

headlines
of the near
future

What follows is a scenario for the seventies, events that will probably happen—in some cases undoubtedly happen—although not necessarily in the order presented. Contingencies can be planned for but their exact timing can only be guessed at. Various sources were drawn upon in creating the scenario including the work of Ray Bradbury, Herman Kahn, Olaf Helmer, and Nigel Calder. An inventory of the ages of world leaders and crucial world problems was also made. Recent history also served as a guide. The result is a plausible history of the global future between now and 1980, one scenario out of scores of possibilities. Something of the texture of the world we are moving into is suggested by these forthcoming frontpage stories, nonetheless, and in this lies the value of looking forward into our decade.

1972

February: Chiang Kai-shek dead in Taiwan; new regime is created that seeks to "modernize" Formosa. Ten year plan to replace most ideographs with Roman letters is announced. Major effort is made to organize "overseas" Chinese—the millions in southeast Asia, the tens of thousands in America—into a series of formalized trade associations.

March:	Safe cigarettes invented: Lorillard stock advances 20 points in one day.
July:	Chicago firm begins marketing robot "house-keepers": mechanical mice to vacuum rugs and clean floors, automated kitchens that prepare hot meals according to consumer specifications, etc.
November:	Team of Muskie and Adlai Stevenson III defeats Republicans for Presidency.

1973

January:	J. Edgar Hoover resigns post as head of FBI.
June:	Astronauts find evidence of sub-cellular life on the moon—two billion years ago.
July:	Jackie divorces Ari; she plans to marry David Brinkley.
September:	New Jersey becomes first state to legalize marijuana.
November:	Stones break up. New music stirs U.S.; Cheyenne native rock-and-tom-tom group tops charts.
December:	Peace settlement reached in Middle East; version of Allon plan adopted on a "phase-out" basis; Israel-Jordan to become joint secular state.

1974

March:	Mao-Tse-tung suffers heart attack in China. Succeeded by Chou En-Lai. Red Guard "party" forms to challenge authority of the government, cultural revolution becomes an underground movement.
April:	Hovercraft "grass highway" bonds approved by Congress: Boston-Richmond route.
May:	Haile Selassie dies in Washington hospital. His death removes last obstacle to United States of East Africa, a new nation made up of the former states of Ethiopia, Kenya, Uganda, Rwanda.
July:	South Sudan secedes from Arab Federation; civil

war erupts as rebels receive encouragement and aid from Addis Ababa.

October: Houston doctor discloses discovery of selective memory-erasing drug.

November: Reagan defeated by 350,000 votes.

1975

February: Rescue in space; Russians save Americans endangered on orbiting space platform.

April: U. of Oklahoma student disorders reach insurrection proportions; social science building destroyed, 4 police, 18 students killed.

June: "Electro-pop," completely synthetic beverage, starts a new food craze; Electro-snax, Electro-suppers are marketed.

August: First space hospital (4 "beds") established by U.S.S.R.

September: Socialists return to power in Britain.

1976

May: Cabinet restructure in U.S., new secretaries of Education, Environment.

October: Sex-selection industry booms. Chemical treatments enable prospective parents to predetermine sex of offspring.

November: Allard Lowenstein defeats Buckley in N.Y. Senate contest.

1977

January: Temporary lunar base set up by U.S.—6 men, 2 months.

June: Famine conditions worsen in India, Java. Communist revolution develops.

October: Sexual intercourse allowed in Yale sex ed. classes. Harvard follows suit.

November: Brazilian church secedes from Rome; "second reformation" as Dutch, some Americans, also walk out.

December: Tito dies in Yugoslavia, unsuccessful leftist coup to oust hand-picked successor.

1978

March: Religious revival reported in Africa: Nigeria, Dahomey, Ivory Coast, Guinea become Baha'i countries.

July: Japanese firm announces opening of sea-chains, series of floating cities to accommodate 10,000 people each; located in Polynesia.

August: Police force retired in Seattle; replaced by paid, plain clothes community people.

1979

February: First "time traveller." Start of ten-year hibernation for Minneapolis man.

September: Radio signals from vicinity of 41 Y Cygni indicate intelligent life in the universe.

October: Laser "arrays" used by commercial ships to navigate Antarctic waters; business firms start pilot plants on southernmost continent.

December: U.S. court system reformed. New features include "maximum wait law"—no more than 30 days between arrest and trial—and "obsolete statute law" —any law on the books is retired after 20 years unless specifically renewed by legislative act.

ROBERT THEOBALD
J. M. SCOTT

chronology of events: 1970s-1990s

Early seventies	Planning party formed, created from among the most aware members of Democratic and Republican parties.
Throughout seventies	Continuing decline in the efficiency of industrial-era infrastructure.
Throughout seventies	Many colleges and universities collapse.
Throughout seventies	Decline of cities, revivification of smaller decentralized communities.
Throughout seventies	Ecological thinking replaces economic thinking.
1975	Statement on desirability of world citizenship being coupled with national citizenship by 500 liberal-humanists.
1976	Planning party wins elections.
Mid-seventies	Neo-Luddite revolt leading to high levels of inefficiency in operation of technological infrastructure.

Mid-seventies	Consumer revolt against misleading advertising, planned obsolescence.
Mid-seventies	Critically high levels of tension between abundance-regions and scarcity-regions.
Late seventies	Significant attempts to create world parliament.
1979	Scientists Synergy. Those involved refuse to circulate deliberately distorted or falsified information with two major effects: a) overwhelming victory of Planning party in 1980 followed by development of fundamentally different style of politics. b) increased cooperation and transfer of ecofacts between abundance-regions and scarcity-regions.
Early eighties	Terran Communication Center developed in Hawaii.
Early eighties	Problem/Possibility Institutes come into existence.
1984	Creation of Orwell Foundation celebrating the fact that situation in this year was not as bad as might have been expected.
Mid-eighties	Distribution of ecofacts becomes free in America, spreads to all abundance areas. Information movement replaces money movement.
Mid-eighties	INTER, OUTER and SITUATIONAL communication styles understood.
Mid-eighties	Creation of significantly new ways of structuring knowledge.
Early nineties	Growing crisis due to declining sense of

responsibility in decentralized communities: decrease in pace of economic growth in scarcity regions after earlier significant increase, distortions in information flows.

basic tools for your future imagining

If you really want to do so you can now begin to imagine, with others, your future world. You can have decided by now whether the future is basically random, basically determined or some complex meshing of the two. You are now at a point where you can decide what type of world you would like to live in—and the routes you would like to use to get there.

But imagining a functioning world is still not easy. The utopian writers of the past have tended to imagine worlds in which human beings were simple rather than complex and where the world remained the same over extended periods of time. There are few writers who have built into their books a sense of change. A few of the volumes you might want to look at to obtain the time dimension are:

Stranger in a Strange Land. *Robert Heinlein. This volume explores new patterns of human relationships several centuries in the future.*

Dragonflight *and* Dragonquest. *Anne McCaffrey. Two volumes which explore, in the guise of an adventure novel, the situation man has reached today.*

Teg's 1994. *Robert Theobald and J. M. Scott. Perhaps the most conscious attempt to describe a route from the present breakdown to a more human system, a system which inevitably contains some flaws.*

These volumes will give you an idea about the way in which books dealing with the future can be structured. You may know others from your previous reading in such fields as science fiction. This part of the book is designed to help you gain more ideas about the aspects of society and the future you will need to cover if your work is to be complete.

The paper by A. H. Maslow sets out some of the aspects which determine the shape of a society. A filing system created for my wife's work and my own is included as a useful method of classifying data.

Richard Cellarius and John Platt have developed a listing of areas that are critical to the future of man. You will not want to deal with all the aspects that they mention but you will certainly want to be sure that you have not unintentionally excluded any of them. Finally, included is a futurist bibliography compiled by Dennis Livingston for one of his classes.

This material is not included here to convince you that imagining the future is impossibly complex. These resources are placed here for the times when you actually need them: you should not try to absorb them all at once. You can begin to imagine your own future now: for example, many college classes now include the creation of scenarios for the future as part of their studies.

Even if your efforts do not satisfy you fully, you will necessarily be far more aware of the patterns of assumptions out of which you operate—some of your unconscious ideas will become known to you. Once you are aware of the beliefs out of which you make your decisions, you will be better able to decide whether they are actually suitable for the world in which we presently live.

One of my major reasons for writing this book is that I

believe that each of us has greater capabilities than he presently realizes. While no one of us is presently capable of creating a fully satisfactory scenario, I am certain that if we cooperate we can begin to imagine together the world we want.

The Whole Earth Catalogue had as its motto: "We are as Gods and we'd better get good at it." Man is, for better or worse, in control of the evolution of this planet. The profession of world problem solver has been created—it is one of the few areas in which there are plenty of openings. You are invited to get busy!

A. H. MASLOW

some fundamental questions that face the normative social psychologist

This paper is based on notes given out at the beginning of the Spring 1967 semester-long seminar for seniors and graduate students. In addition to furnishing a common background of assumptions, rules and problems for the assigned reading and papers, I hoped also that these notes would help keep the group in the realm of empirical and scientific endeavor.

The catalog description of the proposed seminar read: *"Utopian Social Psychology:* Seminar for graduate students in Psychology, Sociology, Philosophy or any of the social sciences. Discussion of selected Utopian and Eupsychian writings. The seminar will concern itself with the empirical and realistic questions: How good a society does human nature permit? How good a human nature does society permit? What is possible and feasible? What is not?"

The following is the text of the notes.

Note that the description of the seminar implies practical-

From *Journal of Humanistic Psychology,* vol. 8 (Fall 1968). Reprinted courtesy of the Journal of Humanistic Psychology © 1968 and Bertha Maslow.

ity, actual attainability, rather than dreams, fantasies, or wish fulfillments. In order to stress this point, not only must your paper describe your good society, but it must also have some specification about the methods of achieving it, i.e., politics. Next year the title of the course will be changed to "Normative Social Psychology." This is to stress that the empirical attitude will prevail in this class. This means that we will talk in terms of degree, of percentages, of the reliability of evidence, of missing information that needs to be obtained, of needed investigations and researches, of the possible. We will not waste our time on dichotomizing, on black or white, either/or, on the perfect, on the unattainable, or on the inevitable. (There is no inevitable.) It will be assumed that reform is possible, as are also progress and improvement. But *inevitable* progress toward the attainment, in some future moment, of a perfect ideal, is not likely, and we will not bother talking about it. (Deterioration or catastrophe are also possible.) In general, merely being against something will not be sufficient. Better alternatives should be presented at the same time. We will assume a holistic approach to the problem of reforming or revolutionizing or improving an individual man or the whole society. Furthermore, we will assume that it is not necessary to change one first before the other can be changed, i.e., the man or the society. We will assume that they can both be worked at simultaneously.

Make the general assumption that no normative social thinking is possible until we have some idea of *the individual goal,* i.e., the kind of person to aim to be and by which to judge the adequacy of any society. I proceed on the assumption that the good society, and therefore the immediate goal of any society which is trying to improve itself, is the self-actualization of all individuals, or some norm or goal approximating this. (Transcendence of self—living at the level of Being—is assumed to be most possible for the person with a strong and free identity, i.e., for the self-actualizing person. This will necessarily involve consideration of societal arrangements, education, etc., that make transcendence more possible.) The question here is: Do we have a trustworthy, reliable conception of the healthy or desirable or transcending or ideal person? Also this normative idea is itself moot and debatable. Is it possible to improve a society without having some idea of what one considers to be an improved human being?

We must also have some notion, I assume, of the *autonomous social requirements* (which are independent of the intrapsychic or of individual psychological health or maturity). I assume that the idea of personal improvement, one person by one person, is not a practicable solution of the problem of improving the society. Even the best individuals placed under poor social and institutional circumstances behave badly. One can set up social institutions which will guarantee that individuals will be at each other's throats; or one can set up social institutions which will encourage individuals to be synergic with each other. That is, one can set up social conditions so that one person's advantage would be to another person's advantage rather than the other person's disadvantage. This is a basic assumption and is debatable, and ought to be demonstrable. (I propose for discussion my article, Synergy in the Society and in the Individual, 1964, also the notes on synergy, pages 88–107, in my *Eupsychian Management.*)

1. *Is the Norm to be universal (for the whole Human species), or national (with political and military sovereignty), or subcultural (with a smaller group within a nation or state), or familial and individual?* I assume that universal peace is not possible so long as there are separate and sovereign nations. Because of the kind of wars which are possible today (and which I think are unavoidable so long as we have national sovereignty) any normative social philosopher must assume in the long run limited sovereignty of nations, e.g., like that proposed by the United World Federalists, etc. I assume that the normative social thinker will be automatically working toward such a goal at all times. But once this is assumed, then the questions come up of improving the nation-states as they now exist, of local subdivisions like the states within the U.S., or subcultural groupings in the U.S., like the Jews or the Chinese, or, finally, the question of making an oasis out of the individual family. This does not exclude even the question of how a single person can make his own life and his own environment more Eupsychian.

I assume that all of these are simultaneously possible; they do not in theory or in practice mutually exclude each other. (I suggest as a basis for discussion The theory of social improvement; The theory of the slow revolution, in my *Eupsychian Management,* pages 247–260.)

2. *Selected or unselected societies.* For my conception of Eupsychia see page 350 in *Motivation and Personality* (Maslow 1954). Also Eupsychia, The Good Society, *Journal of Humanistic Psychology* (Maslow 1961). Also scattered sections in my *Eupsychian Management.* My definition of Eupsychia is clearly a selected subculture, i.e., it is made up only of psychologically healthy or mature or self-actualizing people and their families. Through the history of Utopias, this question has sometimes been faced and sometimes not. I assume it *always* has to be consciously decided upon. In your papers you must specify whether you are speaking about the whole human species, unselected, or about a selected-out smaller group, with specified entrance requirements. Also you must address yourself to the question of exiling or assimilating disruptive individuals if you do have a selected Utopian group. Must individuals be kept in the society once they have been selected or born into it? Or do you think you need provisions for exile or imprisonment, etc.? For criminals, evil doers, etc.? (I assume on the basis of your knowledge of psychopathology and psychotherapy, and of social pathology, and of the history of Utopian attempts, that any unselective group may be destroyed by sick or immature individuals. But since our techniques of selection are still very poor, my opinion is that any group trying to be Utopian or Eupsychian must also be able to expel dystopian individuals who slip by the selection techniques.)

3. *Pluralism. The acceptance and use of individual differences in constitution and in character.* Many Utopias proceeded as if all human beings were interchangeable and were equal to each other. We must accept the fact that there are very wide ranges of variation in intelligence, character, constitution, etc. Permission for individuality or for idiosyncrasy or individual freedom must specify the range of individual differences to be taken into consideration. In the fantasy Utopias there have been

no feeble-minded people, no insane, no seniles, etc. Furthermore, there is frequently built in, in a covert fashion, some norm for the desirable human person which seems to me far too narrow in view of our actual knowledge of range of variations in human beings. How fit all kinds of people into *one* set of rules or laws? Do you want to allow for a wide pluralism, e.g., of styles and fashions in clothes, shoes, etc.? In the U.S. we now permit a very wide, though not complete, range of choice among foods, but a very narrow range of choice among fashions in clothes. Fourier, for instance, founded his whole Utopian scheme on the full acceptance and use of a very wide range of constitutional differences. Plato on the other hand had only three kinds of human beings. How many kinds do you want? Can there be a society without deviants? Does the concept of self-actualization make this question obsolete? If you accept the widest range of individual differences and the pluralism of characters and talents, then this is a society that in effect accepts much (or all) of human nature. Does self-actualization mean in effect the acceptance of idiosyncrasy or of deviants? To what extent?

4. *Pro-industrial or anti-industrial? Pro-science or anti-science? Pro-intellectual or anti-intellectual?* Many Utopias have been Thoreauvian, rural, essentially agricultural (e.g., Borsodi's School of Living). Many of them have been a move away from and against the cities, machines, the money economy, division of labor, etc. Do you agree? How possible is decentralized, ruralized industry? How possible Taostic harmony with the surroundings? Garden cities? Garden factories? i.e., with housing always attached so no commuting? Must modern technology necessarily enslave human beings? There certainly are small groups of people in various places in the world who are moving back to agriculture, and certainly this is feasible for small groups. Is it feasible for the whole human species? But also some intentional communities were and are built around manufacturing rather than agriculture or handicrafts.

There is sometimes seen in anti-technology, anti-city philosophies a sort of covert anti-intellectualism, anti-science, anti-abstract thought. These are seen by some people as desacralizing, divorced from basic concrete reality, bloodless, opposed to beauty and emotion, unnatural, etc. (Maslow 1966; Polanyi 1958).

5. *Centralized-central, planning-socialistic or decentralized-anarchic societies.* How much planning is possible? Must it be centralized? Must it be coercive? Most intellectuals know little or nothing about philosophical anarchism. (I recommend *Manas.*) One basic aspect of the *Manas* philosophy is a philosophical anarchism. It stresses decentralization rather than centralization, local autonomy, personal responsibility, a mistrust of large organizations of any kind or of large accumulations of power of any kind. It mistrusts force as a social technique. It is ecological and Taoistic in its relationship to nature and to reality, etc., How much hierarchy is necessary within a community, e.g., a kibbutz or a Fromm-type factory, or a partnership-owned farm or factory, etc.? Is command necessary? Power over other people? Power to enforce majority will? Power to punish? The scientific community can be taken as an example of a leaderless Eupsychian "subculture," decentralized, voluntary yet coordinated, productive, and with a powerful and effective code of ethics (which works). With this may be contrasted the Synanon subculture (highly organized, hierarchically structured).

6. *The question of evil behavior.* In many Utopias this question is simply missing. It is either wished away or overlooked. There are no jails, nobody is punished. Nobody hurts anybody else. There is no crime, etc. I accept as a basic assumption that the problem of bad behavior, of psychopathological behavior, of evil behavior, of violence, jealousy, greed, exploitation, laziness, sinfulness, malice, etc., must be consciously confronted and managed. ("The short and sure path to despair and surrender is this, to believe that there is somewhere a scheme of things that will eliminate conflict, struggle, stupidity, cupidity, personal jealousy"—David Lilienthal.) The question of evil must be discussed both intrapersonally and in terms of the societal arrangements, i.e., psychologically *and* sociologically (which means also historically).

7. *The dangers of unrealistic perfectionism.* I assume that perfectionism, i.e., thinking that ideal or perfect solutions may be demanded, is a danger. The history of Utopias shows many

such unrealistic, unattainable, nonhuman fantasies (e.g., let us all love each other. Let us all share equally. All people must be treated as equals in all ways. Nobody must have any power over anybody else. Application of force is always evil. "There are no bad people; there are only unloved people"). A common sequence here is perfectionism or unrealistic expectations *leading to* inevitable failure *leading to* disillusionment, *leading to* apathy, discouragement, or active hostility to all ideals and all normative hopes and efforts. That is, perfectionism very often (always?) tends ultimately to lead to active hostility against normative hopes. Improvability has often been thought impossible when perfectibility turned out to be impossible.

8. *How to handle aggression, hostility, fighting, conflict?* Can these be abolished? Is aggression or hostility in some sense instinctive? Which social institutions foster conflict? Which minimize it? Granted that wars are unavoidable in a human species divided up into sovereign nations, could force be conceivably unneeded in a united world? Would such a world government need a police force or an army? (As a basis for discussion, I suggest Chapter 10, Is Destructiveness Instinctoid? in my *Motivation and Personality,* and my paper, Some Parallels between the Dominance and Sexual Behavior in Monkeys and the Fantasies of Patients in Psychotherapy, Maslow, Rand & Newman 1960). My general conclusions are: that aggression, hostility, strife, conflict, cruelty, sadism certainly all exist commonly and perhaps universally on the psychoanalytic couch, i.e., in fantasy, in dream, etc. I assume that aggressive behavior can be found in everyone as an actuality or a possibility. Where I see no aggressiveness at all, I suspect repression or suppression or self-control. I assume that the *quality* of aggression changes very markedly as one moves from psychological immaturity or neurosis up toward self-actualization or maturity in that sadistic or cruel or mean behavior is a quality of aggression found in undeveloped or neurotic or immature people, but that as one moves toward personal maturity and freedom, the quality of this aggression changes into reactions or righteous indignation and into self-affirmation, resistance to exploitation and domination, passion for justice, etc. I also assume that successful psycho-

therapy changes the *quality* of aggression in this second direction, i.e., changing it from cruelty into healthy self-affirmation. I assume also that verbal airing of aggression makes actual aggressive behavior less likely. I assume that social institutions can be set up in such a way as to make aggression of any quality more likely or less likely. I assume that some outlet for violence is more necessary for young males than for young females. Are there techniques for teaching young people how to handle and express their aggressions wisely, in a satisfying fashion, and yet not in a fashion harmful to others?

9. *How simple should life be?* What are the desirable limits to the complexity of life?

10. *How much privacy for the individual person, the child, the family must a society allow?* How much togetherness, community activity, fellowship, sociability, community life? How much privacy, "let-be," nonintrusiveness?

11. *How tolerant can a society be? Can everything be forgiven? What cannot be tolerated? What must be punished?* How tolerant can a society be of stupidity, falsehood, cruelty, psychopathy, criminality, etc.? How much protection must be built into the societal arrangements for, e.g., aments, seniles, the ignorant, crippled, etc.? This question is also important because it raises the question of overprotection, and of hampering the ones who don't need protection, which may lead to hampering the freedom of thought, discussion, experimentation, idiosyncrasy, etc. It also raises the question of the dangers of the germ-free atmosphere, of the tendency in Utopian writers to somehow remove all danger as well as all evil.

12. *How wide can the range of public tastes be that must be accepted? How much tolerance for what you disapprove of? How much tolerance for degrading, value-destroying, "low tastes." How about drug addiction, alcohol, LSD, cigarettes? How about the tastes on TV, movies, newspapers?* It is claimed that this is what the public wants, and probably this is not too far off the statistical truth. How much will you interfere with what the statistical public wants? Do you plan equal votes for superiors, for geniuses, for the talented, the creative, the capable on the one hand, and feebleminded on the other hand? What

would you do with the British Broadcasting Corporation? Should it always teach? How much should it reflect the Neilsen ratings? Ought there to be three channels for different kinds of people, five channels? Do the makers of movies, TV shows, etc., have any responsibility for educating and improving public taste? Whose business is this? Or is it nobody's business? What should be done, for instance, about homosexuals, pederasts, exhibitionists, sadists, and masochists? Should homosexuals be allowed to solicit children? Supposing a pair of homosexuals carry on their sexual life in complete privacy—should the society interfere? If a sadist and a masochist please each other privately, is this public business? Should they be allowed to advertise publicly for each other? Should transvestites be allowed public exposure? Should exhibitionists be punished or limited or confined?

13. *The problem of the leader (and the follower), the capable, the excellent, the strong, the boss, the entrepreneur.* Is it possible wholly to admire and love our (factual) superiors? Is it possible to be post-ambivalent? How protect them from envy, *ressentiment,* "the evil eye"? If all newborn infants were given complete equality of opportunity, all sorts of individual differences in capacity, talent, intelligence, strength, etc., would appear during the life span. What to do about these? Should greater rewards, greater pay, more privileges be given to the more talented, the most useful, the ones who produce more? Where would the "gray eminence" idea work, i.e., paying the powerful people *less* (in money) than other people, while perhaps paying them off in non-monetary terms, i.e., in terms of higher need and meta-need gratifications, e.g., being permitted freedom, autonomy, self-actualization. How possible is the vow of poverty (or at least simplicity) for leaders, bosses, etc.? How much freedom should be given to the entrepreneur, to the person with the high need for achievement, to the organizer, to the initiator, to the person who enjoys running things, being boss, wielding power? How get voluntary self-subordination? Who will collect the garbage? How will the strong and the weak relate to each other? The more capable and the less capable? How achieve love, respect and gratitude for authority (policeman, judge, lawmaker, father, captain)?

14. *Is permanent contentment possible? Is immediate contentment possible?* As a basis for discussion I suggest my section on Low Grumbles, High Grumbles and Meta-grumbles in my *Eupsychian Management,* pages 236–246. Also various writings of Colin Wilson on what he calls the "St. Neot margin." Also, *Work and the Nature of Man* (Herzberg 1966). It can be assumed that contentment is for practically all people a transient state, no matter what the social conditions may be, and that it is useless to seek for permanent contentment. Compare with concepts of Heaven, Nirvana, the benefits expected from great wealth, from leisure, retirement, etc. Parallel to this the finding that solving "lower" problems brings not so much contentment as more but "higher" problems, and "higher" grumbles.

15. *How shall males and females adapt to each other, enjoy each other, respect each other?* Most Utopias have been written by males. Would females have different conceptions of a good society? Most Utopians also have been either obviously patriarchal or covertly so. In any case throughout most of history females were regarded as inferior to males in intellect, in executive capacity, in creativeness, etc. Now that females, at least in the advanced countries, have been emancipated and self-actualization is possible for them also, how will this change the relationships between the sexes? What kind of change is necessary in the male in order to accommodate to this new female? Is it possible to transcend the simple dominance-subordination hierarchy? What would a Eupsychian marriage be like, i.e., between the self-actualizing male and the self-actualizing female? What kinds of functions, duties, what kinds of work would the females do in Eupsychia? How would the sex life change? How would femininity and masculinity be defined?

16. *The question of institutionalized religions, personal religions, the "spiritual life," the life of values, the meta-motivated life.* All known cultures have a religion of one sort or another, and presumably always have had. For the first time non-religion or humanism or non-institutionalized personal religion is possible. What kind of religious or spiritual or value-life would exist in Eupsychia, or in a small Eupsychian community? If group religions, religious institutions, the historical religions continued, how would they be changed? How would they differ

from what they were in the past? How shall children be reared and educated toward self-actualization and beyond to the value-life (spiritual, religious, etc.)? Toward being good members of a Eupsychia? Can we learn from other cultures, from the ethnological literature, from the high synergy cultures (Maslow 1967).

17. *The question of intimacy groups, of families, brotherhoods, fraternities, fellowships.* There seems to be an instinctoid need for belongingness, for roots, for a face-to-face group in which affection and intimacy are given freely. It is pretty clear that these would have to be smallish groups, certainly not over 50 or 100. In any case it is unlikely that intimacy and affection is possible between millions of people, and therefore any society must organize itself from below upward starting with intimacy groups of some sort. In our society it is the blood family, at least in the cities. There are religious fellowships, sororities, fraternities. The T-groups and encounter groups practice candor, feedback, honesty with each other, efforts toward friendship, expressiveness, and intimacy. Is it possible to institutionalize something of this sort? An industrial society tends to be highly mobile, i.e., people tend to move around a lot. Must this cut the roots and the ties to other people? Also—must these groups be cross-generational? Or can they be peer groups? It looks as if children and adolescents are not capable of complete self-rule (unless perhaps if specifically brought up toward this end). Is it possible to have some nonadult peer groups living by their own values, that is, without fathers, mothers, without elders?

Problem: is intimacy possible without sex?

18. *The effective helper: the hurtful helper. Effective non-helping (Taoistic non-interference). The Bodhisattva.* Assuming that in any society the stronger would want to help the weaker, or in any case, would have to, what is the best way to help others (who are weaker, poorer, less capable, less intelligent)? What is the best way to help them become stronger? How much of their autonomy and responsibility for themselves is it wise to take upon yourself if you are the stronger or older person? How can you help other people if they are poor and you are rich?

How can a rich nation help poor nations? For discussion purposes, I will define arbitrarily the Bodhisattva as a person, a) who would like to help others, b) who agrees he will be a better helper as he himself becomes more mature, healthy, more fully human, c) who knows when to be Taoistic and noninterfering, i.e., non-helping, d) who *offers* his help or makes it available to be chosen or not chosen as the other person wishes, and, e) who assumes that a good way to self-growth is via helping others. This is to say that if one wishes to help other people, then a very desirable way to do this is to become a better person oneself. Problem: How many non-helping persons can a society assimilate, i.e., people looking for their own personal salvation, hermits, pious beggars, people who meditate alone in a cave, people who remove themselves from society and go into privacy, etc.?

19. *Institutionalizing sex and love.* My guess is that the advanced societies are now moving toward beginning the sex life approximately at the age of puberty without marriage or without other ties. There are "primitive" societies that do something of the sort, i.e., pretty complete premarital promiscuity plus a post-marital monogamy or near-monogamy. In these societies the marriage partner is chosen hardly at all for sexual reasons since sex is freely available, but rather as a matter of personal taste and also as a partner in the culture, e.g., for having children, for economic division of labor, etc. Is this a reasonable guess? What does it imply? There has already appeared a tremendous range of variation in sexual drive or sexual need, especially in women (in our culture). It is unwise to assume that everybody is equally strongly sexed. How is it possible to accept in a good society a wide range of difference in sexual appetite?

Sexuality, love, and family folkways are now in very rapid transition in many parts of the world, including many Utopian communities, e.g., promiscuity groups, group marriage, "swap-clubs," non-legal marriages, etc. (See for instance the novels of Robert Rimmer.) Many kinds of arrangements are being suggested and actually tried out. The data from these "experiments" are not yet available, but will be one day and will then have to be considered.

20. *The problem of choosing the best leaders.* In our society there are many groups, e.g., adolescents, that seem often to prefer bad leaders to good ones. That is, they choose people who will lead them to destruction and to defeat—losers rather than winners—paranoid characters, psychopathic personalities, blusterers. Any good society that hopes to grow must be able to choose as leaders those individuals who are best suited for the job in fact, in actual talents and capacity. How can such good choices be enhanced? What kinds of political structure make it more possible for, e.g., a paranoid person to have great power? What kinds of political structures make this less possible or impossible?

21. *What are the best social conditions for bringing human nature to full humanness?* This is a normative way of phrasing the study of personality-culture. The new literature of social psychiatry is pertinent here, and also the new literature of the mental hygiene and the social hygiene movement, the various forms of group therapy that are now being experimented with, the Eupsychian educational communities like Esalen Institute. This is the point at which to bring up the question of how to make the classroom more Eupsychian—the schools, universities and education in general—and then on to each of the other social institutions. Eupsychian management (or theory-Y management) is an example of this kind of normative social psychology. In it society and each of the institutions within the society are defined as "good" to the extent that they help people toward fuller humanness, and they are defined as bad or psychopathogenic to the extent that they diminish humanness. At this point as well as at other points the questions of social pathology and of individual pathology must undoubtedly be discussed.

22. *Can a health-fostering group itself be a path toward self-actualization?* (See the materials on the Eupsychian factory, on Synanon, the international community, etc.) Some people are convinced that the interests of the individual *must* be opposed to the interests of a group, an institution, an organization, a society—civilization itself. The history of religions show frequently a split between the individual mystics whose private

illuminations set them *against* the church. Can a church foster individual development? Can the schools? Factories?

23. *How is "idealism" related to practicality, "materialism," realism?* I assume that lower basic needs are prepotent to higher needs, which in turn are prepotent to meta-needs (intrinsic values). This means that materialism is prepotent to "idealism" but also that they both exist and are psychological realities which must be taken into account in any Eupsychian or Utopian thinking. (See my *Theory of Metamotivation,* 1967.)

24. *Many Utopias have visualized a world composed exclusively of sane, healthy, and effective citizens. Even if a society selects only such individuals originally, yet some will become sick, aged, weak, or incapable. Who will take care of them?*

25. *I assume that the abolition of social injustices will permit the unmistakable appearance of "biological injustices,"* of genetic, prenatal, and natal inequalities, e.g., one child is born with a healthy heart while another is born with a bad heart— which of course is not fair. Neither would it be fair that one is more talented or intelligent or strong or beautiful than another. Biological injustices may be harder to bear than social injustices, where alibis are more possible. What can a good society do about this?

26. *Is ignorance, misinformation, concealment of truth, censoring, blindness necessary in the society or any portion of it?* Are certain truths reserved for the governing group? Dictatorships, benevolent or not, seem to require some concealing of truth. What truths are considered dangerous, e.g., to the young, etc.? Jeffersonian democracy *needs* full access to truth.

27. *Many actual and fantasied utopias have relied on a wise, benevolent, shrewd, strong, effective leader, a philosopher-king. But can this be counted on?* (See Frazier in Skinner's *Walden Two* for a modern version.) Who will pick this ideal leader? How guarantee that this leadership will not fall into the hands of tyrants? Are such guarantees possible at all? What happens when the good leader dies? How possible are leaderlessness, decentralization of power, retention of power by each individual and leaderless groups?

28. *At least some of the successful Utopian communities, past and present, e.g., Bruderhof, have built into the culture candor mechanisms for private or public confession, discussion of each other, mutual honesty, truthfulness and feedback.* Currently this is true of the T-groups (encounter groups) of Synanon and Synanon-like groups of Eupsychian (Theory Y) factories and industries, various types of therapy groups, etc. See *Esalen* brochures; *The Tunnel Back: Synanon* (Yablonsky 1965); pages 154–187 in my *Eupsychian Management; The Lemon Eaters* (Sohl 1967); the back files of *The Journal of Applied Behavioral Sciences,* of *The Journal of Humanistic Psychology,* etc.

29. *How integrate enthusiasm with skeptical realism?* mysticism with practical shrewdness and good reality-testing? idealistic and perfect and therefore unattainable goals (needed as compass directions) with good-natured acceptance of the unavoidable imperfections of means?

REFERENCES

Herzberg, F. *Work and the Nature of Man.* New York: World, 1966.

Manas. P.O. Box 32112, El Sereno Sta., Los Angeles, Calif., 90032.

Maslow, A. H. *Motivation and Personality.* New York: Harper & Bros., 1954.

Maslow, A. H. Eupsychia, the Good Society. *Journal of Humanistic Psychology* 1 (1961): 1–11.

Maslow, A. H. Synergy in the Society and in the Individual. *Journal of Individual Psychology* 20 (1964): 153–164.

Maslow, A. H. *Eupsychian Management: a Journal.* Homewood, Ill.: Irwin-Dorsey, 1965.

Maslow, A. H. *Psychology of Science: a Reconnaissance.* New York: Harper & Row, 1966.

Maslow, A. H. A Theory of Metamotivation: the Biological Rooting of the Value-Life. *Journal of Humanistic Psychology* 2 (1967): 93–127.

Maslow, A. H.; Rand, H.; and Newman, S. Some Parallels Between the Dominance and Sexual Behavior in Monkeys and the Fantasies of Patients in Psychotherapy. *Journal of Nervous and Mental Disorders* 131 (1960): 202–212.

Polyani, M. *Personal Knowledge.* Chicago: Univ. of Chicago Press, 1958.

Skinner, B. F. *Walden Two.* New York: Macmillan, 1962.

Sohl, J. *The Lemon Eaters.* New York: Dell, 1967.

Wilson, C. *Introduction to the New Existentialism.* Boston: Houghton Mifflin, 1967.

Yablonsky, L. *The Tunnel Back: Synanon.* New York: Macmillan, 1965.

filing
categories

Individual Activity → Directly motivated → Sense heightening, Sex, Drugs, Art, Entertainment, etc.

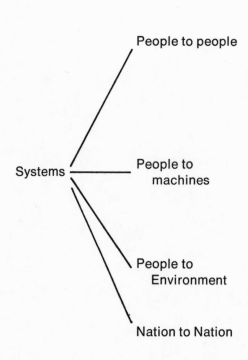

People to people

Health
Justice/Law
Education
Race
Religion
Government/Politics
Consentives

Systems

People to machines

Capital
Distribution of product (physical, advertising)
Distribution of income
Taxes
Marketives
Labor

People to Environment

Demography
Ecology
Patterns of Habitation

Nation to Nation

International organizations
War, Subversion

	Analyses of Technological Change
	Proposals to change socioeconomic system
Process of change	Economic issues
	Life cycle of individuals
	Life cycle of institutions
	Plans/Planning/Research/Prediction
	General theorizing
	Space
	Languages, symbolic and mathematical
	Transportation
Technology	Production (food, ecofacts)
	Power
	Medical, Drugs
	Psychology

RICHARD CELLARIUS AND JOHN PLATT
UNIVERSITY OF MICHIGAN

classification of crisis research studies by project areas

This is an attempt at a classification by *areas and projects* rather than by *urgency* and *intensity* of crisis problems. (The latter classification was suggested in Tables 1 and 2 of "What We Must Do" by Platt, in *Science,* November 28, 1969, pp. 1115–1121.) It is an attempt to see some of the great bones and nerves instead of the usual speech-maker's gross outline of our problems.

The classification is into six broad disciplinary groups with 25 narrower areas of Divisions, like the Divisions of NDRC in WW II. The decimal sections and subsections of particular project areas would need to be restructured and subdivided much more carefully by interdisciplinary committees of experts in the fields involved. In the list here, some areas have been subdivided more carefully, to serve as possible examples. Many subdivisions may represent potential multi-billion dollar industries, some of whose beginnings can already be seen. But others may represent almost intangible changes of attitudes or habits, equally or more important for survival.

In each of the divisions and subdivisions, it would be worth making a careful inventory of such aspects as (1) present knowledge resources; (2) present research effort, including local and national agencies and their scale; (3) promising or far-out solutions that are being neglected, with evaluations; (4) needed research effort, agencies, and scale; (5) estimated payoffs for better solutions, in dollars or in crisis-prevention potential. In areas where no existing organization has such a mission, this would take strong staff work and a number of conferences on a scale comparable to the recent National Academy studies on the prospects and needs of the various fields of science.

i: physical technology and engineering (crisis-related)

1 ENERGY SOURCES

1.1 Nuclear
    1.11 Nuplexes—agro-industrial complexes
        1.111 Air-conditioning for tropical cities and farms
    1.12 Radioactive disposal
1.2 Conventional power plants
    1.21 Cleaner technology (minehead gasification, etc.)
    1.22 Pollution
1.3 Novel sources and conversions
    1.31 Turbine or steam cars
    1.32 New batteries and fuel cells
    1.33 Special solutions for poor countries

2 STRUCTURES AND REPLACEMENT

2.1 Housing and architecture
2.2 Public ways (roads, airports, rail lines and terminals)
2.3 City planning and regional planning
2.4 Replacement of structures: speed and aesthetics
2.5 Special fast-building, low-cost solutions
2.6 Reduction of inefficiency; assembly-line and systems approaches

3　TRANSPORTATION

3.1　Auto/traffic problems; safety; pollution; noise; new engines

3.2　Air/adequacy; convenience; safety; noise

3.3　Rail/restoration; speed; quality

3.4　Marine/new devices for speed and economy

3.5　Novel solutions/minibuses; systems approach

4　NATURAL RESOURCES

4.1　Water supply

　　4.11　Conservation/regional ecology; management design

　　4.12　Pollution/waste disposal; recycling; thermal pollution; monitoring

　　4.13　Nuclear desalination

4.2　Fossil fuels

　　4.21　Economics for various countries/substitution methods

　　4.22　Forecasts

　　4.23　Low-level extraction

4.3　Minerals

　　4.31　Recovery and recycling

　　4.32　Nuclear extraction from low-level rock

5　ELECTRONICS AND COMMUNICATIONS

5.1　Communications and TV for underdeveloped countries

5.2　Satellite education and world communication

5.3　New communications and printing methods/microlibraries

5.4　Large-scale data handling/management; census; researchers; banking; selling

5.5　Knowledge storage, indexing, retrieval/access for the world

5.6　Applications to crime, rights, justice/privacy

5.7 Special applications/person-to-person communications; medicine; household automation; identification and credit

6 GENERAL PHYSICAL AND ENGINEERING PROBLEMS

6.1 Military technology
   6.11 Civilian spin-off
   6.12 Pollution and dangers/monitoring
6.2 Weather control
6.3 Ocean resources and use
6.4 Special technical problems in underdeveloped countries
6.5 Reliability, maintenance, repair, recycling engineering/ systems approach
6.6 Technological forecasting

ii: biotechnology

7 POPULATION PROBLEMS

7.1 Better contraceptive methods/blocks to research and testing; side effects; social and political aspects
7.2 Genetic surveys of populations
7.3 Population pressure research
7.4 Forecasting

8 FOOD AND FAMINE

8.1 New grains and agriculture
8.2 Microbiology sources
8.3 Food from oceans/fish farming; saline agriculture; ocean farming
8.4 Genetic copying of animals
8.5 Novel sources/digestion of grass; new biology; systems approach

9 ENVIRONMENTAL PROBLEMS

9.1 Low-level monitoring of pollution

9.2 Biological handling of pollution

9.3 Ecological survey/local; global; monitoring methods

9.4 Ecological control/improved methods in agriculture; fishing; hunting

9.5 Ecological education and philosophy

9.6 Ecological balance/systems analysis; forecasting

10 HEALTH: BASIC RESEARCH

10.1 Microbiology

10.2 Development and differentiation

    10.21 Regeneration of organs

10.3 Reproduction

10.4 Neurosciences—biopsychology and behavior

10.5 Theoretical biology

    10.51 Population analysis and statistics

    10.52 Evolution and genetic change today

    10.53 Theory of living systems and hierarchical flow systems

10.6 Biotechnological forecasting

10.7 Medical education/world medical education and services; large-scale methods

11 HEALTH: THERAPY

11.1 Disease research and cure/cancer; heart and stroke; neurological; aging, etc.

11.2 Low-level diagnosis/systems approach; continuous optimization of health

11.3 Artificial organs and transplants

11.4 Psychopharmacology and drugs/world survey; long-range effects; poisons

11.5 Psychiatry and mental health/sanitoriums

11.6 Nutrition/measurements; prenatal and infant

11.7 Large-scale survey/forecasting

11.8 Public health/health services; hospitals; underprivileged communities

11.9 Special problems of underdeveloped countries

iii: behavior and personal relations

12   BEHAVIORAL RESEARCH

12.1 Operant-conditioning research

12.2 Responsive-environment studies

12.3 Child development and training/early enrichment

12.4 Dimensions of personality/psychological testing

12.5 Psychotherapy/crisis management; rehabilitation

12.6 Behavior change and learning with interpersonal games

13   EDUCATION

13.1 Classroom teaching/new materials and methods; class management

13.2 Programmed instruction and computer assisted learning

13.3 Educational testing

13.4 Special skills/language teaching; vocational

13.5 Universities/structures; communities; education for careers and change

13.6 Adult education/life problems; retraining

13.7 Teacher education/community knowledge services; world education

13.8 Special problems of underdeveloped countries

14   SMALL GROUPS

14.1 Methods of responsive living

14.2 Family and neighbor relations/new community housing and institutions

14.3 Group interactions/schools, churches, small business, civic problems

14.4 Group-living experiments/religious; behavior-theory; group economics and law

14.5 Child-care communities/slums; suburbs; housing and organization

14.6 Theory and philosophy of individual-group relations, emotional health, etc.

14.7 Special new roles/confidant; economic adviser; group therapist; ombudsman

iv: social structure (national)

15   ECONOMICS

15.1 Inflation/removal without unemployment; relation to credit and computers

15.2 Aids to urban restructuring/Urban Devel. Corps; cutting drain from ghettoes

15.3 Problem-solving inventions and organization

   15.31 Aids and incentives for the poor/guaranteed income; negative tax

   15.32 Financing education

   15.33 Helps to other problems/transport; pollution; crime

15.4 Economic payoffs and methods for needed governmental restructuring

15.5 Large-scale long-range analysis and theory/descriptive; normative

16   ORGANIZATIONS

16.1 New management methods/innovative and adaptive management; democratization

16.2 Improving information handling and decision making

16.3 Computerization

16.4 Participatory problems and humanization

16.5 Systems analysis/planning, programming, budgeting

16.6 Small organizations/business; civic groups; schools; churches; cooperatives

16.7 Special problems of underdeveloped countries

17   MASS COMMUNICATIONS

17.1 Press

17.2 Radio-TV

17.3 New media/records; neighborhood and small group publications

17.4 Mechanisms for increased diversity and freedom/lock-ins

17.5 Masscomm as community and world education

17.6 Role in change/adult adaptation; images of change and future; amplification of crises

17.7 Cultural upgrading

17.8 Theory of effects/systems analysis; forecasting change

18   POLITICS

18.1 Improvement in public administration and management

18.2 Responsiveness/ombudsmen; participation; role of elites and checks on them

18.3 Incorporation of technical advice and planning

18.4 Reduction of community hostilities

18.41 Acculturation/adulthood; urbanization; rapid change

18.42 Education for tolerance and democracy

18.43 Information handling before and during crises

18.44 Mediation

18.45 Crisis management

18.5 Social indicators of choice and stress/opinion polls

18.6 Mechanisms of stability and change

18.7 Systems analysis and theory

19   URBAN PROBLEMS

19.1 Structures/housing; streets; transport; zoning; planning

19.2 Inflow-outflow/people; food; water; garbage and sewage; communications

19.3 Creation of new cities

19.4 Political and community structures
19.5 Law and justice
19.6 General welfare/family relations
19.7 Aesthetic and cultural satisfactions
19.8 Megalopolis-state-national relations/councils of governments

20 LARGE-SCALE CHANGE

20.1 Population pressures/mitigation; use patterns; redistribution incentives
20.2 Quality of life/recreation; aesthetics; differentiation; minority groups
20.3 Social indicators
20.4 Systems analysis/forecasting; theory of change; megalopolis-ecumenopolis
20.5 Analyses and philosophy of individual-group relations in modern society
20.6 Law and justice in high-interaction world/prisons; police; positive incentives
20.7 Special problems in underdeveloped countries
20.8 Reward systems for social inventions and improvements

v. world structure

21 PEACE-KEEPING STRUCTURE

21.1 United Nations revisions
21.2 Crisis damping
21.3 New feedback stabilization mechanisms/fast communications; feedback to elites
21.4 Non-zero-sum game theory research
21.5 Contingency plans for new peace-keeping mechanisms
21.6 Local war mediation and control/arms reduction
21.7 Arms control and disarmament
21.8 Military-industrial lock-ins and conversion to new roles and feedbacks

21.9 Systems analysis of alternative world structures (international group)

22   ECONOMIC DEVELOPMENT

22.1 Mechanisms of investment and growth
22.2 International monetary stabilization
22.3 Housing, large-scale
22.4 Managerial education and skills
22.5 Systems analysis
22.6 Special problems of underdeveloped countries

23   UNDERDEVELOPED COUNTRIES

23.1 Population leveling/policy; methods; education; economics; social optimization
23.2 Food
23.3 Health
23.4 Power
23.5 Education, large-scale/local and world language; TV
23.6 Easing of change/preservation of values; independence
23.7 Damping of racial and national hostilities/education; commercial payoffs
23.8 Governmental and political restructuring
    23.81 Mechanisms of change
    23.82 Pressures of technology
    23.83 Education for democratic management
23.9 Systems analysis and forecasting/new planning structures

vi. channels of effectiveness

24   POLITICAL AND ECONOMIC SUPPORT OF CRISIS STUDIES

24.1 Case studies of social innovation
24.2 Government support of studies
24.3 Organization of interdisciplinary centers for crisis studies

24.4 Support and coordination of nongovernmental studies/ coordination structure

24.5 Political and economic channels for application and action

24.6 Technical advisory service to legislature and industry

24.7 Self-supporting research developments/new companies and industries

24.8 Diplomacy and education for broad support of studies/ PR; "something for all"

25 SYSTEMS ANALYSIS

25.1 Mapping of problem areas and studies/resources; progress; feedback

25.2 Theory of crisis-organization structure and growth

25.3 Large-scale long-range systems analysis/hierarchical jump theory; global eco-system; ecumenopolis

25.4 Match of new innovations to long-range directions

25.5 Match of world education to long-range directions and self-determination

25.6 Democratic theory of group and social choices, and checks and balances, in the process of complex change

25.7 Philosophical structure integrating these changes and studies/long-range evolutionary; normative; personal-behavioral; human benefit and self-fulfillment

DENNIS LIVINGSTON

bibliography

GENERAL FUTUROLOGY

Note: This is a selective list of (mostly) recent books on the general subject of alternative futures, omitting particular slices such as technological change, warfare, space, etc.

Ayres, R. U. *Technological Forecasting and Long-Range Planning.* McGraw-Hill, 1969.

Bauer, Raymond, et al. *Social Indicators: a First Approximation.* MIT, 1966.

————, with Richard S. Rosenbloom, Laurie Sharp, and the assistance of others. *Second-Order Consequences: a Methodological Essay on the Impact of Technology.* MIT, 1969.

Beckwith, Burnham Putnam. *The Next Five Hundred Years: Scientific Prediction of Major Social Trends.* Exposition, 1968.

Bell, Daniel, ed. *Toward the Year 2000: Work in Progress.* Houghton Mifflin, 1968.

Bright, James R., ed. *Technological Forecasting for Government and Industry: Methods and Applications.* Prentice-Hall, 1968.

Calder, Nigel, ed. *The World in 1984,* 2 vols. Penguin, 1965.

Cetron, Marvin. *Technological Forecasting: a Practical Approach.* Gordon & Breach, 1969.

Chase, Stuart. *The Most Probable World.* Harper & Row, 1968.

Council of Europe, Directorate of Political Affairs, Division for Long-Term Planning and Policy. *Long-Term Planning and Forecasting in Europe: Long-Term Forecasting in Europe 1968–1970.* 1970.

Dunstan, Maryjane, and Patricia W. Garlan, eds. *World in the Making: Probes for Students of the Future.* Prentice-Hall, 1970.

Fabun, Don. *The Dynamics of Change.* Prentice-Hall, 1967.

Feinberg, Gerald. *The Prometheus Project: Mankind's Search for Long-Range Goals.* Doubleday, 1969.

Ferkiss, Victor C. *Technological Man: the Myth and the Reality.* Braziller, 1969.

Forrester, Jay. *World Dynamics.* Wright-Allen, 1971.

Gabor, Dennis. *Inventing the Future.* Seecker & Warburg, 1963.

Helmer, Olaf, and Ted Gordon. *Social Technology.* Basic, 1966.

Hetman, Francois. *The Language of Forecasting.* Sedeis, 1969.

Jantsch, Erich. *Technological Forecasting in Perspective.* OECD, 1967.

Jouvenel, Bertrand de, ed. *Futuribles: Studies in Conjecture.* Droz, 1963 (vol. 1) and 1965 (vol. 2).

———, *The Art of Conjecture.* Basic, 1966.

Jungk, Robert, and Johan Galtung, eds. *Mankind 2000.* Norwegian Universities Press, 1969.

Kostelanetz, Richard, ed. *Social Speculations: Visions for Our Time.* Morrow, 1971.

McHale, John. *The Future of the Future.* Braziller, 1969.

Michael, Donald N. *The Unprepared Society: Planning for a Precarious Future.* Basic, 1968.

Ofshe, Richard, *The Sociology of the Possible.* Prentice-Hall, 1970.

Polak, Fred L. *Prognostics.* Elsevier, 1970.

Prehoda, Robert W. *Designing the Future: the Role of Technological Forecasting.* Chilton, 1967.

Sheldon, Eleanor, and Wilbert Moore, eds. *Indicators of Social Change: Concepts and Measurements.* Sage, 1968.

Theobald, Robert. *Teg's 1994.* Swallow, 1971.

Toffler, Alvin. *Future Shock.* Random House, 1970.

Young, Michael, ed. *Forecasting and the Social Sciences.* Heinemann, 1968.

GENERAL INTERNATIONAL
POLITICAL FORECASTING

Abt, Clark C. "The Impact of Technological Change on World Politics." *The Futurist* 2 (April 1968): 21–25.

Bestuzhev-Lada, Igor V., and D. Yermolenko. "The Scientific Forecast of International Relations in the Light of Lenin's Teachings." *International Affairs,* February-March 1970.

Black, Cyril E., and Richard A. Falk, eds. *The Future of the International Legal Order.* Princeton, 1969–: *Trends and Patterns,* 1969; *Wealth and Resources,* 1970; *Conflict Management, The Structure of the International Environment,* and *Toward An International Consensus,* all forthcoming.

Deutsch, Karl W. "The Future of World Politics." *Political Quarterly,* January 1966, pp. 9–32.

Foreign Policy Association, eds. *Toward the Year 2018.* Cowles, 1968.

Galtung, Johan. "On the Future of the International System." *Journal of Peace Research,* no. 4 (1967), pp. 305–333.

Greenberg, Stuart. *Forecasting in International Relations.* George Washington University, 1970.

Haas, Ernst B. *Collective Security and the Future International System.* Social Science Foundation, Denver University, 1968.

Herz, John. *International Politics in the Atomic Age.* Columbia University, 1957.

————. "The Territorial State Revisited: Reflections on the Future of the Nation-State." *Polity* 1 (Fall 1968): 11–34.

Hoffman, Stanley. "Obstinate or Obsolete? The Fate of the

Nation-State and the Case of Western Europe." *Daedalus* 95 (Summer 1966): 862–915.

Kahn, Herman. "The Alternate World Futures Approach," in Morton A. Kaplan, ed., *New Approaches to International Relations.* St. Martin's, 1968.

————, and Anthony J. Wiener. *The Year 2000: A Framework for Speculation on the Next Thirty-Three Years.* Macmillan, 1967.

McClelland, Charles A. *Research Potentials and Rules in Predicting International Futures.* Holloman AFB, 1968.

Morse, Edward L. "The Transformation of Foreign Policies: Modernization, Interdependence, and Externalization." *World Politics* 22 (April 1970): 371–392.

Rosecrance, Richard. "Bipolarity, Multipolarity, and the Future." *Journal of Conflict Resolution* 10 (September 1966): 314–327.

Rubin, Theodore J., E. M. Krass, and A. H. Schainblatt. *Projected International Patterns.* General Electric Tempo (67 TMP–79A), 1967: *Overview of the Environmental Information System* and *Final Technical Report.*

Rummel, Rudolph. "Indicators of Cross-National and International Patterns." *American Political Science Review* 63 (March 1969): 128–147.

————, et al. *Dimensions of Nations.* Northwestern University, 1967.

Russett, Bruce M., et al. *World Handbook of Political and Social Indicators.* Yale, 1964.

————. "The Ecology of Future International Politics." *International Studies Quarterly* 2 (March 1967): 12–51.

————. "Is There a Long-Run Trend Toward Concentration in the International System?" *Comparative Political Studies* 1 (April 1968): 103–122.

Sakharov, Andrei D. *Progress, Coexistence and Intellectual Freedom.* Norton, 1970.

Seaborg, Glenn T. "The Birthpangs of a New World." *The Futurist* 4 (December 1970): 205–208.

Syracuse University Research Corporation. *The United*

States and the World in the 1985 Era, and Appendices 1 and 2; *Science and Technology in the 1985 Era,* and Appendix (Committee Reports). Clearinghouse for Federal Scientific and Technological Information, 1964.

Tanter, Raymond. *Explanation, Prediction, and Forecasting in International Politics.* University of Michigan, 1969.

Wright, Quincy. *On Predicting International Relations, the Year 2000.* Social Science Foundation, University of Denver, 1969.

PROJECTIONS OF UNITED STATES FUTURES

Almon, Clapper. *The American Economy to 1975.* Harper & Row, 1967.

Baier, Kurt, and Nicholas Rescher, eds. *Values and the Future: the Impact of Technological Change on American Values.* Free Press, 1969.

Barach, Arnold B. *U.S.A. and Its Economic Future.* Free Press, 1964.

Basuik, Victor. *Technology, the Future, and American Policy.* forthcoming.

Brzezinski, Zbigniew. *Between Two Ages: America's Role in the Technetronic Age.* Viking, 1970.

Gross, Bertram M., ed. *Social Intelligence for America's Future: Explorations in Societal Problems.* Allyn & Bacon, 1969.

———. "Friendly Fascism: a Model for America." *Social Policy* 1 (November–December 1970): 44–53.

Hill, Robert L., ed. *America 1980.* Graduate School Press, 1965.

Hopkins, Frank Snowden. "The United States in the Year 2000: a Proposal for the Study of the American Future." *The American Sociologist* 2 (August 1967): 149–150.

Masters, Roger D. *The Nation is Burdened: American Foreign Policy in a Changing World.* Alfred A. Knopf, 1967.

Lecht, Leonard A. *Manpower Needs for National Goals in the 1970s.* Praeger, 1969.

Pfeffer, Richard M., ed. *No More Vietnams? The War and the Future of American Foreign Policy.* Harper & Row, 1968.

Rogers, Carl R. "Interpersonal Relationships: U.S.A. 2000." *Journal of Applied Behavioral Science* 4 (July–September 1968): 265–280.

Seabury, Paul, and Aaron Wildavsky. *U.S. Foreign Policy: Problems and Perspectives for the 70s.* McGraw-Hill, 1969.

Theobald, Robert. *An Alternative Future for America: Essays and Speeches by Robert Theobald.* Swallow, 1970.

Tugwell, Rexford G. "U.S.A. 2000 A.D." *The Center Magazine* 1 (November 1968): 23–33.

U.S., National Goals Research Staff. *Toward Balanced Growth—Quantity With Quality.* Government Printing Office, 1970.

Waskow, Arthur I. "Looking Forward: 1999." *Our Generation* 5 (March–April 1968): 26–51.

PROJECTIONS OF SOVIET UNION FUTURES

Amalrik, Andrei. *Will the Soviet Union Survive Until 1984?* Harper & Row, 1970.

Braverman, Harry. *The Future of Russia.* Grosset & Dunlap, 1966.

Hamil, Ralph. "The Cloudy Future of Communism." *The Futurist* 4 (December 1970): 213–215.

Shapiro, Leonard. *The USSR and the Future.* Praeger, 1963.

Tatu, Michael, et al. "The Future of the Soviet Union: a Symposium." *Interplay* 2 (May 1969): 4–9.

PROJECTIONS OF UNITED KINGDOM FUTURES

Beloff, Max. *The Future of British Foreign Policy.* Taplinger, 1969.

Brech, Ronald. *Britain 1984: An Experiment in the Economic History of the Future.* Humanities, 1966.

Calleo, David. *Britain's Future.* Horizon, 1969.

Hugo, Grant. *Britain in Tomorrow's World.* Columbia University, 1969.

Northedge, F. S. "Britain's Future in World Affairs." *International Journal* 23 (Autumn 1968): 600–610.

PROJECTIONS OF FUTURES OF OTHER COUNTRIES AND REGIONS

Association for Peace. *The Middle East in the Year 2000: A Project.* Association for Peace (Israel), n.d.

Barach, Arnold B. *The New Europe and Its Economic Future.* Free Press, 1964.

Bertram, Christoph. "Models of Western Europe in the 1970s—the Alternative Choices." *Futures* 1 (December 1968): 142–152.

Bertrin, Leonard. *Target 2067: Canada's Second Century.* Macmillan of Canada, 1968.

Buchan, Alastair. *Europe's Future, Europe's Choices.* Columbia University, 1969.

Commission to Study the Organization of Peace. *The United Nations: The Next Twenty-Five Years.* 1969.

Djilas, Milovan. "There'll Be Many Different Communisms in 1984." *New York Times Magazine,* March 23, 1969, p. 28.

Eayrs, James, and Robert Spencer, eds. "Latin America in the 1970s." *International Journal* 24 (Summer 1969): whole.

Eldridge, H. Wentworth. "Futurism in Planning for Developing Countries." *AIP Journal* 34 (November 1968): 382–384.

Gasteyger, Curt. "Europe in the Seventies." *Atlantic Community Quarterly* 5 (Fall 1967): 317–335.

Kahn, Herman. *The Emerging Japanese Superstate: Challenge and Response.* Prentice-Hall, 1970.

Lowenthal, Richard, ed. *Issues in the Future of Asia: Com-*

munist and Non-Communist Alternatives. Praeger, 1969.

Mazuri, Ali A. "Africa on the Eve of Tomorrow." *Bulletin of the Atomic Scientists* 25 (November 1969): 15–19.

Patyn, C. K. "The Future of the Atlantic Alliance." *Atlantic Community Quarterly* 6 (Winter 1968–69): 512–519.

Suyin, Han. *China in the Year 2001.* Basic, 1967.

Wakaizumi, Kei. "Japan Beyond 1970." *Foreign Affairs,* April 1969, pp. 509–520.

futurology journals and organizations

JOURNALS AND SPONSORING ORGANIZATIONS

Analysen und Prognosen: Uber die Welt von Morgen
ZBZ Mitteilung
Zentrum Berlin für Zukunftsforschung (ZBZ)
Hohenzollerndamm 170
D–1000 Berlin 31, Germany

Analyse et Prevision
SEDEIS
205 Boulevard St. Germain
Paris 7, France

Bulletin of Social Forecasting
Istituto Ricerche Applicate Documentazione e Studi (IRADES)
Via Paisiello 6
00198 Rome, Italy

Documentation Bulletin on Future Research 2000
Wolters-Noordhoff Publishing
Box 58
Groningen, The Netherlands

Futures: the Journal of Forecasting and Planning
Iliffe Publishers

32 High Street
Guildford, Surrey, England

Future Trends
Gesellschaft fur Zukunftsforschung
Karl-Muck-Platz 1
2 Hamburg 36, Germany

Futuribili
Istituto per le Ricerche di Economia Applicata (IREA)
Via Venti Settembre 1
00187 Rome, Italy

Futuriblirne
Society for Research on Futures
Skovfaldet 2S
DK-8200 Aarhus N., Denmark

Futurum
Carl Hanser Verlag
Munich, Germany

*The Futurist: a Journal of Forecasts, Trends and Ideas
about the Future*
WFS Bulletin
World Future Society: an Association for the Study of Al-
ternative Futures
Box 19285, 20th St. Station
Washington, D.C. 20036

IFRC Newsletter
International Future Research Conference (Secretariat)
Lars Ingelstam
Institutionen for Matematik
Kungl, Tekniska Hogskolan
Stockholm 70, Sweden

Technological Forecasting and Social Change
American Elsevier Publishing
52 Vanderbilt Ave.
New York, N.Y. 10017

2000 Amenagement du Territoire Avenir

59, Avenue Denfert-Rochereau
75-Paris 14, France

OTHER GENERAL FUTUROLOGY ORGANIZATIONS

Association Internationale Futuribles
52 Rue des Saints-Pères
Paris 7, France
> This group has established the International House of Futuribles, same address, to serve as an information bureau for "futuribles" organizations and to provide a library, meeting rooms, and research services for scholars.

Commission on the Year 2000
American Academy of Arts and Sciences
Boston, Mass.

Hudson Institute
Quaker Ridge Road
Croton-on-Hudson, N.Y. 10502

Institute for the Future
Riverview Center
Middletown, Conn. 06457

Mankind 2000 International
Istituto Ricerche Applicate Documentazione e Studi
(IRADES)
Via Paisiello 6
00198 Rome, Italy

Program for the Study of the Future in Education
School of Education
University of Massachusetts
Amherst, Mass. 01002
> There is available from this group a *Future Studies Bibliography* and a *Future Studies Syllabus,* both 1970.

Science Fiction Research Association

7 Amsterdam Ave.
Teaneck, N.J. 07666

For more complete listings of futurology organizations see:

Council of Europe, Directorate of Political Affairs, Division for Long-Term Planning and Policy. *Long-Term Planning and Forecasting in Europe: Long-Term Forecasting in Europe 1968–1970.* 1970.

Jantsch, Erich. *Technological Forecasting in Perspective.* OECD, 1967.

Umpleby, Stuart. *The Delphi Exploration: a Computer-Based System for Obtaining Subjective Judgments on Alternative Futures.* University of Illinois, 1969.

team chants

Give me an F, Foreseen,
      a U, Unchanged,
      a T, Trends,
      a U, Upward,
      an R, Relax,
      an E, Ego,
A Fast, Up, Tough, Up, Raise, Eon.
F–U–T–U–R–E.

Stuck with an F, Foreseen,
      a U, Unchanged,
      a T, Total,
      a U, Unable,
      an R, Rethink,
      an E, Empathy,
A Fear, Us, Them, Us, Reap, End.
future?

I'm given an F, Foreseen,
      a U, Uprooted,
      a T, Total,
      a U, Utopia,
      an R, Relax,
      an E, Ego,
a Float, Un, Trip, Un, Rare, Ease.
F*U*T*U*R*E!

We'll create an F, Flexible,
a U, Unified,
a T, Transition,
a U, United,
an R, Rethink,
an E, Empathy,
A Find, Use, True, Use, Real, Era.
FUTURE